East End, West End

East End, West End

Bernard Delfont
with Barry Turner

MACMILLAN LONDON

First published 1990 by
MACMILLAN LONDON LIMITED
4 Little Essex Street London WC2R 3LF
and Basingstoke

Associated companies in Auckland, Delhi, Dublin, Gaborone,
Hamburg, Harare, Hong Kong, Johannesburg, Kuala Lumpur,
Lagos, Manzini, Melbourne, Mexico City, Nairobi, New York,
Singapore and Tokyo

ISBN 0-333-51190-5

A CIP catalogue record for this book is available from
the British Library

Typeset by Rowland Phototypesetting Limited
Bury St Edmunds, Suffolk

Printed in Great Britain by
WBC Print Ltd., Bridgend, Mid Glam.

For Carole and the family

Chapter 1

My first memory of childhood is of standing in a police station. I had been found in the street, crying my eyes out and calling for my mother.

Getting lost in a crowd is not, I suppose, an unusual experience for a three-year-old, least of all for a known wanderer with an irresistible urge to find out what was round the next corner. But given that I was in a strange city in a strange country, speaking a language which my rescuer obviously did not understand, the event does take on a certain dramatic significance.

The policeman stopped me crying by sitting me on a high chair and feeding me jelly sweets in rapid succession. How long we kept up this routine I have no idea but it must have been for an hour or two because, as I was told later, having looked for me in all the obvious places my parents panicked themselves into believing I had been stolen.

I was beginning to enjoy my new surroundings when a familiar figure appeared. In fractured English my father laid claim to Boris Winogradsky, his Russian-born younger son, lately arrived with his mother and his brother Lovat, at Tilbury docks. With many apologies to the police for distracting them from more important duties (though I, for one, could not imagine what these could be) my father took me back to a room over a shop in Brick Lane, just off the Mile End Road, the place my parents called home.

London's East End in the early years of the century was a refuge for the dispossessed. I doubt there was anyone in our neighbourhood who was not a first-generation immigrant. Most were Jews from Imperial Russia, the scapegoat victims of that country's descent into chaos. When families got together the talk inevitably turned to friends and relatives who had stayed behind and who, as often as not, had died in the pogroms.

1

My birthplace was a little town called Tokmak in the Ukraine. The traditional view in my family is that Tokmak was not far from Odessa on the Black Sea but nobody can be sure just how far because the name no longer appears on any map. My guess is that having been deserted by its younger citizens, Tokmak eventually sank without trace. It happened to quite a few Jewish communities in that part of the world.

I was born on 5 September 1909, just two years and nine months after brother Lovat, better known as Lew. My father Isaac was then twenty-five and my mother Golda three, four or five years younger, her age drifting with her notoriously hazy memory for dates. The birth certificate which might settle the matter has long since disappeared, even assuming it ever existed. Ukrainian bureaucracy was not too particular in such matters.

It was a marriage of opposites. While my father was a romantic drifter, a man of ideas without much notion of how to apply them, Mother was an organiser with a strength of purpose. The name she surrendered on her wedding day – Izenstadt, or iron city – suited her better than the gentler-sounding Winogradsky, literally 'the town where wine is made'. What brought my parents together was a passion for amateur theatricals. Both had good voices which they were liable to put to use at the first hint of encouragement. Their act, a lively rendition of popular folk songs, toured the surrounding villages earning them the few extra kopeks that made life bearable.

My father's regular job was to run a drapery store which enjoyed a brief spark of excitement on market days. Otherwise it was a simple and tedious life.

But here he might have stayed had he been allowed to live in peace. It could not be. Times were hard and for every tightening of the screw the Jews were held to blame. It was bad enough being poor but to be beaten up for the poverty of others was sheer insanity.

I have little doubt that Mother took the initiative. Three of her brothers had already settled in Britain and letters back suggested that two of them were doing quite well. Anyway, prosperous or no, Jewish family tradition ruled that a helping hand would be offered. There was a language barrier, of course, but it was not so high as we might assume. Thousands of Russian and Polish refugees preceded my family to Britain, and there were well-established communities in London, Manchester, Leeds and other big industrial cities. London's

East End alone contained over one hundred thousand of my compatriots.

It was assumed we could get by in Russian, at least to begin with, but just to make sure my parents started to speak more Yiddish. Penetrating the mysteries of English was a challenge thankfully deferred.

The plan was for Father to travel ahead with whatever small savings he had collected and to send for the rest of us when he had found a home and a job. There was never any question that he would succeed. London had an aura of prosperity second in brightness only to New York where, as we all knew, vast fortunes were made by Europeans within hours of them stepping off the immigrant ship. Such naïvety had its value: without it we might never have got beyond the next village.

It is hard now to imagine what it must have been like for an unpractised traveller of my father's generation and upbringing to set off across Europe. Even the concept of distance and of how long it took to get from A to B was hazy in the extreme. Years later an English friend told me about a worker on his family farm who decided to emigrate to the States at about the same time as my father was on his way to London. Born and bred in the heart of the Norfolk countryside the man was understandably nervous at the prospect of a long and tiring journey. His wife did her best to comfort him. 'Don't you fret yourself; we can stay overnight in Norwich.'

My father would have understood. He thought all his problems would be over once he got to Hamburg, one of the main exit ports from Central Europe. Instead, he had hardly begun his adventure. Like other migrants with their savings in their pockets, he was prey to every villain on the waterfront. Even if he did not fall for the old trick of buying a cheap ticket for a non-existent boat he undoubtedly lost money somewhere along the way – probably by gambling. Never able to resist a bet, a characteristic he passed down to me, he was bound to fall victim in his first encounter with professional card-sharps. He was still learning the hard way when, six months later, the family was reunited in London.

By his own account, my father's voyage across the North Sea was an experience never to be repeated by a sane person. He could not have been out of sight of land for more than three days but it was long enough to create for him the indelible impression that all waves are thirty feet high and that boats are made for sinking. Pressed into

3

steerage with twice as many passengers as the shipper was supposed to carry and unable to change his clothes or wash in clean water, the journey was as unhealthy as it was uncomfortable. Landing at Tilbury was a merciful release.

Most, if not all, of his fellow passengers were seeing England for the first time. So this was the place they had chosen to call home. Shoved and squeezed down the gangway and crushed together on the quayside, their bags and cases piled up about them, they must have doubted their own senses.

The noise was bad enough with everyone shouting over the thunderous rumble of carts and barrows on cobblestones. But the smell! Every day upwards of a hundred tons of horse manure were dropped on to the streets of London. The stench, made more pungent by clouds of coal smoke, not to mention the petrol fumes, brought a nostalgic longing for fresh air. If the smells of the old East End could be revived it might serve as a reminder to today's environmentalists that we have already come a long way.

The newcomers who had most to fear were those without sponsors. There was no problem getting into the country; those were the days when immigration was a free-for-all. Anyone with the resources and strength of purpose to reach this country had the right to stay, if not to automatic citizenship. But without friends to give them a push-start, life could be bleak. It was not unusual to see whole families, fresh off the boat, out on the Mile End Road with nowhere to stay the night.

The Jewish community made a noble effort to look after its own. As a last resort, the destitute could always turn to the Jewish Board of Guardians or the Jews Temporary Shelter for a few days' food and lodging. It was not much but it was kosher. The Jews Temporary Shelter was in Mansell Street which runs down to Tower Bridge. I drove past the shelter a little while ago and saw from the gold-coloured name-plates that it is now offices for financial consultants and investment companies.

Father was lucky in so far as he did have a relative to meet him. Brother-in-law Herschell, the poorest of the three, was waiting on the far side of the customs shed. Unfortunately, the wealthier brothers-in-law had more pressing business to attend to. It seemed that Father's initiation into the British way of life was to start on the lower rungs of the ladder.

Herschell lived in Brick Lane close by the Whitechapel market and a short walk from Spitalfields where the sweat shops made clothes for the West End. Started by the Huguenots, taken over by the Jews and now dominated by the Indians, the East End garment business has long had an appeal to immigrants of an entrepreneurial turn of mind. It holds out the chance of setting up an independent business – to be one's own boss. That was what my father wanted above all else.

But first he had to make enough money to bring over his wife and children. While he looked for work he stayed with Herschell and his family in their tiny flat. He went to night school to learn English and when he came home he had to wait until everybody had gone to bed before he could make room on the floor for his mattress.

Eventually he found a job as a trouser presser at eight shillings a week. On the strength of this modest and irregular income he rented a one-room flat over a shop at the brewery end of Brick Lane. Then, with what was left of his savings he bought sea passages for Mother, Lew and myself, a wise move since women travelling without their men were particularly prone to ticket sharks. There were even stories of white slavers who sought out and ensnared lonely females.

Our mother was too level-headed to fall for such wiles. None the less it was a relief to her to be spared the challenge of negotiating with the shipping agents at Hamburg. They were in a seller's market and used it for all it was worth.

I remember nothing of the journey. No doubt I slept most of the way. But I do remember seeing my father for the first time in six months and I retain a distinct sensation of wonderment that so many exciting things could be happening simultaneously. We children were even given new names. According to the identity cards filled out for us at Tilbury where the immigration officials found Russian hard to grasp, Lovat became Lewis and I became Barnet.

I fancy that Mother was less enthralled by her new surroundings. We had left behind a simple life in Tokmak but it was a life centred on a house, a garden and some trees. Now there was no house, no garden and no trees – just one room over a shop. Hardly the brave new world she had been led to expect. Still, they had a bed of their own; it was we children who had to sleep on the floor.

My parents spoke Russian over the meal table or Yiddish if they wanted to keep a secret. But Lew, who was a quick learner, caught on to English almost immediately and refused to speak any other language.

5

In the wonderful way that children have of adapting to their surroundings, we country-born boys took to the city, or our part of it, as if it was one huge toy. As the older brother, Lew was the intrepid pioneer, exploring the streets for new adventures. For all his tough-guy exploits, told to me in florid detail, I gave him my unstinted admiration. But my hero-worship was short-lived. Came the day when I was up against superior forces I retaliated in the traditional manner: 'I'll get my brother on to you!' To his credit, Lew rose to the challenge. But one black eye and a bloody nose later, I had to acknowledge that as a bruiser he had his limitations. To add to my humiliation, I had to make up the unlikely story that Lew had run into a wall.

The East End of my boyhood was hard-living but it was not without hope and I never really felt underprivileged. Though we knew hardly anything of British politics – except that they were more liberal than Russian politics – the evidence of change was all around us. For a start, slum property was recognised for what it was – dark, dirty and degrading – and much of it was falling before an army of demolition workers. Just behind Brick Lane an area of some fifty acres was cleared by the London County Council to make way for a new estate of working-class homes. Known as the Boundary Estate because it straddled the boroughs of Shoreditch and Bethnal Green, the neat tenement blocks of two- and three-room flats were set out like spokes of a wheel. The hub was Arnold Circus with its hillock of greenery topped by a bandstand like a cherry in a fruit cake. On summer Tuesdays the crowds gathered to hear the music, with the Winogradskys invariably occupying a patch of grass close to the bandstand. It was then that my parents talked longingly of climbing a step up the social scale.

'Don't we deserve something better?' enquired my mother with invincible logic. 'Have we come all this way to live over a shop?'

With a little help from his friends, Father got our name on to the council waiting list for 'improved' accommodation. He must have struck lucky because within months we were offered a ground-floor flat on the Boundary Estate in Henley Buildings. The entrance was through a short alleyway and up some stone steps. The numbers of the flats were printed on the wall in large figures. There was a lot of white tiling around which was kept spotlessly clean by house-proud residents. On one side of Henley Buildings was a line of small workshops, part of the Boundary Estate development, which offered

accommodation at a modest rate to two- or three-man businesses –
nearly all Jewish.

This love of being one's own boss even if it meant working harder
and earning less than many who were on a fixed wage was a devoutly
held wish of the typical Jewish immigrant, however modest his
origins. He found it hard to come to terms with large companies
employing thousands of workers. He did not like the idea of surren-
dering his independence to an all-powerful and generally unseen
boss.

In many ways this was fortunate because work in the factories or
on the docks was hard to come by. Those who had jobs were naturally
opposed to sharing what little they made with refugees fresh off the
boat. In the East End there was not much choice beyond owning or
working for a small business. The typical employee was one who
had hopes of setting up on his own or who had already tried and
failed.

My father moved quickly from the first to the second category. As
always with him, he started well with a good idea. Not having any
recognised skills beyond those of a humble shopkeeper, he steered
away from the quality trades like tailoring and printing but stopped
short of unskilled occupations at the lower end of the garment trade
where the profit margin was wafer thin. What he needed was a living
where he would use his personality and maybe satisfy his ambition
to entertain.

My parents practised their stagecraft at the Mile End Pavilion,
better known as the Yiddisher Theatre, where there was always an
audience for the old songs of home – home being Russia. But that
was no way to get rich. If Father had had the money, or the backing,
I am certain he would have taken over a music hall, no doubt putting
himself at the top of the bill. Fortunately, perhaps, mainstream music
hall was awash with tenors, while openings for managers who were
short on experience and spoke with a heavy accent were few and far
between.

But there was another area of entertainment where the undercapi-
talised entrepreneur might make an impact. All over town the seekers
after diversion were being drawn towards the penny gaffs – often no
more than a single room with rows of chairs set out in front of a
screen on to which were projected moving pictures.

The great virtue of the early movies was that everybody could
enjoy them. It did not matter about language because there were no

7

spoken words. No wonder the cinema was a favourite East End entertainment.

Father was by no means the first to try his luck as a cinema promoter in the Mile End Road. There were at least two established competitors, one of whom he had worked for as a part-time assistant doing everything from collecting the takings to sweeping up the orange peel. The experience taught him a few basic rules, like making sure the dust cover was off the projector lens before starting the film, and convinced him that the business was ripe for expansion.

He leased himself a building (a converted shop), rented some second-hand equipment, painted a few bright signs promising thrills in plenty and opened for business. The poor man never stood a chance.

While he was undoubtedly right to believe that he was part of an expanding industry in which there was room for all, his rivals did not take the same optimistic view. For them, my father was an unwelcome intruder who had to be discouraged from stealing their customers. Entering what was then a free-for-all market in which films were sold (at between four and six pence a foot) or rented to the highest bidder, Isaac Winogradsky was fobbed off with old prints of poor quality. The public stayed away in droves.

In fairness, I can believe that Father was in large measure responsible for his own downfall. With his happy-go-lucky and commercially naïve temperament he probably misread the trend in the movie business. With the appearance of larger, purpose-built cinemas there was a strong move towards an organised distribution system and exclusive booking contracts.

To survive, Father needed a deal with one of the circuits like Provincial Cinematograph Theatres (later absorbed into Rank) which set up with the intention of opening a cinema in every major town. But while screen entertainment moved on to bigger and better features shown in plush surroundings, my father kept up the unequal battle with faded reruns of *The Great Train Robbery* and *Rescued by Rover*.

The last straw was the London County Council's attempt to license cinemas in the same way as music halls and to ban Sunday performances. This took away the best part of the Winogradsky income for reasons that my parents could not even begin to understand.

'So what have we done wrong?' wailed my mother. 'If they want us to be religious should we close on Saturdays?'

8

After this venture Father went back to the rag trade. His return to twelve hours a day pressing trousers in a basement workshop coincided with the beginning of the Great War. Not for a moment did he or his friends consider offering themselves as recruits, though there were many pressures to do so. The gratitude they felt to Britain for taking them in did not extend to sacrificing their lives for Russia, Britain's ally, the country that had driven them from their homes. For the Jewish immigrant communities, Russia was *the* enemy and would remain so until memories of the eastern pogroms were swept away by a mightier wave of anti-Semitism.

Technically, the enforcement of general conscription in mid 1916 overrode all personal convictions but, by an irony of fate, my father escaped the net. Like thousands of others, he had left Russia without a passport for the good reason that if he had applied for one it would have immediately made him liable for military service and put a stop to his plans to emigrate. That made him a stateless person. He was in Britain but not of Britain and so was excluded from the rights and commitments of full citizenship. This was to cause problems later for me as much as for Father but while the war was in full spate being a non-person had its advantages.

The war intruded little on my young life though I imagine I saw more action than most children. Living within a bomb's throw of the London docks we were the near misses for raiding Zeppelins. These clumsy, slow-moving airships looked harmless but the damage they inflicted was real enough. Not far from Henley Buildings, a stick of bombs wiped out an entire street, killing a dozen people.

There was a makeshift warning system consisting of a man wielding a wooden clapper, which meant that a raid was expected in about half an hour. Where his information came from I have no idea. Perhaps he just stood there, looking up into the sky. If the warning came when we were at school, the teacher settled our fears with a spot of community hymn singing. There was no question of running for cover since there was no cover within running distance. At the all-clear, we resumed our studies as if what had just happened was the most natural thing in the world.

Once, the clapper was followed by several loud explosions which rattled the windows. Our singing died away and we sat at our desks waiting, listening. Eventually, on the all-clear, we were told to go home. I ran all the way. The courtyard to Henley Buildings was flaked with glass and there was water rushing into the gutter from a broken main. I threw myself in at the door of number eleven and shouted for my mother. She called back but I could not see her. There were not many hiding places but I was stumped for a moment until I located her under the bed. With me on my knees, bending my head to talk to her upside down, I tried to assure her that the danger had passed. She was not convinced. To be on the safe side I was urged to join her, just for a few minutes.

Thereafter, if we were at home when there was a warning, we made tracks for the security of Old Street underground station. I have a clear recollection of spending one entire night walking to and from Old Street in Pavlovian response to the signals from the air-raid warden.

Then, suddenly, we were whisked away to Reigate to live in a tiny cottage near the Downs. The reason for this dramatic move was lost on me at the time though I now realise that the impending birth of brother Leslie must have had a lot to do with it. Father stayed in the East End but came down by train for weekends. I doubt that we were in Reigate for more than a few weeks but it was long enough for me to discover that to be Jewish was to be different. While it is true to say that we were not a particularly religious family (visits to the synagogue were a rarity) we were at home in the Jewish East End without feeling all the time that we had to prove ourselves. But Reigate was like a foreign country. As the only two Jewish children in the local school, Lew and I were objects of curiosity. What was wrong with us?

My father was understanding. 'Look at it this way. To be one among many is to be a rarity; and a rarity has great value.'

But I was still glad to get back to Henley Buildings and to the school which I knew if not exactly loved.

Why do I say that? It was not that I was unhappy at Rochelle Street School; I made friends easily and enjoyed lots of laughs. Perhaps that was my trouble. The fruits of learning were not for me: I was more interested in having fun. In the way that youngsters have of blaming their failings on their elders, I must point the finger at my form teacher, the multi-talented Mr Silverstein whose infallible technique for holding the attention of an unruly class was to show what he could do in the way of funny walks and grotesque faces. I was not much good at reproducing his gallery of famous look-alikes (though in the effort to rise to his heights of caricature I nearly dislocated my jaw) but I did find that I had a natural talent for silly walks. Such was my devotion to practising the man with rubber legs and his equally unfortunate friend, the man with two left feet, that kindly neighbours were disposed to offer words of sympathy to my parents.

'Such a nice boy but maybe a little strange? I'm sure you do your best.'

I was not deterred.

Rochelle Street School was a short walk from Henley Buildings. Built to the standard Victorian pattern of a central assembly hall surrounded by classrooms on two levels there were separate entrances for boys and girls and a wall down the middle of the playground to keep us apart. The pupils and teachers were mostly Jewish. On the other side of Arnold Circus was a somewhat larger school where the pupils and teachers were mostly Gentile. Inevitably there was rivalry but as far as I can remember it was always good-natured without any hint of racial acrimony. In fact, I can honestly say that with the exception of the school in Reigate, where Lew rescued me from bullying and collected a black eye in the process, I have never experienced anti-Semitism in Britain. But I sympathise strongly with those who have and if I was asked to identify the source of my strongest emotion I would say that it is an abiding hatred of all forms of discrimination.

The verdict of my seniors that I was a boy of modest abilities shocked my older brother who, early on in life, revealed an enviable capacity for self-promotion. Lew, according to Lew, was someone special who had every intention of coming out on top. He was certainly a quick learner with a natural bent for figures. There was talk of him moving on from elementary school to secondary education, a rare privilege in those days, but the scholarship that would have made this possible was withheld for the same reason that stopped Father from going into the army – the Winogradskys were not yet fully signed-up British citizens. Had my father applied for naturalisation all his children would have automatically become British. But that would have cost him money and there was none to spare.

Lew left school at fourteen, the legal minimum age for starting work. I went one better and left school at twelve. It was remarkably easy. I just did not go any more.

The events which set me off on my record-breaking run of truancy started with our move to a house in Grafton Street which was still in the East End, but further out on the Mile End Road. The change of address did not signal a change for the better in the family fortunes. For one thing, the property in Grafton Street was a hotchpotch of sad little dwellings, long since discounted by the rent collector who called by occasionally, more in hope than in expectation. Then again, the house was not exactly spacious. Occupying the middle rooms we were sandwiched between two other families, one above, the other below.

The effort to economise, which I suppose is what motivated our departure from Henley Buildings, put a great strain on Mother's spirit of neighbourliness. When frustration spilled over into anger she took it out on the people upstairs. The rows were frequent and loud.

'Why can't we be friends?' I asked. 'They don't do any harm.'

Mother sniffed derisively. 'They're Polish,' she declared emphatically, as if that settled the matter.

Father was more tolerant but he could afford to be. He was out at work all day and in the evenings there were powerful distractions from domestic affairs such as roller skating and trying to calculate which horse was likely to win the big race at Kempton Park. My first truly intellectual exercise was interpreting the method used by my father when marking up his racing paper to signify the strengths and weaknesses of the various runners. I use the same system to this day.

Which brings me back to my education. After settling in at Grafton Street it was decided to keep Lew at Rochelle Street School where he was the star turn, while transferring his lacklustre younger brother to the ranks of Stepney Jewish School. The régime there was more rigorous than anything I had so far experienced. Compelled to pay attention, sit up straight, march in time as part of a neat line when moving about the school and at all times to have clean fingernails, I longed for the carefree days of Mr Silverstein.

I had no doubt that Mr Silverstein would not have objected to a farthing sweepstake on the weekend football results. Or, if he had objected, he would not have identified me as the promoter. At Stepney Jewish, the staff had an eye for the miscreants. Moreover, I made it easy for them by overplaying my hand. Having enjoyed one or two quite profitable weeks I tried to bring in more business by increasing the first prize to a full sixpence. Come the end of Friday break I still had a queue of eager backers and a fistful of handwritten team slips.

The teacher called me out to the front. 'Winogradsky. What have you got in your hands?'

'Nothing, sir.'

'Just show me your hands.'

I held out my left hand.

'Now the other.'

I held out my right hand, tightly clenched.

'Open it.' He took the slips and then read out: 'Chelsea, Tottenham Hotspur, Manchester United . . .'

Minutes later I was in the company of the headmaster, nervously anticipating the inevitable verdict. He was a humourless man given to uttering moral precepts as if he had a direct line to Moses.

'The gambler who loses destroys himself,' he told me. 'But the gambler who wins is twice cursed for he leads others into his sinful ways.'

Any bookie's runner would have told him differently but he was not in the mood for contradiction. Once again I was told to hold out my hands. I had a sudden fear that he was about to cane me where it would hurt most.

'Please, sir,' I said, 'don't hit me on my warts.'

Three on each hand and then I had to stand in a corner for what seemed hours.

I might have done better to have kept quiet.

After that, I took to finding excuses for staying at home. Nobody seemed to mind. It might have been otherwise if I had shown promise as a scholar but as it was the school disposed of a problem and my parents gained an extra pair of hands about the house. With Mother preoccupied with a lively infant (Leslie was then four), trying to feed a ravenous family on short rations and taking in sewing to make ends meet, she could do with all the help she could get.

The odd jobs I was allocated consisted largely of shopping trips to the corner grocery and to Blundells, the big departmental store on the Mile End Road where we bought some furniture on the hire purchase. With her mortal fear of falling for ever into debt, Mother hated the very idea of paying on the never-never. She was persuaded against her better judgement only on condition that she did not have to appear at Blundells to deliver the weekly instalments. It was a responsibility I gladly took on not least because, acting on her instructions, I had to perform the task like a secret agent, taking care not to be seen by any of the neighbours as I slipped into the store by the back entrance, clutching an envelope of coins as if it held plans for saving the nation.

I continued to get into scrapes but they were generally minor ones like buying chocolate biscuits (my favourite) on the weekly grocery slate until over-indulgence pointed out the discrepancy to my mother. One of my most serious misdemeanours was to steal from Uncle Herschell. I had been sent to deliver a message and while I was waiting in the kitchen I saw a heap of pennies on the table. I calculated that he would not miss the three coins I slipped into my pocket but he must have had his suspicions even before I left the flat because he insisted on walking back with me to Grafton Street. Once there he had a long conversation with my father in Yiddish while I strained to understand one word in six.

Eventually, Father turned to me. 'Did you take the money?'

I mustered every ounce of conviction. 'No.'

'Take off your jacket.'

I did so, handed it over, and watched the two men go through my pockets. They found the usual grisly hoard of boyhood collectibles but no coins.

'Take off your trousers!'

We went through the same routine. Standing there in my shirt and underwear I was still determined to gamble to the limit. Sadly, Father understood me only too well.

'Take off your shoes!'

I was rather proud of the switch I had engineered while pausing to tie a lace. But the game was up. I had underestimated Father's powers of deduction, a mistake for which I suffered a hefty belting. I thought of going back to school but the pain and the mood soon passed.

Life was never dull; there was so much to discover. When I was not out with equally inquisitive friends exploring the streets, my favourite haunt was a music hall known as Ye Olde Paragon, which many years later was to become one of the ABC chain of cinemas controlled by EMI (chief executive, Bernard Delfont). I used to do a lot of hanging about outside Ye Olde Paragon. If it was a thin house and the doorman liked the look of you there was a fair chance of a 'bunk in' to the gallery free of charge. I remember the great acts of the early twenties, but the Paragon was not in the same league as the major Moss Empire or Stoll theatres which played all the top performers, nor the London Theatres of Variety, owners of the

Holborn Empire and the Palladium, nor even the Syndicate Variety theatres with their middle-of-the-road acts.

At the Paragon we had to make do with Peel and Curtis.

PEEL: Good evening, ladies and gentlemen. I'm very pleased to be with you in this splendid emporium. Now I'd like to begin with a little recitation entitled 'Get Off the Kitchen Sink Grandmother, You're Too Old to be Riding the Range'.

CURTIS: I'm not having it.

PEEL: What do you mean, you're not having it?

CURTIS: It's a scandal.

PEEL: What is?

CURTIS: (*Pulling a candle out of his pocket*): This is.

PEEL: I don't wish to know that. Kindly leave the stage.

After Peel and Curtis there was usually a cyclist or a juggler, followed by another comedy act – Haig and Escoe, who did their entire act sitting on a park bench. Their last big gag brought the curtain down.

He would say to her, 'May I hold your Palm Olive?' and she would reply, 'Not on your Life Buoy!'

All I can say is that I cherished every moment of Peel and Curtis and Haig and Escoe whose acts I must have seen more than a dozen times in less than a year. They gave me my first feeling that I must be a part of show business.

On occasion, the Paragon boasted a mixed programme of live acts and two-reel film features, the former covering for the setting-up of the projectors and the preparation of elaborate sound effects like the roll of oil drums to give the audience the full force of the Battle of Jutland. I liked the comedies and serials, especially *The Perils of Pauline* and *The Exploits of Elaine*, starring Pearl White, whose adventures attracted a ready audience in the Mile End Road long after the lady had matured to a less energetic form of acting.

I was at an age when the charms of young women lost out to their tendency to soppiness. But Miss White, who, single-handed, could escape from a pit of poisonous vipers or extricate herself from a wafer-thin ledge over a thousand-foot precipice, was an obvious

15

exception to the rule. As for more conventional actresses, those who clutched hand to mouth and recoiled in terror whenever a mouse jumped out of the cupboard, I confess to a certain interest in their tendency to drape themselves in diaphanous costumes. It began to dawn on me that there was a world beyond Grafton Road.

Another pointer in that direction was our bi-monthly visit to Uncle Maurice whose cabinet-making business had prospered to the extent that he was able to afford a house in Stoke Newington, the first step on the way up for the Jewish immigrant who had made good. Thereafter it was but a short jump to Golders Green and ultimately to Hampstead, the pinnacle of respectability and a foretaste of heaven.

I did not like Stoke Newington which, for me, represented a stiff, starchy suit and silence at meal-times. For all his commercial acumen, the sombre Uncle Maurice was hardly a walking example of the joys of success. Still, it was made clear to me that comforts and pleasures could be had for ready cash. It was all a matter of attracting money to the right hands: mine, of course.

Spending so much time at the Paragon naturally it occurred to me that I might make my fortune on the stage. But I was not too clear as to what precisely I could do to hold an audience. Improvisations for home entertainment suggested a modest voice and a capacity for good humour which stopped some way short of rivalling Peel and Curtis or Haig and Escoe.

While practising juggling with balls of squashed newspaper it occurred to me that another well-trodden route to vast wealth was to set up as a press baron. Never one to go slow on a good idea I founded the *Grafton Street Gazette*, appointing myself proprietor and editor-in-chief. When there was no real news to speak of I made it up. It was not exactly Fleet Street at its best and I anticipated customer resistance but my parents' objection to the enterprise was less to do with journalistic ethics than the amount of glue needed to create my newspaper. They returned from a few days' holiday in Southend to find sideboard, table, chairs and much of the floor pasted up with newsprint. My fledgling business was closed forthwith.

For weeks I consoled myself by collecting sales catalogues of items we could not possibly afford as a reminder of what might be achieved by raw ambition, given a little encouragement from the adults.

My first taste of real work came with my fourteenth birthday. I was hired at fourteen shillings a week as office boy to a Houndsditch chinaware company called Lazarus and Rosenfeld, a large company with branches in America, Germany and Czechoslovakia. I spent most of my time running messages and posting parcels and cables to our customers in Britain and abroad. I was also in charge of the stamps and a petty cash box. The hardest part of the job was stamping letters so that a stamp was precisely in line with the corner of its envelope.

The chief cashier was very particular in such matters: 'You must think of every letter as an advertisement for the efficiency and dependability of this firm,' he told me.

To drive the message home, each stamp carried a perforated L & R symbol.

I was also taught how to pack chinaware into parcels. I set my mind to thinking how I might make the job more exciting.

Lew, meanwhile, had left his regular job with a women's clothing firm to set up a family partnership. Entirely on Lew's initiative he and Father started an embroidery workshop which actually made money. It might have gone on doing so if Father's health had stood up to the long hours and if Lew had not had the urge to break out into an entirely different line of business.

The boy who was good with figures and who looked set for a prosperous career in the garment trade announced that he wanted to be a dancer.

The family thought he was mad but when he pointed out how much he could earn by matching his nimble feet to a syncopated rhythm, the idea began to make sense.

And what Lew could do, I could do too. My days at Lazarus and Rosenfeld were numbered, though not for the reasons I anticipated.

Chapter 2

A s for many people the swinging sixties began and ended with
the Beatles, so for most of my generation the roaring twenties
was just another way of saying the Charleston. Not for us the thrills
of West End night life: the drinking clubs and wild parties were
reserved for the bright young things with money to burn. But the
Charleston was for anyone who could move an arm or kick a leg. It
also helped to have a sense of rhythm, a lot of energy and a total
disregard for dancing conventions as expressed in the foxtrot and the
stately waltz.

The Charleston came in from America in 1925. Having taken some
ten years to cross the Atlantic, it soon made up for lost time. One
day nobody had heard of the Charleston, the next day everybody
was talking about it, the day after that everybody was dancing it – or
so it seemed to those of us who were caught up with the excitement
of the craze.

A curiosity of the Charleston was the way in which it lent itself to
individual performance. You might start with a partner but as the
tempo built up and the action accelerated, it was the style to break
apart for a display of virtuosity which could stop other dancers in
their tracks. This made the Charleston a natural for competitions in
which star dancers could show the rest how it was done. Such was
the popularity of the Charleston as a spectator entertainment that
some of the more inventive performers took it up as a living. One
such was Lew Winogradsky. His brother followed close behind him.

Whereas in most families the devotion of two teenage boys to the
pleasures of the dance-halls might have raised eyebrows, our parents
were enthusiastic fans. Their fondness for the stage was in our favour,
I suppose, but also there was clear evidence in the number of prizes
borne home in triumph that Charleston competitions could be a
paying proposition. Even if we did not have much use for a silver-

knobbed walking-stick (the product of one of my early triumphs at the Tottenham Palais) nor yet for the three bottles of Johnnie Walker which I carried off at East Ham, these trophies were easily convertible into cash. A victory in a Charleston competition was invariably followed by a visit to the Portobello Road.

For a few months I managed to combine the excitement of competitive dancing with the dull routine of my regular job at Lazarus and Rosenfeld. It was hard going. At the back of my mind I had the vague idea of becoming a professional dancer – of following in Lew's footsteps – but, at sixteen, I was still in need of a push to start me on my way.

Meanwhile, I found a way of putting a spark into my clerical duties. Just along from Lazarus and Rosenfeld was a street bookie, a familiar figure in busy thoroughfares in the days before betting shops. Though everybody knew him and knew what he was up to he carried out his business with all the furtiveness of an international spy. He had to, otherwise he was liable to be arrested. Such was the popularity of gambling, the police were willing to turn a blind eye, but they insisted on a pretence of undercover activity to save face. I took great pleasure in the whole elaborate charade. The furtive approach, a muttered conversation, the palming of a slip of paper and a few coins, all added to the thrill of the wager.

I found out all about street bookies from my father who had been a devoted customer and, from their point of view, a profitable one since his early days in the East End. He taught me the formula for winning a lot from a little. You made a selection over three or four races but bet only on the first – in my case three pence each way – with instructions that if that horse came in ahead, part of the winnings should go on your choice for the second race and so on. The bookie who had his pitch near Lazarus and Rosenfeld soon got used to my 'any to come' selections – three pence each way on Speed of the Wind in the two thirty with any to come three pence each way on Raging Tiger in the three o'clock with any to come three pence each way on Slow Coach in the four o'clock. It was a neat trick if you could pull it off. Trouble was, I needed practice – or so my early run of losers seemed to suggest – and my modest income did not allow for the necessary investment. I had to find a way of raising some capital – a few shillings would do – but it was not the sort of proposition I could put to friends or family.

I soon found the answer. It came to me as I was going about my daily routine. As the office boy in charge of the post I had access to a large box of stamps for letters and parcels and a much smaller box of cash for cables and telegrams. While there was no chance of me misappropriating stamps (each was perforated with the distinctive L & R) or indeed the money which had to tally with the post office receipts, it occurred to me that there was a chance of linking the two sides of the operation to my financial benefit.

When next I went to the post office to despatch a telegram I paid for it partly in cash, partly in stamps. This was against the rules of the company though not of the post office who were content to take payment in their own currency, as it were. The clerk gave me a receipt which simply specified the amount spent. So it was that I was able to steal from my employer by holding back some of his cash. It was not exactly a foolproof scheme, as I was soon to discover, but in the short run it brightened up my life and made my bookmaker happy.

The turning point came with an administrative bungle made by one of my superiors. Handed an expensive overseas cable I paid for it with four shillings in cash and three shillings worth of stamps, stuck on the back of the form. I presented it to the counter clerk and waited for my receipt. Instead, he handed back the cable.

'You can't send this.'

'Why not?'

'There's no address, that's why.'

I stared at the cable. Suddenly I was a very nervous boy.

The clerk must have noticed and misinterpreted my concern. 'Don't worry, son. All you've got to do is take it back and get your boss to fill it in properly.'

But that was precisely my dilemma. I couldn't return the cable without a convincing explanation as to why it carried a three-shilling block of L & R stamps. And for the life of me, the only explanation that came to mind was the obvious one.

I walked the long way back to the office. When I was far enough away not to be recognised by passers-by, I took the cable from my pocket, tore it into small pieces and dropped them down a drain. It was a terrible waste and it put paid to any hopes I might have had of cleaning up on the St Leger but it was the only way.

Summoned to give an account of the disappearing cable, I wove a fanciful story of how the flimsy paper had been torn from my hand by a sudden gust of wind.

'I chased after it, but it went into the gutter and just as I was catching up with it, down it went.'

'Down what, exactly?' enquired Mr Lazarus, icily. There was disbelief written all over his face.

'The drain, sir. It went down the drain.'

Well, at least that part of the story was true. And for the moment, anyway, it was no matter that Mr Lazarus doubted my honesty. I had no trouble in accounting for the seven shillings – they were there on his desk – and he did not think of checking the stamps. I left him in a thoughtful mood. Back in the post-room, the chief cashier gave me a long look. It crossed my mind that maybe I was overstretching my luck.

The thought reoccurred a few days later when I learned that I was through to the semi-final of the Charleston competition currently packing them in at Ye Olde Paragon.

The event was billed for a Friday afternoon, not the best time for me, bearing in mind that I was out of favour and that, in any case, time off was granted only in the most dire circumstances. I had a feeling that a Charleston competition would not qualify.

There was only one way forward. I had to skip work.

The next Monday, I was called to account by Mr Lazarus. 'Where were you?'

'I was ill, sir.'

'You look healthy enough to me.'

'I'm feeling better today, thank you, sir.'

The pause was just long enough for Mr Lazarus to decide that lack of evidence would not deter him from asserting his authority.

'Very well, Winogradsky. From now on you can be ill in your own time. You're fired.'

I presented myself to the chief cashier for the closing ritual. As I handed over the cash book and stamps he favoured me with another long look. I started thinking ahead. What would I say to the judge? More to the point, what would I say to my mother?

The chief cashier was speaking. As speeches go, it was not much. Just one word. 'Goodbye.' I couldn't believe it. He had given not a glance at my carefully written but wholly inaccurate figures. All he wanted was to shake my hand and see me to the door. As I was departing, still mesmerised by my good fortune, he held up the cash book, the indelible record of my indiscretions.

'Chin up, Winogradsky. It's all for the best, don't you think?'

21

On the way home, cynicism got the better of me. It was my guess that, like me, my benefactor was taking more out of that company than his salary. The only difference between us was that he was operating on a bigger scale.

I forestalled family enquiries as to how I lost my job by grandly announcing that I had another one. Henceforward, I was to be a professional dancer. I even had cards printed. To anyone who asked, and to quite a few who didn't, I presented my credentials, boldly set out in heavy black type: Barnet Winogradsky, Charleston Champion of the East End.

That I was taken seriously was mostly thanks to Lew who, by my reckoning, had already blazed a trail to fame and fortune by winning the 1926 World Championship at the Albert Hall. The event was organised by the sporting and theatrical impresario, Charles B. Cochran. Fred Astaire was one of the judges.

It was heady stuff for a family of first-generation East Enders but our indomitable mother took it in her stride. What Lew won or earned, he deserved, every penny of it; the same inflexible law applied to me – and to Leslie, though at ten his talents had yet to be revealed.

It was different for the last-born – the one-year-old Rita who achieved distinction by breaking the run of male offspring but was not otherwise expected to prove herself. Convention ruled that the daughter should be transformed into a good wife and mother; to aspire to anything else was near sacrilege.

Urged on by the family, I put my heart into becoming a true professional. I learned tap dancing – largely by watching my rivals from the front of the gallery and then practising on the bedroom lino – and picked up some of the tricks of what was known as eccentric dancing, like throwing one leg behind the other while both feet were off the ground and dropping to the knees by way of taking off for a back flip. After a few weeks I had the beginnings of a routine that would just qualify me for bottom of the bill in third-rate variety. But this is hindsight. At the time I had a loftier view of my entertainment value. I took to reading the *Stage*, *Encore* and the *Performer*, the weekly papers of the variety profession, for opportunities to audition.

The advertisement to catch my eye was for boy dancers in a revue called *League of Neighbours*. I already knew a little about this show because Lew and his partner Al Gold had been taken on as two of its principal dancers. The producer was Thomas F. Convery (Charlie

Cochran set the trend for aspiring impresarios by becoming Charles B. Cochran) and the star was a popular northern comic, Albert Burdon, who got his laughs by playing off the pomposity of some figure of authority, like the chairman of a means test committee.

CHAIRMAN: What are you by profession?

ALBERT: I'm a fret-worker.

CHAIRMAN: A fret-worker?

ALBERT: Aye – if there's any work going I fret and fret.

CHAIRMAN: Have you ever done any work?

ALBERT: Yes, once, on the railway.

CHAIRMAN: On the railway? What doing?

ALBERT: You know the man that goes round tapping the wheels with a hammer?

CHAIRMAN: Yes.

ALBERT: Well I helped him listen.

CHAIRMAN: Are your relatives in business?

ALBERT: Yes – in the iron and steel business. Me mother irons and me father steals.

I was convinced that *League of Neighbours* was my opportunity for the big time.

The auditions were held in a room off Oxford Street. There were some forty hopefuls gathered, nearly all of them from dance schools where the Charleston competitions were not widely regarded as a suitable training for a stage career. Another difference between us was in manner and style. I was the boy from the East End, streetwise and cocksure but without any claims to sophistication. My new friends started from the other side of the track. They talked and joked like smart people who took their social superiority for granted. And they were so light on their feet. Not delicate exactly (never believe that there is anything soft about dancing) but a bit feathery in the way they pranced around. I was enormously impressed and did my best to fit in though my voice was ill suited to a high-pitched flute and I drew the line at calling everyone 'Darling'.

23

The audition was a two-minute dance of our choice. I did my Charleston routine to a piano accompaniment which compensated variety for pace and with nine others was told to report back at three o'clock to sign contracts.

Over tea and buns at Lyons Corner House, the conversation with the other favourites was about how much Thomas F. Convery was likely to pay for our services. I had the advantage, or so I imagined, of knowing that Lew had already struck a deal. It was inconceivable to me that his brother should be lower in the pecking order, though I kept this to myself. When we lined up for the afternoon formalities I anticipated a breakthrough.

The three in front of me had contracts pushed in front of them which they signed without comment. Then it was my turn. Facing me behind a trestle table was one of Convery's assistants, an older man (why were production assistants always so much older in those days?) in an oversized suit who could smoke a cigarette down to the butt without ever taking it out of his mouth.

'Name?'

'Barnet Winogradsky.'

He pointed to where I was supposed to sign the contract. 'OK, you're in. You start Monday at three pounds a week.'

Three miserable pounds! That was way below what I considered to be my market value.

He pointed to where I was supposed to sign the contract.

'I'm not accepting three pounds. I want fifteen pounds a week.'

The production assistant allowed the cigarette to hang on his lower lip. 'Is that right?' He tilted his chair. 'You want fifteen pounds,' he said sweetly. 'You can have fifteen pounds. But not as a chorus boy and not from Thomas F. Convery. Now, get out!'

I heard him say just one more word – 'Next' – before I was back on the street wondering if I needed to improve my sales technique.

It was in search of wisdom that I got in touch with Albert Sutan, later better known as the comedian Hal Monty. He was a near-contemporary of mine, another East Ender, who danced his way into show business. He was not exactly in the first division but he was making a living.

'You're aiming too high,' he told me.

'So what do I do?'

'Start at the bottom, like the rest of us. There are plenty of bookings if you know where to look.'

He made sense but I needed clearer guidance.

Albert had an idea. 'I've got two bookings for next week. I can't do both. Why don't you go to Gravesend in my place?'

'How do I know they'll want me?'

'That's the easy part,' said Albert whose knowledge of how the world worked was beginning to make a powerful impression. 'You go as me. They've never seen Albert Sutan so how will they know the difference?'

Chastened by my failure to join the *League of Neighbours*, I took a suitably modest view of my accomplishments but I was pretty confident of passing muster as an Albert Sutan dance-alike. Anyway, it was worth a try.

'It's six pounds for the week,' said Albert. 'Four for you and two for me.'

That settled it. It was a better rate than Thomas F. Convery was offering, if only for one week.

Gravesend may well have boasted a theatre but if so, I never found it. What I did find, and I had to check twice to believe I was in the right place, was a hut pretending to be a theatre. It had a pebbledash front with a crenellated tower on each side, built high to distract attention from the corrugated iron roof over the auditorium.

Inside were rows of spring-back seats which could have done service as mousetraps. Heating and ventilation were non-existent and when it rained, the metal roof gave a whole new dimension to theatrical acoustics.

Barnet Winogradsky alias Albert Sutan opened the show. My energetic dancing was supposed to set the mood for the juggler, the baritone ('The Road to Mandalay' and excerpts from Gilbert and Sullivan) and the stand-up comic, all of whom were fighting a losing battle long before I entered their lives. The hint of defensiveness is intentional. There were those who claimed, uncharitably, that I was solely responsible for a disastrous week. My version is that we all made our contribution.

My problem was timing. I had a two-minute act for a ten-minute spot. A brief and chaotic rehearsal did nothing to warn me of the predicament and it was not until just before I went on that I realised the fix I was in. Since the manager was the type to demand value for money – ten minutes was what he wanted and ten minutes was what he was going to get – my only chance was to pray for an encore. After a first session of throwing myself about the stage, I could tell

25

this was not going to be easy. The applause was of a volume which suggested that the audience had had enough. But the manager was in the wings and I did not fancy losing my and Albert's money. So I gave them the encore they didn't want, and when that was over I gave them another and with four minutes to go I gave them two more to make the round ten minutes. I went off in total silence.

The manager aimed a passing shot: 'Is that what you call an act?'

I was too exhausted to reply. I had just enough strength to get to the dressing-room. And I still had the second house and five more days to go.

Back in London I had a few words for Albert Sutan who still seemed to think that he had done me a favour. While I was unable to disillusion him on that score (he showed no remorse as he took his money) I did manage to persuade him that our style of eccentric dancing was best suited to a double act.

'We'd need an agent,' said Albert, who had a strong grasp of the priorities. 'And it's no use calling ourselves Winogradsky and Sutan; we have to think up a stage name people can remember.'

Lew had solved the last problem by cutting off two sides of the family name and calling himself Grad which others quickly converted to Grade. That left me with Wino, which even in those days had unsavoury implications. Stumped for anything better I decided to follow Lew's example – show business, I was sure, had room for two Grades – while Albert anglicised his name to Sutton.

So it was that as Grade and Sutton we put together an eight-minute act (even as a partnership we couldn't think of enough steps to satisfy the demands of Gravesend) and went to see Syd Burns, a big name among agents whose latest triumph was a young comedian called Tommy Trinder, the best, it was said, since Max Miller.

'If we want to get to the top, we have to aim at the top,' declared Albert.

I did not doubt him for a moment. My confidence was further boosted when Syd Burns, having agreed to let us audition for him in his office, proclaimed our act to be 'not half bad' (which Albert assured me was praise indeed) and promised us immediate work. But reaction set in when I heard that our first job was a weekend booking at Thames Ditton for two pounds all in, including travel. Even that small sum eluded us. Understanding all too well the psychology of young entertainers and their irrational belief in luck, the theatre manager had furnished the dressing-room with a one-armed bandit. By the end of the evening we had lost our fee, with interest.

I wish I could say that we learned from this experience but neither of us was much good at holding on to money – what little we had. After my contribution to the family budget the competing claims on my income were mostly of a sporting nature with the inevitable wager sometimes reducing but more often increasing the cost of each event.

Girls were not an expensive item, largely because I did not get to meet very many. It was not for the want of trying. Every time I went dancing I did my best impersonation of Douglas Fairbanks, but when on the rare occasions I found a partner who would let me take her home, the romantic interlude was brief and inglorious. Having made our way to her parents' house we would sit together on the window-sill debating the next move.

'Let me come in.'

'No. Mum will hear.'

'She won't. I'll be quiet.'

Perseverance brought a small reward.

'Well, all right. But just for a little while.'

It was never more than ten minutes, side by side on the sofa, with the occasional lunge from me leading to a quick kiss and fumble. I knew there had to be more to love but while waiting for the revelation I was happy to look for excitement elsewhere.

Like many other Jewish boys, I was brought up to revere the name of David Mendoza, a boxing champion from the days of bare fist fighting, who set the standard in the one sport in which Jews have traditionally excelled. Known by his supporters as the 'Light of Israel' he was one of the folk heroes of the East End whose achievements were held up as an example almost a century after his death. I have lost count of the number of friends who tried to emulate Mendoza. I watched them all, in victory and defeat, at the Blackfriars Ring or the Holborn Stadium or at lesser venues where a match of whatever quality could be guaranteed to draw a crowd. I had two good friends in the East End boxing fraternity, Lew Pinkus and Jack Donn. Jack and I were at school together though in those days he was known as Isaac Goldberg. Variety was not the only business where names could be a problem.

It was the production side of boxing that interested me as much as anything. A big fight was theatre in its most dramatic form and it is surely no coincidence that the theatrical impresarios of the day, like

27

Cochran, also put their money into sporting events. In fact, the first I ever heard of Cochran, who was later to enter my life in a more direct way, was as the promoter of the fight between the heavyweight champion Joe Beckett and the Frenchman Georges Carpentier. This was in 1919 at the Holborn Stadium where Cochran built up interest in the fight by charging the then unheard-of price of twenty-five guineas for ringside seats, and five guineas to stand. It was because the prices were so outrageous that the fight caught on. And it was all over in seventy-three seconds. It is said that one patron, having paid for one of the best seats, missed the blow that felled Beckett because he bent down to pick up his hat. But Cochran came out of it a richer man and the envy of his rivals. I guess that he made more from the Beckett–Carpentier match than from most of his theatrical enterprises.

The same flair for showmanship was characteristic of another great sportsman, Herbert Chapman, the football manager who came down to Arsenal in 1925 after achieving a hat trick of league championships for Huddersfield, a club that was virtually unknown until it was blessed with the Chapman magic.

He was a true impresario who easily transferred my allegiance from West Ham, the first loyalty of East End boys, by his aggressive buying of star players like the Sunderland scorer Charles Buchan who was promised one hundred pounds for every goal (he chalked up nineteen in his first season). But Chapman created more than a top-class team. He was always ready to try out ideas. Highbury Grove was the first ground to be floodlit and Arsenal players were the first to appear with numbers on their backs. It doesn't sound much now but then it was controversy all the way. I loved every moment. Chapman's outstanding coup was to persuade London Transport to rename the tube station nearest Highbury Grove after the home team. What marvellous advertising. Arsenal tube station is as much a memorial to the Chapman genius as the Cup Final triumph – against Huddersfield of all clubs – in 1930.

More people went to matches than ever before or since but I don't recall any of the hooliganism that is commonplace today. Not that we were at all shy of expressing our feelings. Great roars of conflicting advice descended from the terraces on to the heads of players and, more particularly, the referee, who had to be wrong whatever he did. It was, I felt, a harder life than treading the boards and perhaps for this reason I took pleasure from the Saturday match. Here was inspiration from great performers who staked their popularity every time they went out on to the field. As I drifted away with the crowd after the final whistle, it was always with the strengthened conviction that I too could promote myself out of the ordinary if I really set my mind to it.

It was thirty years later when I had long since sacrificed live football to the working weekend that brother Leslie tried to revive my interest.

'You remember what it was like in the old days? It's the same now. Even better. You don't even have to stand any more.'

As a director of Leyton Orient, Leslie was naturally an enthusiast. But there was more to this conversation. He was leading up to something.

'You work too hard. You don't give yourself a chance to relax.'

'What do you want me to do? Support Leyton Orient?'

'You could join me on the board. Then you'd have a seat in the directors' box.'

The cost of this privilege was higher than I had anticipated – a straight purchase of five thousand pounds worth of shares and an interest-free loan of twenty-five thousand. And this for a club which was languishing in the Third Division. But Leslie had a point. The pressures of show business were beginning to wear me down. I decided to unwind with Leyton Orient.

At my first match as I waited with the other directors for the kick-off, one of the officials came into the bar and sidled up to the chairman.

'They're coming in slowly,' he said. 'It won't be near capacity.' The chairman looked serious. As a producer with one or two marginal shows on my hands, I knew how he felt. There was no getting away from it, football and show business had something in common. At the interval, the directors gave each other long looks. There were murmurs of a bad first half and doubts voiced about one of the star players who was thought to be performing below par. Again, the thought occurred, this is much like show business. And when, in the closing seconds of the match, the chairman was slipped a note showing the attendance figures and told, 'It's down on last week, probably the weather,' I saw the ghost of Herbert Chapman and I knew for a certainty that football was exactly like show business. Saturday with Leyton Orient would be not so much a relaxing break as a rerun of every other day in my life.

I did a five-year stint as a director of Leyton Orient. The first three years were a glorious rise from the bottom of the League to the dizzy heights of the First Division. I could take no credit for this but because my first appearance at the club coincided with its change of fortune I was popularly assumed to be the behind-the-scenes architect of success. I had only to arrive at the ground for a crowd to gather round my car pressing me for autographs and calling for three cheers for Bernie.

Then we started the long slide back to the Third Division, an apparently unstoppable fall from grace for me as much as for the club. Now, instead of cheers, I had to get used to boos and catcalls. When my car was badly scratched I decided it was time to get out. By way of making the parting easier I told my fellow directors I would forget about the twenty-five-thousand-pound loan. As I made for the door, the chairman called after me: 'What do you want me to do with your shares?'

I forced a smile. I think he understood.

To return to my teenage years, there is one other sport I must mention. Racing greyhounds after a mechanical hare only began in 1926, though within a year there were so many tracks the National Greyhound Racing Society was formed to standardise the rules. Since races were held in the evening, under floodlights, the opportunities for ordinary punters to attend were far greater than with horse racing.

Naturally, I was often to be seen at White City and West Ham, with rarer appearances at Harringay, Wimbledon and Catford.

The discovery that a night at the dogs could be as exciting as a day with the horses coincided with the realisation that there is no such thing in life as a safe bet. Despite the best advice from old hands, I finished one evening minus a week's wages. I was terrified to go home before I had thought of a reasonable excuse so I made my way to the Charing Cross Road in search of friends from the lower reaches of show business. One of them would surely put me up. A favourite meeting point was the Express Dairy on the Charing Cross Road, a coffee bar which stayed open all hours, largely for the benefit of out-of-work performers who wanted to catch up on the gossip and stay close to their agents, all of whom had offices in the area.

On this occasion I found a sprinkling of regulars but no one who was in a position to be my host for the night. There were not many of us who had spare rooms or even a spare sofa and as the Charleston Champion of the East End, I had too much pride to contemplate sleeping on someone's floor.

I was talking to another young dancer about the usual problem –
how to escape from the bottom of the bill – when he nodded towards
the door.

'There's Johnny Riscoe. He could fix you up; if he's feeling
generous.'

Johnny was rather grand, a young up-and-coming comedian who
was earning good money and was able to live independently. I put
the question.

He smiled benignly. 'Sure,' he said, 'be my guest.'

It was a kind gesture but I fancy that he enjoyed the chance to
bestow a favour on a newcomer. It confirmed him as a leader of the
pack. But I thought, I mustn't make this too easy. If I'm not careful
it will look as if I am on for every free handout. So having thanked
him most politely, I enquired, 'By the way, Johnny, do you have a
bathroom?' It was ungracious of me and I deserved the park bench,
but I did savour his double-take as he registered the sheer cheek of
the boy. And he still let me stay the night.

My initiation into variety continued in its bruising fashion. If there
seemed to be no end to the succession of third-rate bookings I suppose
I should have been grateful that there was also no end to the
succession of producers willing to chance their arm on tatty revues.

The technique for putting together a show was an early interest of
mine. The usual starting point was a whisper that another producer
was selling off the wardrobe and scenery from a show that had either
failed or run its course. Buying a few props at a knock-down price
was a signal to the agents that work of a sort was on hand. They were
soon buzzing around the producer pushing the claims of the slow
movers on their client list – those on the way up and the even greater
number on the way down. The star names did not need pushing.
Anyway they were long past being interested in provincial towns that
were not part of the Moss or Stoll circuits. The producer of the sort
of show in which I served my apprenticeship had to rely on spotting
crowd-pulling talent that the big boys had missed. Nine times out of
ten, he was out of luck.

One such was Manville Morton who, having made money on a
provincial tour of his revue *That's Cheerful*, tried for double or quits
with a sequel, ominously entitled: *Sure Thing*. Years later I was
reminded of the dangers of tempting providence when I went to New
York to see a revue called *Alive and Kicking*. A critic had savaged
it with a single phrase: 'Dead and Buried'. No critics came to *Sure*

Thing but if they had, the best they could have found to say about the show was that the talents of the chorus girls were, in all respects, above the average.

The rest of the line-up was barely adequate. At the top of the bill was a comedian called Billy Hayes who specialised in the tongue-twisting songs made popular by Wilkie Bard, songs like 'She Sells Sea Shells on the Sea Shore', 'The Leith Police Dismisseth Us' and 'Stewed Prunes and Prisms', as sung by a beauty consultant (Hayes in drag) to those of her patients with over-sized mouths:

> Stewed prunes and prisms,
> Stewed prunes and prisms!
> That will make your mouth so small
> People won't know you've got a mouth at all.
> You don't need to study
> The -Ologies or -Isms,
> But just screw up your lips
> Like a solar eclipse
> And say 'Stewed prunes and prisms'.

Then he told of the lady with the large mouth who kept saying 'Stewed prunes and prisms' till her mouth became so small that she had to open it with a shoe-horn in order to eat a banana.

Elsewhere on the bill we had the Jocelyns' Magical Act, Rennie Stallard (the Welsh Nightingale) and Grade and Sutton who as usual appeared at the beginning of each half.

We opened in Deal where, taking into account that it was early October, about midway between the summer season and the Christmas holiday, we did reasonable business. After that it was downhill all the way. At Woking the conductor was drunk and the local replacement did not live up to expectations; at Faversham they had just had a bad week and the audiences stayed away, presumably to recuperate; at St Alban's, Morton's partner walked out taking whatever spare cash he could lay his hands on. This left us with a single date – the Bijou Theatre at Rye. As our train arrived we saw the cast of the previous week's entertainment leaving from another platform. Recognising fellow martyrs they shouted from the carriage windows. I couldn't hear what was said but their thumbs down needed no interpretation.

Rennie Stallard could certainly hit the high notes, but 'Land of My

Fathers' in Welsh was not what they wanted to hear on the south coast. There were shouts from the audience and pennies were thrown on to the stage. The reappearance of the chorus in a high-kicking dance helped to concentrate attention but not for long. In the interval there was a fight in the bar. I did not see how anyone could blame us for what happened outside the auditorium but the manager was made yet more nervous and spent the entire second half at the rear of the stalls walking up and down giving out sighs of anguish.

After Billy Hayes died the death and the curtain fell to raucous jeers, Manville Morton called us together on stage. 'The show is cancelled from tonight. I don't have another date. I'll pay you up to the end of the week. I'm sorry.'

And that was the last anyone heard of *Sure Thing*. Grade and Sutton announced their availability but there were no takers. Back in London we made straight for our agent, Syd Burns, who gave us a sympathetic hearing.

'Don't worry,' he said. 'You'll get your break.'

'So where are we going wrong?'

Syd thought for a moment before coming up with the stock excuse for those glued to the bottom rung of the ladder. 'The name is wrong. I should have seen it before. Two Grades is one too many. People get confused.'

'So what do we call ourselves?'

He surveyed the walls covered with posters and autographed photographs. 'There's a big act in America, two boys like yourselves. They call themselves the Dufor Boys.' He took up a pencil and scribbled a few variations on a large pad. Then he sat back in his swivel chair and considered the alternatives. 'I've got it. Delfont. You can call yourselves the Delfont Boys.'

So that was settled. We went into his office as Grade and Sutton and came out as the Delfont Boys.

It was a new beginning.

Chapter 3

Almost immediately the offers of work started coming in, starting with two weeks with the Alfredos Orchestra. Doubtless there was more to it than our change of billing but I do believe that having a stage name we felt comfortable with increased our confidence and made us a sharper and more entertaining act.

The routine we settled on was to open together in a high-speed display of eccentric dancing, weaving and writhing our way through a succession of muscle-stretching contortions. Then Albert did his solo and I followed with my version of the Charleston. Our finale was a slow motion dance to the death, fighting with knives against flickering lights to give the effect of jerky movements as in a silent movie. We borrowed the idea from Nervo and Knox (later of the Crazy Gang) who naturally favoured a comic variation. Though a simple piece of trickery, it never failed to win applause.

The Delfont Boys went down well on a tour of the number two spots – towns like Grimsby, Scunthorpe and Greenock – where audiences were notoriously hard to please. After about a year we were promoted to the Moss circuit of number one dates – Brighton, Birmingham, Manchester, Liverpool, Newcastle and the Glasgow Empire, the last a tough proposition for English performers whose voices betrayed their origins but easier for 'dumb' acts like the Delfont Boys.

For the first time in my life I really felt myself to be part of the show business fraternity. I loved the musty smell of the theatres, the stage door gossip, the nod of recognition from the star of the show (it was too much to expect conversation with such eminences though Harry Tate once bid me 'Good evening', an experience which kept me happy for a month and when I worked with Sir Harry Lauder at Aberdeen he gave me a friendly pat on the back).

Life took on a regular pattern: a week in one town was much like a week in any other town. We arrived by train and made straight for the theatre. We had two heavy cases of props to drop off but more to the point we were eager to check how we came out on the poster billing. The Delfont Boys were invariably at the tail end but honour was saved and our self-esteem boosted by several degrees if we appeared in a large typeface. In this as in so many other matters we were entirely at the mercy of the theatre manager. If he had seen and liked our act we could usually rely on a respectable showing. But that was the limit of his benevolence. For instance, we knew without asking which dressing-room was ours. It was the one at the top of the stairs at the end of the longest corridor. There was no point in complaining if the lights were dim or if there was nothing to sit on. Our lowly status dictated that we had to make do.

Having checked out the theatre, the next priority was to make friends with our landlady. Every stage memoir of the pre-war years contains a horror story of theatrical digs but I have only the fondest memories of boarding out in the provinces. It could be that my formative years in the East End had prepared me for a modest assessment of home comforts but it is more likely that as a fast-growing youngster my regard for the theatrical landlady was centred on her kitchen. If her cooking was up to scratch and the portions were generous, I had no other favours to ask.

At best the menu consisted of breakfast of porridge, bacon and eggs, toast and butter with as much tea as we could drink; a lunch of soup, roast beef and Yorkshire pudding followed by treacle tart or plum duff; a high tea of cakes and toast and, to round off the day, a fish and chip supper after the show. And all for twenty-five shillings a week.

We soon got to know the best digs, though getting in was another matter. There were superior landladies who refused all but the top names. That was all right by us. We simply told ourselves that if we weren't good enough this time around, the day would come . . .

At the end of the week, each guest was expected to sign the book and, if he wanted to come back, to pen a suitable compliment to the landlady in the column headed 'Remarks'. For the initiated this was also a way of passing on coded messages such as LDOK meaning that the charms of the landlady's daughter were to be recommended. At digs in Glasgow the entry appeared so often the landlady was moved to ask what it meant, only to be told that the acronym referred to the quality of her dinners. Suitably flattered she pressed newcomers to add their endorsement. 'Don't forget the LDOK, will you, dear?' It was only when a polite but elderly actor of the old school thanked her kindly but said he was long past that sort of thing that she began to have doubts.

If on a scale of generosity and kindliness landladies were among the high scorers, theatre managers rarely got off the base line. They ruled like petty dictators. All power was in their hands. When for some reason a theatre manager took against a performer a stiffly worded report to the Moss or Stoll head office could put his career into reverse, sending him back to the number two dates and on down to the depths of variety – wakes week in Halifax.

There is no sense of personal grievance in all this. Given the limitations of our act, the report cards for the Delfont Boys were unfailingly complimentary.

But in our dealings with the managers we left nothing to risk. Pomposity was treated with the respect it did not deserve. Mostly we kept out of the way, trying not to catch the manager's eye.

The only time we were pleased to see him, or, in the larger theatres, his deputy, was on Friday evening between performances. This was when 'the ghost walked' or to put it more prosaically, when we were paid. It was always in cash, counted out in front of us from the contents of a black tin box.

On a good week Albert and I could make fifteen pounds between us. After deducting our agent's 10 per cent and paying for lodgings, I still felt well off, the more so because what was then my favourite pastime, sitting in the cinema, was free of charge to performers who were appearing locally. All I had to do for a ticket was to present my card at the box-office. How this concession came about I have no idea but whoever thought of it was responsible for keeping me out of mischief in the afternoons.

Most mornings I slept in and if there was any time after breakfast I wandered the shops. A show poster in a window was a guarantee of a 10 per cent discount, an attractive bait to buy what I might otherwise have done very well without. On the other hand, the only real extravagance was buying a saxophone and this, I told myself, was more an investment than a purchase. I persuaded Albert to follow suit, though in his case the money went on a trumpet.

We practised together until immoderate criticism from fellow lodgers persuaded us we had better stick to dancing. After several months, my complete repertoire consisted of a single tune: 'That's

My Weakness Now'. Later, when I hit a bad patch, I sold the instrument for half the price I paid for it. I was never tempted to repeat the experiment.

The day came when Syd Burns thought we were ready for another step up. He arrived unexpectedly in Birmingham with the news that the Moss booking agent was willing to try us out on London audiences. This was not an automatic passport to the West End. We are talking of the days when there was a music hall for just about every stop on the underground. Performers could work for more than a year in London without appearing twice in the same theatre or appearing at all within two miles of Shaftesbury Avenue.

But we were not in the least worried. After a fair run of the provinces we told each other that it was only a matter of time before the Palladium and the Alhambra beckoned. Meanwhile, we were happy to ply our talents at the Stratford, Hackney and Shepherd's Bush Empires.

We felt like royalty as we stepped off the train at Euston though, having spent all on a celebratory thrash, the effect was somewhat muted by the long walk to the East End. The suitcases weighed a ton. For two stars in the making it was not much of a homecoming.

London variety increased my earning power. A good dance act was worth up to thirty pounds a week at a time when youngsters of my age but with a better education thought themselves lucky to be making a tenth as much. But we worked hard for our money – performing twice nightly for six days with at least two matinées – and we had to bear the insecurity of not quite knowing where our next date was coming from.

When there were no bookings and after days of hanging about the Charing Cross Road without hearing a word from Syd Burns, I took to growing a moustache. Immediately an offer came through, I shaved it off. In a perverse way, I thought it an achievement that over two years I was unable to sprout a full foliage – I was never out of a job long enough.

The high spots of 1928 were appearances at the Holborn Empire, the Alhambra and the Palladium. The Holborn Empire was the most luxurious of London's variety halls. Even the gallery had proper seats with a padded leather covering instead of the usual wooden benches. But to enjoy the full palatial splendour of the place you had to see it from the centre stalls or the front of the dress circle. The walls were of polished marble dressed with crimson hangings, the rich red carrying through to the plush seats, a thick pile carpet and the curtain. The Holborn Empire could seat two thousand with comfort – and I do mean comfort.

It was Max Miller's favourite theatre though his style of comedy – almost a conspiracy between him and his audience to take everything the wrong way – seemed to call for a cosier, more intimate setting. But this was Miller's genius, to turn a vast audience into a gathering of close friends who knew how to take a nod and a wink. He would offer jokes from two books – the white book (clean) and the blue book (rude). The clean jokes invariably featured his wife.

'I always have a wonderful time when I go on my holidays because I haven't got one of those wives who says, "Where've you been? How much have you spent? Who've you been with?" She doesn't say that – she comes with me. No, listen . . .'

The rude jokes were really quite tame double meanings. 'It's the way I tells them,' he would assure his audience and he was right. It was all in the delivery.

'I was down the club the other day and they wanted me to give a talk. You know, to the lads. So they said, "What are you going to talk about?" and I said, "Sex." No, stop it, listen, what are you laughing at now? Anyway, I went back to the wife and I said, "I'll be out next Wednesday. I'm giving a talk at the club." And she said, "What about?" Well . . . No, listen . . . I couldn't tell her, could I? So I said, "Flying." Really, that's what I said.

'Anyway, it went well. It really did. A few days later, someone who heard me met my wife in the street. He told her, "Your husband knows a thing or two. He gave a smashing talk." Well, my wife, she couldn't believe it. She couldn't, lady. No, wait. She said, "What, him? What does he know? He's only been up twice. The first time he was sick and the second time his hat blew off." Ere . . .'

The Delfont Boys shared the bill with Max Miller just once – not at the Holborn Empire but at the Alhambra, another of the extravagantly designed Edwardian theatres that made the customer feel privileged to be let in. The Alhambra had had a curious history. With the decline of the music hall after the First World War, it had gone over to ballet and had kept to the serious side of the business until 1922 when the management decided that music hall, now called variety, was worth a second try. For the next seven years the Alhambra thrived on a quick turnover of popular stars and promising newcomers. In the second group was Gracie Fields who emerged famous from an otherwise forgettable revue called *Mr Tower of London*. That was in 1923.

Apart from the boast of saying we had done it, the excitement of sharing the programme with Max Miller was the prospect of being noticed by the critics. In those days, every national paper covered the big variety shows, giving them as much space as any West End production. Since there was only so much a critic could write about Max Miller who, like everyone else in variety, worked within a recognisable formula, there was always the chance of a mention of a new if lesser act, even one that opened the bill. In the event, we struck lucky with the *Telegraph* critic who gave us three lines, ending with the prophecy, 'The Delfont Boys will go far.'

Someone must have taken him seriously because shortly afterwards we were booked for one week of the Palladium Christmas show. I took this as a clear signal that we had arrived and went around telling everybody the good news. A certain amount of euphoria was justified. After a few patchy years in which the Palladium had played host to revues, circuses, even films without making money, it was thriving as never before under George Black who, with his deputy Val Parnell, was soon to control the entire Moss Empire circuit. Then, as now, the opportunity to play the Palladium was a high distinction for any artiste. How we all revered that theatre.

Thankfully, it has survived and prospered, bucking the trend which led to the destruction of the other great music halls. Today, I look at the Holborn Empire and see the Pearl Assurance offices, at the Alhambra and see the Leicester Square Odeon but I look at the Palladium and see the Palladium, the living proof of the staying power of top-class light entertainment. Long may it thrive.

The Christmas show for 1928 (interestingly, it had no title; presumably the Palladium was its own best advertising) starred the Duncan Sisters (Rosetta and Vivian) an American act popular for their hill-billy songs and Nat Mills and Bobbie, 'The Rare Pair', a husband and wife act who got their laughs by taking everything too literally.

NAT: You've got hold of the wrong end of the stick.

BOBBIE: What stick?

NAT: When I say, 'You've got hold of the wrong stick,' I don't mean there is a stick, I mean there isn't a stick!

BOBBIE: You're talking through your hat.

NAT: What hat?

BOBBIE: When I say, 'You're talking through your hat,' I don't mean there is a hat, I mean there isn't a hat!

NAT: Oh, let's get on with it. (Their catchphrase which they took with them to radio.)

The Delfont Boys opened the second half, not at all a bad position and certainly much better than opening the first half.

I still have the programme – pure nostalgia for those of a certain age. The top price was two shillings and ten pence for the best stalls; a balcony seat was a shilling. An after-show supper could be had for seven shillings and sixpence at the Casanova in Regent Street ('Comfort, Conviviality and Charm') or three shillings at Pinoli's ('Private rooms for club and Masonic functions'). Several advertisements were placed by money lenders – '£100 to £10,000 without security' – a reminder of the problems business people were having in trying to keep going in a recession. Ever mindful of the health and comfort of its patrons, the Palladium was 'scientifically cooled by the Ozonair system of ventilation' and 'disinfected throughout with Jeyes' Fluid'.

The critics gave the show a head start with an enthusiastic welcome to 'super-variety', despite a first-night near disaster when the Three Demons, a cycling team who did their act on a fast revolving table, missed their timing and careered off into the wings. Two of them went back for a second try, leaving their colleague in need of hospital treatment. Judging by the laughter the audience thought it was all part of the show.

There was praise for Rafayette's dogs, an act distinguished by the curiosity of having the trainer off stage, signalling directions from the wings, so that it looked as if fifteen terriers were performing their 'elopement by motorcycle' without human intervention; plaudits for Joe Termini, the 'somnolent melodist'; for Archie Glen, one of the many comedians to portray the 'inebriated gentleman'; and a resounding cheer for the Delfont Boys who, according to one perceptive reviewer, are 'here to show that the new school, in spite of those who yearn for the good old days, is up to variety's highest standards'.

And then – silence. We finished at the Palladium in the last week before Christmas. By the end of January we were still waiting for the summons to greater glory. By the end of February the money was running out and we were ready to take any job. Still – nothing.

During the long hours at the Express Dairy café, waiting for Syd Burns to pop his head round the door, I debated with Albert where we had gone wrong. His theory was that we had priced ourselves out of the market.

'Obvious, isn't it? Now we've been on at the Palladium everyone thinks we'll ask too much.'

I could see what he meant. It would not have been so bad if the Delfont Boys had been promotable to a higher spot on the programme but eccentric dancing was essentially a warm-up act with its natural place at the opening of the first or second half. This was precisely where producers did not like spending money, preferring to concentrate resources on the top of the bill, on names that were sparkling enough to attract business whatever the quality of the supporting acts.

Another factor counting against us was that variety generally was in a poor state of health. Competition from the cinema was beginning to bite but the closure of a succession of variety halls had as much to do with the miserable state of the country. The length of the dole queue was fair measure of the fall in audiences for live entertainment. The unemployed had no money for frivolities. More than once we thought of trying America.

'We'd have to change our name again,' said Albert. 'The other Delfont Boys wouldn't be too happy if we started moving in on their territory.'

A less radical move but one that could serve the purpose of keeping us in funds until prospects at home took a turn for the better, was to work on the continent. Like us, the French and Germans had their economic problems but, according to the grapevine, they were spending more, not less, on entertainment, maybe as a way of forgetting their troubles. Eccentric dancing was still a novelty over the Channel and there was good money for those with an inside track record. Moreover, as a dumb act we didn't have to worry about crossing the linguistic boundaries.

Syd Burns was enthusiastic. 'Look on it as a break. When you come back you'll be fresh for another round of the number one spots.'

All we were short of was an actual booking, an omission that was made good by Syd talking to Rottenburg and Goldin, an agency

41

specialising in exporting variety talent. We were offered a month at the music hall which was to Paris what the Palladium was to London.

Our parents came to see us off on the boat-train.

I had no idea of what I was getting into. Not counting the family trek from Russia which I was too young to remember, I knew nothing of foreign travel, let alone working and living abroad. Few youngsters did. Though I hardly realised it at the time, I learned more in the next three years than ever I could have picked up at school. Travel was my basic education.

One piece of received wisdom that had already made its impression on me was the Parisian attitude to sex. Everybody assured me that I was on my way to sin city. Even my mother, with her frequent admonitions to 'be careful' only served to encourage speculation.

For my part, I felt in urgent need of enlightenment. Just how naïve I was can be gathered from my experience with *The Mustard Club*, a touring revue with a lead singer, a rather attractive girl, who seemed to take a fancy to me. I was standing in the wings waiting to go on when she propositioned me.

'Would you like to come round to my lodgings tomorrow after the show?'

This jolted me but I managed to say, 'Yes. Very much. Thank you.'

She turned to go. I stood as she walked a couple of steps, then she looked back. 'Oh, and bring some Rendells Pessaries with you.'

That's funny, I thought, for a slim girl she's very keen on sweets. The next day, I made for the very best confectioners I knew. Joining a crowd of people at the counter I announced my purchase in a loud, clear voice: 'A box of Rendells Pessaries, please.'

The assistant, an older man, gave me a wry smile. 'You don't want a sweet shop, sonny. You need a chemist.'

After that, you can see why I looked to Paris for a crash course in living.

First impressions were not encouraging. I was struck by the tall buildings and narrow streets, the profusion of balconies (unknown in the East End), the lavish window displays in food shops, the newspaper kiosks, the streetside cafés and the smell of strong cigarettes. But it was all so staid and respectable. Where were the voluptuous women I expected to see on every corner? With his greater knowledge of the world, Albert assured me that I should not judge too quickly.

We made our way to Montmartre, notorious for its low life. It was also the district for cheap hotels, which happened to be our more immediate interest. We booked in to a pension called the Olympic on the rue Fontaine, close by the Moulin Rouge.

That evening we went out to explore the neighbourhood. 'Now what do you think?' asked Albert as we sat over drinks, contemplating our new world from a bar stool.

I looked out on the crowded pavements, the winking lights of clubs and cabarets, the pavements crowded with sharp-eyed men looking for a good night out and doe-eyed women only too happy to help them find it.

I was open-mouthed with wonderment. I may have been a little shocked. 'Well, it's different,' was all I could find to say.

The next day we found our way to the Empire for our initiation into French music hall. We were shown to a dressing-room, small but cosier than those we were used to at home and told to wait until we were called on stage for a run-through of the new acts. So far, communication between two non-French-speaking performers and the non-English-speaking management had been conducted by sign language supported by single words like theatre and artiste familiar to both sides. It was a lengthy but serviceable process and I was fast gaining confidence in my ability to get across a message. Albert cheerfully nominated me as official spokesman for the Delfont Boys.

The first true test of my linguistic skills was provided by a doorman who came into the dressing-room with his hand outstretched.

'*Argent pour le claque,*' he said.

I was lost. I fell back on another familiar theatrical word. '*Reprise, s'il vous plaît.*'

He tried again. '*Argent pour le claque,*' he declared firmly.

I turned to Albert. 'It sounds as if he wants us to pay him to clap.'

'Is that right?' said my ever helpful partner. 'Well, tell him to get lost.'

But somehow I felt that a brush-off would be counter-productive. Instead, I gave the man a few francs which seemed to please him. Later, I found out that the money was not for him but for selected customers in the gallery who, for a small bribe, raised the volume of their applause. The more generous performers were rewarded with shouts for an encore which may not have done much for their self-esteem but certainly encouraged those in the more expensive seats to believe they were getting their money's worth. I concluded that the French could teach us a thing or two about keeping audiences happy.

This view was confirmed when I came to look at the running order of the programme. At the top of the bill was an act unheard of in Britain – not a comedian, or a singer, or dancer but a striptease artiste called Fifi Grande.

Striptease was a popular feature of old variety shows in Paris and had been so since the early part of the century. And it was not only the French who were devotees . . . British and American tourists, who were used to a public code of morality which allowed for outrageously suggestive songs and jokes but excluded any form of nudity, turned up in droves to see what they would almost certainly have condemned back home.

What they saw for the price of their tickets was tame by modern standards – at least in the famous music halls like the Empire, the Casino and the Folies Bergère.

The skill of striptease was to create a scene in which the performer could have some convincing reason for divesting herself of several layers of clothing. An early example was La Puce (The Flea) in which Angèle Herard coyly scratched herself to near nakedness. So popular was this mime that Mme Herard toured the European capitals, adapting her act to meet the local criteria for decency. Wisely, she avoided London where I doubt she would have been allowed to go so far as taking off her shoes.

The successors to Angèle Herard (by the time I was in Paris she had long since retired into matronly comfort) generally played variations on What the Butler Saw. At the Empire we had a splendidly equipped young lady who, in the first half of the programme, appeared as a lady's maid intent on trying on her mistress's clothes and, in the second half, as an innocent in the summer countryside tempted towards a spot of nude bathing. I watched every night from the wings but she never did take the plunge.

While in Paris I met up with Lew who was offering himself as a solo dance act. We went out a few times together, starting late after curtain down, sometimes staying up all night, wandering the clubs of Montmartre until hunger took us into one of the many bistros for a combined supper-breakfast of onion soup and mussels. But where it really mattered I was still the innocent abroad. And my month was nearly up.

I should not have worried. As the Delfont Boys went into their last week at the Empire, we were saved by a booking for a Marseilles cinema which featured variety acts between the films. We went from there to the night-clubs; mostly of the seedier variety where the Delfont Boys were among the few performers to appear fully clothed. The effect on me was dramatic. Any modesty or reserve I had when I left London fell away with remarkable ease. Taking my cue from Albert, who had always fancied his luck as a Casanova, I made clear my availability to any good-looking girl to come my way. I would not say that they lined up for the privilege but in our area of show business the female company was gloriously uninhibited. Abundant favours were on offer – at a price. In quick succession I lost my savings and my illusions.

As the quickening pace of life coincided with a fall in income, the Delfont Boys were often on the breadline. This didn't seem to worry us or, if it did, I don't recall us allowing the occasional lapse into penury to cramp our style. Once, when we could not put together enough centimes to make one franc, Albert went to a cinema manager who had booked us for the following week to ask for an advance on our fee. He took some persuading but Albert put on a performance of such tear-jerking pathos that eventually money changed hands. Emerging from the cinema in triumph, we went off to a nearby bar to celebrate. There we met two girls. By morning we were flat broke again.

It was time to move on. We had a vague idea of making our way back to London, but without the resources for the whole journey we decided to take it in stages, picking up on jobs en route. This was how we found ourselves back in Paris and how we came to meet Paul Spadoni, a booking agent for the German variety circuit. He held out the prospect of up to six months' employment starting with a top theatre, the Winter Gardens in Berlin, followed by the Krystal Palace in Düsseldorf. We took the next train north.

German variety was the variety of excess. To begin with the theatres, they were bigger and more lavish than any I had so far encountered. The largest, the Grosse Schauspielhaus in Berlin was built like a Sultan's palace and had five thousand seats. Performances started at seven and went on until the early hours of the morning, the audience coming and going as the fancy took them. At our first appearance at the Krystal Palace we were disconcerted by a group of revellers who noisily walked out on us. But they were back before our finale, each carrying a hot dog and a mug of cold beer. And when

45

we took our bow they applauded louder than anyone. Non-stop variety was later to become popular in Britain, notably at the Prince of Wales and one or two other West End theatres but here, I think, the change was dictated by the cinema where it was quite usual for customers to stroll in and out of a continuous performance, often seeing the end of a film before the beginning.

German variety acts were something else again. In every programme there had to be a grotesque – a midget contortionist or a fat lady who could bend iron bars with her teeth. Escapology was enormously popular. One man was buried alive on stage, another tied in a sack and thrown into a tank of water. They were both outclassed by a street performer I saw who had to free himself from his chains as he was dragged along behind a motorcycle. No doubt the risks were deliberately magnified but even so it was a desperate way to make a living.

At the Winter Gardens we were on the bill with a weight swallower who seemed to be able to take down the contents of a small foundry. His means of recovery was a heavy chain which disappeared down his larynx along with the rest of his collection of scrap metal. The act, which was accompanied by much coughing and wheezing, certainly kept the audience in its seats, at least until the reappearance of the front end of the chain. Then there was a rush for the bars. I knew how they felt. After watching ten minutes of the Mighty Klein, the need to quench the thirst was overwhelming. No wonder the management regarded him so highly.

Back in the money, I could afford to broaden my experience – another way of saying that I took out more girls. Romance had little to do with it. That I often paid for what I wanted probably suggests that I still had a lot of growing up to do. But with the itinerant life I was leading, any attempt at a genuine relationship was doomed from the outset. Albert was more fortunate in that he had a girlfriend at home but memories of Renee across the water did not deter him from seeking other adventures.

In Berlin the night life was not hard to find. On the Kurfürstendamm and Friedrichstrasse there were clubs to suit all tastes, including quite a few that were new to me. It came as a huge disappointment to discover that the dark-eyed beauty who talked like Marlene Dietrich really meant it when she murmured in my ear that we had more in common than I could possibly imagine. Her real name turned out to be Alfred.

The Kurfürstendamm had the most expensive bars and clubs and the most expensive girls – fifty Deutschmarks for as much debauchery as a fit man could take. The price dropped to twenty marks on Nollendorfplatz but the charms of the not so young ladies were hard to detect. I never did get to try downtown Buschingplatz where the going rate was one mark fifty.

Spending so much time in low dives was, I suppose, living dangerously though it never occurred to me that I was taking any risks. The nearest I came to violence was when a girl took against me for refusing to measure up to her sexual demands. All was going well until she pushed my head between her legs. I was not too sure what I was supposed to do. She sat up and demanded to know what was wrong. What could I say? My embarrassed silence infuriated her. She was a woman scorned. Jumping from the bed she started screaming and throwing things. I followed her round the room trying to quieten her while at the same time putting on my clothes. I had one leg into my trousers when I saw that she was holding a kitchen knife. I did not like the glint in her eye any more than I liked the glint of the steel. Minus my shirt, one sock and my right shoe, I ran for the door and out into the street.

The walk back to my lodgings was the longest walk of my life. At every corner I expected a policeman's hand on my shoulder. But though I may have attracted a few backward glances, I was allowed to go on my way. I should have told myself that I was not the first half-dressed man to be seen wandering out of the red light district.

There was another sense in which Germany educated me in the seamier side of life. This was 1929, remember, a full four years before Hitler came to power but already the Nazis were behaving loutishly, as if they owned the place. In Hamburg, where we played the Alcazar and clubs on the Reeperbahn, the notorious red light district, I saw the Brown Shirts on the march, singing lustily. A rough translation of their song included the line, 'And when Jewish blood spurts from the knife, that will be the day'. It was all too ludicrously melodramatic to be taken seriously.

Centred in Berlin, a city more in love with toleration than with mob oratory, it was easy to understate the menace of Nazism. Whenever top cabaret artistes like Werner Finck ridiculed the posturing of Hitler and his supporters they were rewarded the loudest laughs of the evening. Audiences never tired of Finck's joke about the law student who, answering a question on alternative grounds for acquittal, forgot to mention insanity. His professor tried to jog his memory. 'Come now, you read the papers. You know that every day defendants who are guilty are let off scot-free not because they are minors, not because they acted in self-defence but because . . .' The student was struck by revelation. 'Of course; because they are Nazis.'

But outside the cosy informality of the cabaret, there were signs that Nazism was too deeply rooted to be blown away by laughter. Encouraged initially by an agent who thought he had work for the Delfont Boys, I was thoroughly depressed by the way he closed the conversation.

'You're Jewish, aren't you? Well, if I were you, I'd watch out. In this country, Jews have to be very careful.'

Did they? I simply hadn't realised.

I talked to a young German friend I'd met in Hamburg. 'The Jews have been here for hundreds of years. They're more German than the Germans. You don't think there's any risk, do you?'

He nodded. 'Oh yes, a great risk. If I was Jewish, I'd be very worried.'

I was startled. 'But I thought you were Jewish. You look Jewish.'

'Oh no, not me,' he protested. 'Not at all, not at all.'

I was not prepared to argue. 'It doesn't matter. It's just that I'm Jewish and I thought you were too.'

His face, which had been doleful, suddenly brightened. 'Oh, in that case, I can tell you. Yes, I am Jewish. You understand, it's not wise to be too open about these things.'

After that, we did not meet very often. Maybe I should have been more understanding. After all, he was stuck in Germany while I was free to move on. But the denial was a greater shock than any racial propaganda. For the first time I realised that *they* could win.

The fear was reinforced a few weeks later when the Delfont Boys appeared at the Cazanova in Essen, a centre of the armaments industry where there was a strong Nazi presence. The management treated us with unfailing decency until the last week before Christmas. A big party was held for all those in the show, all that is, except me and Albert. We did not have to think long to get the message.

We were stacked up with offers of work but I was no longer content just to take the money. Along with a growing conviction that I would rather be anywhere else than in Germany came the thought that there had to be more to life than being treated as the junior partner of the Delfont Boys.

At first, I hadn't worried that Albert called all the shots. I was an easy-going sort of chap who would happily comply with the bidding of someone I liked and respected. But of late Albert had been pushing his luck. It was hard enough that decisions were made without reference to me but this I might have tolerated if Albert had been less condescending. He had a way of showing disapproval, usually for some mistake I had made on stage, by aiming a light clip at my jaw, barely touching me but no less irritating for that. He did it once too often.

We were at the Thalia Theatre in Elberfeld, the town made famous by its overhead railway. In the dressing-room after the show, Albert gave his opinion of our performance.

'You missed a step. You nearly had me over.'

The exaggeration annoyed me and I said so.

'Come on,' said Albert, 'you know you did it.'

He raised a fist but this time I got in first. He ended up with a black eye and I had a sore nose.

It was not the end of the Delfont Boys but it was the beginning of the end.

The next dip in our relationship came with Albert's marriage. I could hardly blame Renee for wanting to tie the knot. She had waited patiently at home half suspecting that Albert was up to more tricks than was good for either of them. She wanted to be where she could keep an eye on him.

This was fine for Renee and, once he had got used to the idea, for Albert too but the new arrangement left me as the odd man out. My consolation was that at last we had bookings outside Germany. As a threesome we went to Rotterdam, Antwerp, Amsterdam and Brussels.

One of the inevitable features of the boarding houses in which we stayed was the wafer-thin walls, a likely cause of embarrassment when, as usually happened, my room adjoined that of the young marrieds. I tried not to listen but after a show when the adrenalin was still running, it was near impossible to settle down with a good book. Any sound out of the ordinary caught my attention, as in Brussels late one night when I heard from next door the unmistakable tap tap of a dance routine. What's more, I recognised whose routine it was.

The following morning I took Albert aside for a serious chat. 'What's going on? Are you trying to cut me out?'

Albert shrugged. 'Renee has talent. We're already a team. It makes sense for the money to go into one pocket.'

I suppose I could hardly expect him to look at it from my point of view. We made a quick tally of our assets – the saxophone (mine), the trumpet (his), a typewriter and the band parts. Albert took the typewriter, I took the band parts. By the end of the week I was back in London.

My parents were pleased to see me but after the welcome home I cannot imagine that I was the best of company. Day after day I moped about waiting for the offers that didn't come.

Syd Burns, when at last I plucked up courage to see him, pulled a long face. 'It's tough here. It's all a question of supply and demand. There are too many acts for too few shows, know what I mean? I might get you into the Stratford Empire, just to try you out as a solo act, but I'm not promising.'

The technique was to make me feel grateful for what we both knew was a substandard booking. Not that I really deserved more. As a solo act, I was back with the problem I had before I teamed up with Albert – I simply could not sustain ten minutes of non-stop dancing. When I came off stage at the Stratford Empire, I was near collapse. The muted applause told me that I might as well have saved my energy.

Thinking over the few prospects that were open to me, I made up my mind to have another try at Amsterdam. There were several advantages in retracing my steps. The Dutch had a fondness for the sort of variety where performers interacted to produce a unified show – a bit like pantomime. It was one way of escaping the strait-jacket of a ten-minute solo. Then again, Amsterdam was in easy reach of other towns where variety theatre still flourished – Rotterdam, Antwerp, Brussels. Finally, I could not think of a pleasanter, or cheaper, place to live. I knew a little boarding house not far from the Sengel Canal where the beds were comfortable, the meals substantial and where the landlady was sympathetic to the impoverished of my profession. A home from home, you might say.

No sooner had I settled in than I began to wonder if I had done the right thing. Most days I made my way to the Rembrandtsplein where actors and other show business people gathered at the café Hecks, a handy vantage point for keeping an eye on the National Theatre just across the square. There I drank a slow succession of black coffees. Occasionally, word got to me that a dancer was wanted for a night or two, usually out of town, for a dismal fee which barely paid for my lodgings. For the first time in two years I was unable to send money home. I borrowed heavily and had to sell some of my props to pay off debts. I was sick with depression.

Then Josette came along. She was warm and welcoming, blonde, blue-eyed, not thin but with a figure that showed off sumptuous curves, older than me by ten, maybe fifteen years, the experienced woman – voluptuous and alluring.

We first caught sight of each other across a crowded table. I had rushed back late to the pension for supper, grabbing one of the last empty seats in the dining-room. She was sitting next to a young German musician, who, like me, was a long-term resident. By the way she kept reaching out for his hand, I assumed they were more than friends. But the warm glances in my direction suggested they were not inseparable.

I spent a night of dreamy imaginings. The next morning I was still, as I thought, giddy with desire. In fact, my weak state had as much to do with an encroaching flu bug. I soon went back to bed, this time to feel sorry for myself.

That evening Josette came to my room. She brought me a bowl of hot soup and said she would wait while I drank it. I tried to talk but she told me I had to rest, that I shouldn't exert myself. I felt another attack of dizziness coming on. Was I victim of a delirious dream? Propped up in bed, I watched silently as she busied herself picking up clothes I had strewn across the floor and folding them away in the wardrobe. The last item she came to was my trousers which were thrown over the back of a chair.

'Oh dear,' she pouted, holding the garment up for me to see. 'These need mending.'

I nodded. The ends were frayed and on one knee there was a small tear that was threatening to spread.

Josette made a decision. 'I will mend them for you.' She came over to me and sat on the edge of the bed. 'And when you are well again, you must visit me to collect them.'

These last words were said into my ear as she bent over to give me a light kiss on my cheek. I smelt her perfume and I felt the warmth of her breasts. I couldn't wait to get better.

That was Tuesday. Fulfilment day was Friday. I knew that Josette's room was on the floor above and I thought that I could recognise her steps on the narrow stairway just outside my door. I waited until I was reasonably certain she was above, tidied my hair, cleaned my teeth, put on my dressing-gown and set forth like Casanova, albeit a somewhat enfeebled version of the great lover.

Though I say it myself, I performed more than adequately, at least that in so many words is what Josette screamed at me as she threw me about the bed in a wild bout of athletic lechery. In the moment of climax she crashed her fist against the wall. I thought the room was caving in. Returning, none too steadily, down the stairs I remembered that Josette still had my trousers. Never mind, I thought, there is always tomorrow.

Restored to robust health, I was eager to pursue the affair. Josette needed no encouragement. We went out to the cinema and had meals together. Josette paid. I was mildly embarrassed by her generosity but, full of conceit, allowed my protests to be brushed aside. I promised that as soon as bookings came in for my act, I would lavish money on her. Meanwhile, I would do anything for her, anything at all.

'I want you to meet my aunt,' she said.

I had hardly expected such a modest request. We made a date for dinner later in the week.

Our hostess lived on the edge of town, a ten-minute tram ride from where we were staying. Her house was part of a nondescript three-storey terrace facing on to a dark warehouse. It was not a street I would have chosen to live in. But inside, the house was comfortable if a little sombre with its heavy Dutch furniture. I was led from the front door straight into a side room where there was a table set for a meal. Josette's aunt came in. She was small and stooped, so unlike her niece it occurred to me, and she spoke Flemish, a language I found impenetrable. Josette interpreted the exchange of greetings and we sat down, me to begin eating, the two women to concentrate on their conversation. I had just disposed of a bowl of delicious onion soup when Josette turned to me.

'I must make love to you.'

This was something new in the way of social chat.

'What, now?'

She gripped my arm. I detected a rising note of urgency. 'Yes, now. It must be now.'

'But what about your aunt?'

'Don't worry. I've told her we need to be alone. She understands.'

I glanced at the woman opposite. Tight-lipped and unsmiling she certainly didn't look to me to be the sort who would understand what Josette had in mind. Still, it wasn't up to me to argue the point. I allowed myself to be led upstairs.

After twenty minutes of thrashing and scratching, I was back at the dining table, slightly dazed, trying to focus on a leg of roast chicken. Josette and her aunt resumed their conversation. I thought how remarkable it was that this girl could change mood so abruptly. She did it again before the meal was over. This time I ventured a mild protest but I might as well have saved my breath.

After that the pace of the evening accelerated. We were on our way back into the centre of Amsterdam before I realised I had not said goodbye to the aunt or thanked her for dinner.

It took less than twenty-four hours for me to drop from total happiness to total despair. The next day, Josette was gone. I found out that she had booked into another hotel, a rather classier place than I was used to. I went to find her. She told me to go away. Tormented by rejection, I could think of only one person I could talk to, Josette's former lover, the German musician. I gave him as much of the story as I thought he needed to know.

'You too,' he said when I had finished.

'What do you mean?'

'You went to the house in the suburbs, you met her aunt, you made wild love.'

I hadn't mentioned any of this. 'How did you know?'

'It was the same with me. We were duped. We were both part of a sex show. The room next door had an audience. There were peepholes all along the wall.'

It was an uncomfortable return to earth and a mighty blow to my pride. I had really believed I was in love. For weeks just the thought of Josette gave me a painful twinge.

Back on the Rembrandtsplein, idling the hours away, I was lost for a way out of my predicament. I did not have enough money to get home, I did not have enough money to pay the hotel. I did not have enough money for a cup of coffee which is why I sat at the table with a glass of water in front of me. I made up a list of those who might be persuaded to extend a few more guilders. It was a very short list.

My name was called. A messenger boy was weaving his way across the room. 'Delfont. Anyone here called Delfont?'

I shouted.

53

The boy came over to my table and slapped down a folded slip of paper. I took in the message.

'He wants to see you.'

I recognised the name instantly. Max van Gelder was one of the leading agents in Amsterdam. I was round at his office in five minutes flat. The engagement was for a musical comedy named after and starring the recently anointed Miss Belgium. She lacked stage experience, said van Gelder, but the producer was confident of masking this defect with a liberal display of the attributes that had won her a national beauty competition. The plot centred on Miss Belgium being promised her break in America as long as she could come up with the best male dancer in the world. That was me. My part was simple. All I had to do was stand in the wings and when I heard a ta ra ra and 'Here is Bernard Delfont', rush on stage, do my routine, receive a big kiss from Miss Belgium and go off again as the curtain fell. The show was to open in Antwerp. Was I interested? What a question! I was so eager I signed the contract before talking money. Later I found that the fee was a generous thirty pounds a week for a six-month contract.

It seemed to me that rehearsals went reasonably well and though on the first night I was too keyed up to notice how the show was received, I felt as if my luck was in. At last. Immediately after the opening I rushed back to my room and wrote to my parents. I wanted so much to tell them that all was well, that from the end of the week I would again be sending money home.

On the second night I made an early start for the theatre. As I got closer it occurred to me that I might have lost my way. I could not see any lights. Then I realised the theatre was in darkness. In the foyer, a few of the actors were talking amongst themselves. It didn't take long to get the message. We had closed. Apparently, some important critics had not appreciated an all-Flemish production. Even worse, the promoter of the show had vanished and there was no money for any of us.

I wandered back to my room. The letter to my parents was still on the table. I took hold of it and tore it into small pieces. Then I sat down, put my head in my hands and wept.

Chapter 4

Y ears later when my career took one of its periodic dips, a friend
recommended a sure-fire confidence restorer. Take a piece of
paper, he said, draw a line down the middle – on one side write all
the minus points in life and on the other all the plus points. Seen
from this perspective, he assured me, my troubles would fade into
insignificance. I did as he suggested. It didn't work. Seeing all those
minus points together, a joyless procession running off the bottom
of the page, I was depressed still further. I scrumpled the paper and
threw it away.

I fancy that the exercise would have led to the same result that day
in Antwerp. There was really not much to say in my favour. I had
no job, no money and I would have nowhere to stay. I slept badly.
In the morning I went back to the theatre. I am not sure why; possibly
I hoped to meet up with fellow sufferers who were better equipped
than I to cope with life's misfortunes. But the only person I could
find to talk to was the stage doorkeeper. He chatted on about the
theatre and its shows (more flops than triumphs, I couldn't help
observing) and about the owner who never came near the place but
had another business nearby . . .

'What was that?'

'*Pardon, monsieur*?'

'You said there's an owner who lives in Antwerp?'

'Why, yes.' The stage doorkeeper was clearly amazed that I could
be so ill-informed. 'He is a chemist. He knows nothing of the theatre.
You would be wasting your time.'

But I was not seeking another companion in gossip: I had a more
serious purpose in mind. The stage doorkeeper gave me directions
and I hurried off. It was easy enough to meet the entrepreneur on
whom all my hopes now rested. When I found his shop, he still had

not yet opened for the morning's business. I simply waited for him to turn up.

There was no mistaking my target. A small fussy man whose starched collar and dark suit suggested an exaggerated sense of respectability, he was evidently embarrassed to encounter an out-of-work entertainer on his doorstep. I poured out my story as he fumbled his key in the latch. It was a moving performance climaxing with an impassioned plea for a small loan to ward off the last stages of destitution. A hand outstretched towards the gutter indicated where, in extremis, I might end my days.

He was unmoved. 'What happens in the theatre is not my concern. You must talk to your producer. I can do nothing for you.'

I changed tack. 'Is this how you treat your own kind? Where I come from we would never condemn a fellow Jew to starve in the street!'

That did the trick. The till yielded some crumpled notes, enough to settle immediate debts and to buy a return ticket to Amsterdam.

Back in my familiar lodgings, I settled on a sleep now, pay later arrangement before girding myself for the round of agents and producers. Not a single offer came my way. I fell back on quizzing other artists for ideas. Still nothing.

It was the last day of 1934. Amsterdam was cold and wet, a fitting compliment to my depressed mood. I anticipated seeing in the New Year from under the blanket. But I had reckoned without Sam and Lil. Fresh off a cruise ship where they had doubled as ladies and gents hairdressers by day and dancing act in the cabaret by night, Sam and Lil saw themselves as variety artists in the making. It was an idle dream, as anyone could have pointed out. Lil was tall and scrawny with a pronounced Adam's apple which made her look like a plucked turkey. Her choice of long tight-fitting dresses was supposed to endorse her claim to enduring youth but instead emphasised the crimped lines of a lady well into her prime. Sam was more presentable but, short and barrel-chested, he was not the ideal dancing partner for Lil, at least on stage where the contrast between them was a persistent source of unintentional mirth.

The advantage that Sam and Lil had over we other itinerant theatricals was the accumulated savings of weeks at sea. This tended to win them friends, myself among them, who benefited from the occasional free meal. On New Year's Eve, I was reconciled to my early bed when Sam came up to me and slapped me heartily on the shoulder.

'What's a young fellow like you doing moping about? You should be enjoying yourself.' He gave me a squeeze. His voice shifted down to a confidential tone. 'I wouldn't tell this to everyone but Lil and I are planning a little celebration. Why don't you join us?'

How could I refuse? We went to a subterranean club on the Herengracht close by the red light district where the ladies sat at their windows to promote their charms to passers-by. Like everything else about the place, the wine was rough and cheap but tended to improve on acquaintance. In the space between getting pleasantly drunk and horribly drunk, the band went into one of my dance tunes and I found myself doing a solo to thunderous applause. After a hasty encore I rejoined Sam and Lil who showered me with compliments.

'So talented,' said Lil, giving me one of her tight, refined smiles. 'I don't think I've ever seen such a fine mover.'

'But seriously,' said Sam, who knew where to draw the line, 'we have the makings here of a great act.'

Lil was enthusiastic. 'It'll be great,' she said. 'Just imagine, the three of us – Sam, Lil and Bernie?'

'That's it,' Sam confirmed. 'It's the break we've been looking for.'

They both turned to me. Well, it *was* an idea; not much of one I admit. I did not see Sam and Lil and Bernie topping the bill outside of a children's concert party. But I could not afford to be choosy.

And Sam had settled on a plan.

'First off, we move to Antwerp.' (This struck me as a retrogressive step but I was still listening.) 'Lil's father runs a little hotel there; a nice little place.'

Lil nodded. 'You'll like it there,' she assured me.

Sam went on, 'We can spend a bit of time developing our act and when we're ready we'll audition for the Palais d'Eté.'

I was intrigued. The Palais d'Eté in Brussels was a number one spot. I really could not see it as a venue for our dancing trio. But Sam seemed to know what he was talking about. Buoyed up on the festive spirit I was easily persuaded to push aside the obvious objections. Except one.

'I think you should know,' I confessed sheepishly, 'I don't have any money and I'm behind in paying the landlady.'

Sam and Lil were quick to reassure me.

'No need to worry,' said Sam.

'We'll make you an advance,' said Lil.

'Enough to pay the hotel and have a bit over,' added Sam.

There was a pause. Lil favoured me with another of her thin smiles. 'As we're paying for the hotel and a little bit more, we ought to have some security. What about us keeping your passport for you?'

'Nothing personal,' Sam put in quickly. 'But we might as well have everything neat and tidy.'

I was in no position to argue.

'Then that's settled,' declared my new partner. 'Now, what about another drink?'

It was as much as I could do to hold out my glass.

The return to Antwerp was not as bad as I expected. It was worse. Lil's family connection with the hotel trade proved not to be an advantage. I was closeted in a boxroom which might have doubled for a broom cupboard if there had been a free corner for the brooms. Jammed up against the wall was a table with a china basin filled with cold water. I washed myself and then my socks and went to bed very depressed.

Rehearsals were an embarrassment. My solo was wedged between two demonstrations of ballroom dancing as practised by Sam and Lil on the cruise ships. The kindest observation on their efforts was that they were probably very good hairdressers. Wedging his chin on the narrow ledge that was Lil's bosom, Sam propelled her round the stage in a series of glides and hops which made them look as if they were trying to play the children's game of jumping the lines between the paving stones.

The idea of us getting any sort of booking was quite clearly farcical (the Palais d'Eté had already faded with the New Year's Day hangover) but until I could find employment on my own account, Sam and Lil were my only meal ticket. The empty moments I filled trying to think how I might turn events to my advantage. One scheme required me to write to all the variety agents in London. I dreamed up a list of everyone I had ever heard of then doubled it with names I invented.

'I'm sure we'll get some engagements through this,' I assured Sam. 'All you have to do is to let me have the money for the stamps.'

As con tricks go, it was a modest success. I had hoped to be able to buy a pair of shoes, instead I only made enough for some new socks.

The young Bernard Delfont.

My father, Isaac Winogradsky.

Stepney Jewish School, 1920. I am standing at the back, furthest left.

With Hal Monty (*left*) and Jack Donn, 1931.

The Delfont Boys, 1934.

Delfont and Toko, 1936.

The failure of our mailing campaign (I found it difficult to explain why we didn't get a single reply) prompted Sam to an even wilder scheme which involved my going on ahead to Brussels to act as business promoter. I responded enthusiastically. This was my chance to break out.

Lil must have read my thoughts. 'You won't be needing your passport.' She kept a tight grip on a black handbag which served as a portable file for our act. 'Best to leave it where it'll be safe.'

I had nightmares of being stuck with Sam and Lil for the rest of my life. Not having a regular passport (I was still officially a stateless person) I couldn't go to the British consul for help. There had to be another way. If only, I reasoned, I could land them a booking, however lowly, I would at least have a bargaining counter.

In Brussels, I took a room at the Parisian, a restaurant with a small residential quarter at the back where not so long before the Delfont Boys had resided. I was relieved to find that I was still credit-worthy. But this promising start led nowhere. Two days' foot-slogging brought a unanimous response from the agents – don't call us and don't expect us to call you.

Returning to the Parisian, I was cheered up by the sight of a familiar face, a musician with Syd Seymour and his Mad Hatters, a comedy band act I had known in more prosperous days. After chatting for a while, he offered me a ticket for that evening's show. I thought I knew Syd's act off by heart but I was promised a few variations on the familiar routine including the appearance of a talented Eurasian girl called Toko. Attractive in an innocent sort of way and wildly energetic, Toko was also double-jointed, a great advantage for an eccentric dancer. The only missing ingredient from an otherwise splendid act was a partner – preferably male, good-looking, mature, say, in his late twenties with a generous share of stage magnetism. Immediately after the show I went backstage and introduced myself.

Close to, Toko was younger than I had expected, a mid teenager at most and shy with it. But there was no problem of communication because Toko's mother did all the talking. This redoubtable lady was the archetypal stage-struck parent. Protective of her charge to the point of suffocation (I don't think she had ever let Toko out of her sight) she was fiercely ambitious and a tough negotiator. It took me a little time to catch on to the closeness of their relationship since there was no family resemblance. Toko had an unmistakable Oriental

look while her mother was undoubtedly British through and through
– or, to be more precise, Scottish through and through. The missing
link was a star of international wrestling, known as Yoko Tani.
Matching his prowess in the ring, he had broken down the reserve of
Toko's mother but had not pressed his advantage, having disappeared
from the scene soon after Toko was born.

At any other time I doubt I would have stood a chance of getting
through to Toko. Single and available, I was the sort of male her
mother regarded with intense suspicion. But on this occasion our
interests coincided. It was clear that Toko had gone about as far as
she could go as an item in a band act. To increase her earning power
she needed back-up. Other prospective partners had been looked
over and rejected as too young and inexperienced for the image her
mother had created. But riding in on the reputation of the Delfont
Boys and without dwelling on the recent months of professional
inactivity or my association with Sam and Lil, I came across as a far
likelier proposition.

'Just think of it,' I enthused, drawing a mental picture of the
Palladium in lights, 'Delfont and Toko.'

'It'll be equal shares,' said her mother. 'And I'll look after the
money.'

On the way back to the hotel I bought two bread rolls. Then,
collecting my key, I went the longest way to my room, through the
restaurant, where I scooped up two curls of butter from one of the
empty tables. That took care of dinner.

I had some thinking to do. When Toko returned to London I was
determined to be with her. I had no intention of letting this opportunity slip for want of a passport or cash for the fare home. The
passport came first.

I put through a call to Sam and Lil and was rewarded by Lil on
the other end of the line. She was in flighty mood.

'We've been worried about you. What have you been up to, you
naughty boy?'

My apology was spiced with tales of humiliation and despair at the
hands of the agents (all more or less true). 'It's no use, Lil; there's
no work here. Let me go to London. It's our only chance.'

'I'll talk to Sam about it,' she said, not unkindly, and put down
the receiver.

An hour later she rang back. 'I'm coming to Brussels tomorrow.
Meet me at the station.'

I didn't quite know what to expect so I prepared for the worst with a list of tear-jerking excuses calculated to divert Lil from the warpath. I could have saved myself the trouble. After the first awkwardness of meeting on another failure she went out of her way to be nice, even treating me to a supper which made up for the skipped meals of the past week. But she avoided talking about my passport until we were back at the hotel.

'I've been thinking,' she said teasingly. 'Sam wants me to give you the passport but I'm not so sure.'

I tried to be firm. 'You've been very kind to me, Lil, but you've no right to my passport. I want it back.'

She pursed her lips. 'Aren't you just the touchy one.'

We were walking towards the stairs. She held her key so that I could see the number on the metal tag. 'Come up in an hour and we'll have a chat.'

Why we needed an interlude I was not altogether sure. All it did for me was to give me heartburn. I felt as if I was coming up for a test of endurance with the odds against me lengthening for every minute I had to wait. At precisely on the hour I tapped on her door. Lil was sitting up in bed. She was wearing a frilly nightdress which started just below her shoulders, exposing a generous expanse of pale flesh.

'So you're here,' she said needlessly. 'Would you like a drink?'

I skipped the offer. 'What about my passport?'

I wanted to sound like James Cagney (my only success in mimicry) but my voice broke into a girlish treble. Lil ignored the admission of nerves. She patted the side of the bed. I obeyed the order and sat down beside her, babbling on about London and the opportunities there for Sam, Lil and Bernie to break their run of bad luck here.

'Don't be a silly boy,' she said. 'Of course you can have your passport.' She patted the bed again. 'But you'll have to work for it.'

Lil taught me one lesson. Anything is possible if you set your mind to it. Having recovered my independence, the thought of not being able to raise the money for the fare home never occurred to me.

I ticked off the list of friends and acquaintances whose lending tolerance I had exhausted. This left a select few who just might be persuaded to make a small investment. One of these was Syd Seymour. It was several years since I had worked with him which gave my appeal for help a certain freshness and I knew I could rely on his good nature – up to a point; the point being that the best of his supporting acts was about to desert him in favour of the penniless dancer who was now asking for money. I took the chance on him not making the connection and came away in a happier financial state than I had known in months. When I did pay Syd back it was with double interest – for the cash advance and for the favour of introducing me to Toko.

Back in London I set about the resumption of my stage career with infectious enthusiasm. I was convinced that I was on to a run of good luck. The first booking we had for Delfont and Toko ('Syncopated Steps-Appeal') was from the young George Black whose father controlled Moss Empires. He put us on a tour of the number one spots where we collected excellent notices from the theatre managers as well as from the critics. That I still have one of the report cards, from Aston, October 1936 ('A very smart dancing act in all ways – good routines – modern – very good changes of costume') shows how I must have valued it at the time though no doubt I was a little upset to have my name spelled as Del Fonte. Our fee for the week was twenty pounds.

An added boost to my confidence was the news that I was now the only Delfont in the business. My former partner, Albert Sutan who had every right to fifty per cent of the Delfont Boys, including the name, was now calling himself Hal Monty and was working as a comedian.

To celebrate my return to modest fortune I bought myself a car. It was not exactly in the front rank of new models, but then it wasn't an old model either. The only way of classifying it was as an ASP, All Spare Parts, lovingly meshed together by an engineer whose sense of style outran his knowledge of practical mechanics. It was a big car made more imposing by Toko's mother insisting there should be curtains over the rear windows. But as an investment in image-building, it had its limitations. My gratification when, on visits to the Charing Cross Road, my peers gathered round to admire the sleek coachwork of what was known as the Delfont charabanc turned sour as soon as I tried to make my departure. It took half a dozen stout shoulders behind the car to give me enough acceleration to start the engine.

But it was fun – for a while. The black spot was in 1935 when my father died. He was only fifty-seven. On and off he had been ill for many years and had long since given up any idea of making a little business for himself. But I don't think any of us believed he would not survive. My mother's indomitable personality, the binding force of the family, made us feel about Father the way we felt about ourselves: that whatever the tribulations, we would somehow find a way to beat them. And Father did nothing to disillusion us. Right up to the end he was eager to gossip and swap jokes. When I visited him in Hammersmith hospital I asked him if there was anything I could get him. He beckoned for me to bend towards the bed so that he could whisper, 'I could do with a Guinness.' I came back with the bottle hidden under my coat.

When he was gone, Lew and I, as the two breadwinners, had to decide how to keep the family together. We made a good beginning by persuading our mother to move out of Grafton Street, with its sombre memories, to a smart new flat in Streatham High Road. Pullman Court was one of those community apartment blocks with all services including shops, tennis courts and a restaurant on the premises. Mother was fiercely independent but we were determined that she shouldn't want for anything. We two elder brothers split all the bills between us.

While we were overseeing the move, Rita, who was just nine, went to stay with Toko's mother. She returned to a home that was quite unlike anything she had known before. We were taking a chance that the money would keep coming in but Lew, as ever, was supremely confident. Even when brother Leslie ran into financial trouble trying to set up his own business, Lew took it all in his stride, helping out the seventeen-year-old by paying off his debts and then by getting him a job as an office boy with Florence Leddington, the bookings manager for the Syndicate Halls theatre chain. There could not have been a better grounding for the future top variety agent.

For Delfont and Toko, things were beginning to look up. We were playing the Ambassadors Club when Jack Payne walked in. As the buzz went round that he was in the audience those of us backstage started thinking hard about ways of smartening up our acts. Jack Payne was the premier band leader of his day. He had made his name on radio when the BBC took to featuring half-hours of dance music from grand hotels and supper clubs – Ambrose at the Mayfair, Harry Roy at the Café Anglais, Carroll Gibbons at the Savoy and Lew Stone at the Monseigneur. In the mid twenties, Jack Payne was the resident conductor at the Hotel Cecil, next to the Savoy, one of the smartest West End addresses, which is probably why Shell took over the site for its London headquarters. By then he was leader of the BBC Dance Orchestra with a ten million audience.

He was not the most distinctive arranger – Lew Stone, among others, created a more memorable sound which bears revival – but the very blandness of Payne's music could adapt equally well to the mellow romance of the ballroom as to the hearty jolliness of a music hall sing-along. He was much in demand by all the top booking agents, he paid well and his musicians and supporting company were among the select few who could rely on a steady income, three good reasons for Delfont and Toko to make their mark with Jack Payne that night at the Ambassadors.

We must have done something right because a few days later we had an offer to join the maestro on a two-month tour of South Africa. This was fine by me but Toko's mother nearly wrecked the deal by insisting on coming with us. I had to go back to Jack Payne to negotiate a cut in salary in return for an extra fare. Looking back, I can understand the parental concern. The Eurasian look gave Toko a maturity which belied her age – she was not long past her sixteenth birthday – and there were all those bar-room stories about what happened to nice girls when they were on the high seas. But I think she knew that I was a pretty safe bet. Though I was fond of Toko, off stage we had little in common. No doubt with me at the ripe old age of twenty-seven, my partner thought of me as some older brother but even that may be pushing it too far since we were rarely in each other's company. Socially, I must have spent more time with mother than with daughter.

It was also some comfort to a protective parent to know that South Africa was a very puritanical society. This became clear when the booking agent realised that Toko was under the age of consent. He demanded all sorts of assurances that her innocence would be protected and we had to promise not to refer to her tender years in any of our publicity. After Berlin, Brussels and Amsterdam, I was entering a whole new world of strait-laced respectability.

The formality of the pecking order in the band was part of the same pattern. We all referred to Jack Payne as Mr Payne – Yes, Mr Payne, No, Mr Payne, Whatever you say, Mr Payne. He handed out orders like a sergeant-major and expected to be treated with the respect normally reserved for a four-star general. On the boat, he and his wife had a state room to themselves; the rest of us shared eight to a cabin.

Considering that we travelled all the way across South Africa, from

Johannesburg to Cape Town and back again, I saw very little of the country. The days were spent rehearsing, the nights in earning our money.

Delfont and Toko (by now 'The Aristocrats of Dance') gave good value. We came on immediately after the band had led with the Jack Payne signature tune, 'Say It With Music'. Next on the bill were two comedy twins, like us essentially warm-up acts for the Jack Payne Band, with its seven saxophones, five trumpets, a string bass, banjo, drums and a violin, played by the only musician in this company to make an independent reputation – Cyril Stapleton.

We were back to open the second half which was billed as Jack Payne's Radio Party and included his top-flight acts like impressionist Beryl Orde and singer Gladys Chappelle.

Every night was a winner, a tribute less to our collective talents than to the scarcity value of true showmanship. Though far from being a charmer, Jack Payne was a natural publicist who was always thinking up ideas to attract the press photographers. He was not above marching us through town to advertise the show and, if the budget ran to it, we rode in a parade of cars, all of the same make and colour, with Jack Payne up ahead, in grand isolation, acknowledging the onlookers with a gentle wave, for all the world as if he was an emissary of George V.

And, indeed, we were treated royally, with no limits on the hospitality. It made a change not to go short of food or drink. For me the climax of the tour was a Zulu war dance performed entirely for our benefit. I was surprised to find that these people were mine-workers. When did they find the hours and the energy to perfect such a magnificent spectacle?

'That's what they do to amuse themselves,' I was told. 'There's nothing else for them.'

'What about their homes? Don't they spend any time with their wives and children?'

The man laughed. 'Not often,' he said. 'They have to leave their families back in their homelands. Some of them don't go back for ten years.'

It was another step in my political education. No one talked about white domination; it was assumed as a law of nature. But thinking of what my parents and countless others had gone through as a penalty for their race, the injustice did not have to be spelled out for me. I was not sorry to be going home.

Bearing in mind we were embarking on a three-week voyage in uncertain weather, it was rash of Jack Payne to have agreed to do a show on the very day we were due to land at Southampton. But it was plain silly of him to have a row with Phil Trix. Phil was an acrobatic dancer who did a popular solo in the second half of the show. Pretending to be a sax player in the orchestra, he would jump up in the middle of a number, throw aside his instrument and to everyone's apparent consternation, kick off into a frantic dance round the conductor before nipping back to his place. Believing he was as good a musician as he was a dancer, the audience loved his act. Jack Payne knew this as well as anyone. But it didn't stop him from firing Phil Trix.

Ten minutes after Phil was told he was off the payroll, I was called to Jack Payne's cabin.

'I want you to take over.'

It was not so much a request as an order. But I refused to jump. Less than a day out of Southampton, we were booked at the New Victoria the next afternoon. There would be little chance to rehearse. There was also the question of money.

'I'll pay you the same as I'm paying for Delfont and Toko,' said Payne.

'OK,' I said. 'But I'll have to give Toko half.'

And that was how I entered Britain's top band as a silent sax player. Jack was delighted that I had helped him out, and Delfont and Toko toured with him for nearly two years, becoming one of the longest-running acts in the show.

Few of his musicians remember Jack Payne with affection. He was a tough, some would say a ruthless, operator who worked his band for all they were worth – which was enough to keep him in Rolls-Royces. But he was urged on by the certainty that in show business there is not much that is long-lasting. He knew that the big bands were a passing fashion and when the fashion changed so would the top earners.

As it happened, his troubles started on a personal level. He had a pleasant wife who looked after him and went with him on all his tours but who wasn't very exciting. She was a country girl doing her best to cope with the high life. This wasn't good enough for Jack who always wanted more than he had. He started an affair with Peggy Cochrane, a solo pianist and the only female in his company who was brought in as much for her glamour as for her talent at the keyboard. Of course, it was impossible to keep the affair secret. When it all came out, Jack was taken for an expensive and highly publicised divorce, though that hardly mattered against the tragedy that hit Peggy. Her husband killed himself, apparently because he could not bear to lose her.

But it was the fading popularity of the big bands that made Jack Payne retire from the stage. He went into management and did well for a time representing, among other rising stars, the young Frankie Howerd. It didn't work out. When I saw him briefly in the early fifties it was to advance a loan to see him over a bad patch. I never heard from him again.

After two years with the Jack Payne Band, and coming up for my thirtieth birthday, I took stock of my career. I was making a living, and not a bad living at that, but there was a limit to how long I could go on as a dancer. The routines were beginning to tire me and I could see that Toko, who was still a mere eighteen, would soon need a younger partner. Anyway, I had a strong feeling the popularity of eccentric dancing was on the wane. I kept reminding myself that as an opening act I was closer to the edge than other performers and that the fall, if it came, would be sudden and final.

But what was I to do with the rest of my life?

The best advice came from my good friend Keith Devon, though it was a while before I could be persuaded to believe him. Like me, Keith was an East End boy who danced his way on to the stage, first as a child act with his kid sister, later as a solo tap dancer and finally in partnership with his future wife Audrey Wayne. He was taller than me, slimmer too and he had a wiry strength which stood him in good stead when theatre work was hard to come by. Then he joined his father and brother on the docks, taking any job that was handed out, including working the tunnels, the cold stores under the Thames where the sledge-loads of carcases were moved about by sheer muscle-power.

We first met up when Keith was in his early twenties. (He has never confessed his real age to me but I guess he must be my senior by two or three years.) Spending much of our spare time at the races, trying to invent a betting system that would make us rich, he came to have an exaggerated confidence in my ability with figures. At the same time, though he was too tactful to speak his mind, Keith was not convinced that my future was on the stage.

'Believe me, you're a business man. A natural. Why don't you go into management or set up as an agent?'

As my thirtieth birthday winged into memory, I determined to take Keith's advice. My way in was brother Lew who was already in partnership with his former agent, Joe Collins, now best remembered as the father of two famous daughters, Joan and Jackie. It will surprise no one to know that Lew was the dominant partner in the business. Quite unlike Joe, who was an easy-going character, content to take what came, Lew was out fighting for business. Not for one moment did I imagine that he would do me any favours.

'This is the deal,' he told me. 'We won't pay you a salary but you can have fifty per cent of everything you bring in.'

That took some thinking about. I reckoned that as a start I could sign up five or six acts including Toko and whoever we could find as her new partner. But assuming they were continuously in work (a wildly optimistic forecast) and that they each made on average twenty pounds a week, my 10 per cent cut as agent was worth twelve pounds. Lew was offering half of that, a lot less than I was making as a dancer.

Still, I had to start somewhere and I was not yet ready to launch out on my own.

The last appearance of Delfont and Toko was at the Wood Green Empire. After the last show I stood a round of drinks for the other performers. It was supposed to be a celebration but I couldn't help feeling a little sad and a little nervous. Everybody was standing about not quite knowing what to say when out in the corridor I saw Elsie and Doris Waters (otherwise known as Gert and Daisy) peeking in over the crowd and waving at me. Top of the bill that week at the Wood Green Empire, they enjoyed a huge following for their scatty Cockney conversations on the daily routine – a natural act which came very close to real life. I thought they were marvellous and I was flattered to bits that they should bother to call round to say goodbye.

'We wish you all the best,' said Doris.

'We know you'll be a big success,' said Elsie. 'We bring luck.'

It was good to know that someone was on my side.

Chapter 5

To signal my change of profession I went out and bought myself a trilby hat, the universal headgear of the successful business-man. This helped to compensate a little for the poverty of the office they had given me at Collins and Grade which can best be described as a space with a desk. Fortunately, I wasn't there very often. I was out and about trying to make more than a basic living before striking out to run my own business.

For the first time I was able to take a broad view of the entertain-ment industry. Notwithstanding the popularity of the cinema, live variety was still claiming a big share of the action. The mighty Moss Empires were open for business in all the big cities and though, like the Stoll Theatres, they were equipped for sound films, there was no immediate prospect of them selling out to Hollywood. Nor was there any shortage of rank and file performers – the acrobats, jugglers, magicians, not to mention dancers, eccentric or otherwise – who were needed to fill out a programme.

What was difficult to find was a top of the bill, a star name guaranteed to have the customers queuing round the block. Even if Gracie Fields, say, or Will Hay could be persuaded into the West End, they were not keen on the hard graft of a provincial tour. They could make more money with far less hassle by working in front of the camera at Pinewood or Ealing. Some of the veterans of music hall were going strong – Will Fyffe, George Robey, Harry Tate – and could still pull in the crowds, but newcomers with audience appeal were in short supply.

As a fledgling agent my ambition was to find a star, a performer who could bowl over George Black and Val Parnell who ran the Moss Empires or, more particularly, Cissie Williams, the shrewd and formidable lady who was their bookings manager. I don't think Lew took my efforts very seriously. There were at least two hundred other

69

agents in or around the Charing Cross Road who were shooting for the same goal and their combined score was not impressive. Lew, on the other hand, was doing good business talent-spotting speciality acts in clubs and circuses across Europe. He did not push for me to follow his example. Perhaps for this reason, I stuck to my guns though with a growing despondency as the weeks rolled uneventfully by.

It was Keith Devon who came to my rescue. He happened to be walking past the office one day when he bumped into Billy Revill who managed the pianist, Charlie Kunz. Charlie was a phenomenon but not yet widely recognised as such. He had started out as a band pianist before developing his own distinctive style of gentle, easy listening which made him a popular recording artist. Any collector of early 78s will have a few Charlie Kunz records on their shelves. But while Charlie was well known in living-rooms up and down the country, he had not yet played the top music halls which is why Billy Revill was pausing outside the offices of Collins and Grade. He was thinking of changing agents, he told Keith Devon, and had heard good reports of Lew Grade as a hungry young business getter.

Keith had to agree. 'No doubt about it, Lew is good. One of the best. But have you met Bernie Delfont? Now he really is something. I'd put money on Bernie at any time.'

'Really?' said Billy. 'I've never met him. Still, if you say so . . .'

Two minutes later he was knocking on my door.

Charlie Kunz was not the easiest performer to sell to the variety circuits. His talent was unquestioned but what the recording companies were able to hide and what the booking managers could not help but notice was the absence of any stage charisma. To say that Charlie was painfully shy is putting it mildly. He went out of his way to avoid direct contact and when he was forced to hold a conversation it was in a voice so soft and diffident that it needed a practised ear to understand him. Some time later I was urged by theatre managers to persuade Charlie to finish his act with a singalong. Audiences expected it, I was told, and they went home disappointed if they were robbed of the chance to bellow out the old favourites. I put this to Charlie who, much to my surprise, agreed to give it a try. I went to see him achieve the miracle. When the spot came for him to roll out the melodies we all knew and loved, he half turned on his piano stool to give his audiences a sidelong smile.

'I wonder . . . dare I ask? If you feel that you would really like to . . . perhaps you might care to join me . . .'

Somehow they got the message. But I don't suppose it really mattered because by then Charlie Kunz was uncontestably at the top of the bill.

Getting him there is another story. I took the gamble on going straight to Cissie Williams. This was a cheeky thing for an untried agent to do. A new boy was expected to wait his turn which usually meant years of footslogging before being invited into the presence. I managed to force a short cut by sheer perseverance – I sat outside her office for hours at a stretch just to fix an appointment. In the end she had to take notice. Of course, having Charlie Kunz on offer was a great help. Miss Williams agreed to see what he could do.

The act was simplicity itself. On stage was a Steinway – with Charlie, it was always a Steinway – and a piano stool. Nothing else. Charlie came on, gave a little bow, sat down and started playing. It was an effortless performance, so laid back that it could make the largest theatre feel cosy. He went through all his favourites ending up with a selection from *Showboat*. As the last note faded, he sat staring ahead for a few seconds, then got up, directed another barely perceptible nod towards the stalls and made his exit.

Cissie Williams was mesmerised. 'Does he ever say anything?'

I had to admit that Charlie was a man of few words, most of them spoken in a whisper.

The bookings manager took her time contemplating the rarity of a solo artist who did not want to bend the ear of his audience. 'Well, there's one thing to be said for him,' she declared. 'At least he won't overrun.'

The deal was a series of dates to see if Charlie could draw audiences. The question was soon answered. He started by sharing the top of the bill. On his next tour, he *was* the top star. I had a valuable property on my hands.

Lew was not as pleased as I thought he might be. Shrewd as ever, he had a dark suspicion that Charlie Kunz had come to me by a devious route.

'Are you *sure* he wanted to see you?' he asked more than once.

'I was highly recommended,' I assured him. It was nothing less than the truth.

With all the confidence of beginners' luck I was eager to finish my apprenticeship with Collins and Grade and to start up on my own. All I needed was a float to cover basic expenses for a few weeks. Lew's sympathy stopped short of practical help.

'Understand my position,' he pleaded. 'How can I lend money out of the business to set up my own brother as a competitor? What would Joe say?'

My feeling was that Joe would not say very much. He was happy enough if the agency turned in a modest profit when in fact it was making a handsome surplus, a state of affairs not altogether unconnected with the success of Charlie Kunz.

'I suppose you'd take Charlie with you,' said Lew, touching on the weak spot in my argument for special consideration.

I had a rough idea what was coming. I waited for Lew to propose a deal.

'I tell you what I'll do. You can have three hundred pounds on condition Charlie Kunz stays with Collins and Grade.'

It was not the most generous of offers but I was in no position to improve the terms and I did want to strike out on my own. At the back of my mind was the thought that Charlie, like most other variety artists of the day, insisted on a non-exclusive contract with his agent. Whatever Lew and I agreed between us there was nothing to stop Charlie from walking out of Collins and Grade. Not that I had any intention of encouraging him to do such a thing. It was just that after a decent interval, once I was established, I had every excuse for renewing an old friendship.

I took a one-room office in Queen's House next to the Empire in Leicester Square. Downstairs was a cigar shop where a friendly proprietor became a frequent source of short-term credit. I bought some second-hand furniture and a typewriter for the secretary, when I could afford her.

I had two strokes of luck which saw me through the early months. The first was to persuade Carl Heinmann, who controlled eight Mecca dance-halls, to let me take over the bookings for his cabaret spots. It was easy enough to make an approach. I had played several of the Mecca halls in my dancing days and knew the sort of acts that went down well. Once Carl Heinmann agreed to give me a try I set off in pursuit of performers I had met on my European travels, mostly speciality acts not seen before in this country. The novelty factor must have worked in my favour because it was not long before I had an exclusive contract with Mecca. My debt to Carl did not stop there. When cash was tight and I needed to widen my scope, he offered to put up two hundred pounds for a share of the business. I was happy enough to accept. In fact, his investment paid off generously, for when, a short time afterwards, I wanted to buy him out, he would not drop one penny below three thousand pounds, to which I agreed.

My second piece of luck was to avoid paying rent on the office. I am still not quite sure how or why I was blessed in this way, but I can make a shrewd guess. Having got firmly into the habit of not paying any bill until I had been sent two reminders, I started on the assumption that it would be at least a month before I had to contribute to my landlord's income. When that time had passed and nothing had been heard from him, I could not have been more delighted. But after another month and still no word I began to worry and after three months I was getting nervous.

I was put out of my agony by the delivery of a handwritten note from the landlord saying that he knew rent was owing but I was not to worry about it. He added, 'It's good to know there's someone there who looks after the place.'

I looked round the office, at the faded wallpaper, the rickety desk and the wafer-thin carpet. It wasn't worth much but for free it was a bargain. I thought it was a miracle that someone was looking after me.

Over a year later, when I moved to more spacious premises in Astoria House in Shaftesbury Avenue, the debt was still unpaid. I can only assume that he had trouble with the Inland Revenue and was prepared to forgo income to conceal ownership of a valuable asset. Either that, or he was my guardian angel, heavily disguised.

The change of address was part of a wider plan to move into production. This had always been my aim even if I was a little vague on details – like what to produce and where. The first priority was to find someone who could support me and eventually take over on the agency side of the business, someone with an eye for talent and a sharp financial brain. The prime candidate, though he wasn't aware of it at the time, was a young agent who had the office next to mine in Queen's House.

Billy Marsh was cool and unflappable, a fixer in the best sense. He was just what the Delfont agency needed. Getting him was another matter. I happened to know that he was making ten pounds a week, which was about twice what I had in mind, at least for a start.

I rang him at the Theatre Royal, Norwich on the last night of a tour held together by one of Billy's acts, the Ganjou Brothers and Juanita, an extraordinary turn in which three muscle-bound dancers, dressed as Regency bucks, threw the elegant Juanita from one to the other in a frenzy of acrobatic excess. I had an excuse for giving Billy a ring. Having booked the show I was genuinely interested in the box-office. After he had told me the figures I asked if he wouldn't mind calling by to see me the following Monday.

The meeting was brief and to the point.

'There's a desk over there,' I told him. 'It's yours if you want it.'

The idea seemed to appeal because he stayed on beyond the end of the week even when he found there were only four pounds in his pay packet. A good part of the reason, I suspect, was Billy's determination to prove that he could do whatever he set his mind to do.

There were the inevitable setbacks. One of the acts I handed over to him was Bert Wright and Zena, an eccentric pair of acrobatic dancers, the very opposite of the Ganjou Brothers. Billed as 'the agile ancient', Bert was in fact a youngish man who disguised himself as a frail octogenarian to stagger through alarming feats with the athletic Zena. With the experience of the Ganjou Brothers behind him, I thought Billy would have no problem in handling Bert Wright and Zena. But I reckoned without Bert's exaggerated respect for astrology.

'What's your birth sign?' he asked Billy at their first meeting.

Unprepared, Billy spoke the truth. 'Gemini.'

Bert was appalled. 'That's no good to me. I can't work with a Gemini. I'll have to get another agent.'

On his way out he gave Billy some comfort. 'You'll get on,' he said. 'But not with Bert Wright and Zena.'

Billy then had to confess to me that he had lost one of our better paying clients. This was not the end of the story, which came forty years later when Billy visited Brinsworth House, the Entertainment Artists' retirement home in Twickenham, of which he is a life governor. There, sitting in a deep chair, was Bert.

'Hello, Gemini,' he greeted Billy. 'Didn't I say you'd get on?'

The upside of Billy's early weeks in the agency was his part in winning back Charlie Kunz. The shy pianist took a liking to Billy, who knew how to manage his affairs without having to keep a running discourse.

Billy Revill set out the terms of the deal. 'Just ring him with the dates. If he says "yes" he'll be there. If he says "no", don't ask twice.

When he's on stage the wings must be clear. He hates having anyone in his eyeline. Oh yes, and don't bother to go to see him at his home more than twice a year.'

The hard work with Charlie was finding dates that suited his pattern of life, since he did not enjoy straying far from home. He was popular throughout the war, easily weathering an absurd rumour that he was a fifth columnist who was using his broadcast concerts to pass coded messages to the Germans. Perhaps it would have been difficult to sustain his appeal into the fifties when popular music was thrown into one of its periodic revolutions but we never had the chance to find out. Sadly, Charlie was struck by arthritis in his hands and retired early.

Having sorted out the agency side of the business, I was keen to get to grips with my first production. *Hello America* was based on the simple idea of gathering together all available American acts (which meant those already in this country) and putting them together in one programme. It was not exactly a showcase of new talent but I did have Wilson, Keppel and Betty, one of the best speciality acts in the industry. Finicky critics might have pointed out that the act was not really American – Jack Wilson was born in Liverpool and Joe Keppel in Ireland – but they had started in American vaudeville. Their parody of ancient Arabian dancers, bringing to life the angular figures on an Egyptian frieze, hardly varied in forty years and by the time I engaged them they were halfway through their career. But familiarity made no difference to their popular appeal.

Defying superstition, I bought the sets and costumes of a rival show that had failed disastrously. The price was a giveaway but the producer was grateful for any income. I knew how he felt.

Hello America opened at the Walthamstow Palace before setting off on a year's tour of the provinces. The profit was less than magnificent but it was sufficient to encourage me to chance my arm again – as soon as opportunity allowed. But when that would be was anybody's guess because by now the country was at war.

In late September 1939 the order went out for all able-bodied men up to the age of forty-one to register for military service. Lew and Leslie signed up. I tried to but was rejected. The reason took me by surprise. It was not that I was in poor health or otherwise unfit to serve. My disqualification was more impersonal.

'We've nothing against you,' said the recruitment officer. 'Except that you're not British.'

It was true. Having come over from Russia with my parents I was technically an alien – a friendly alien but an alien none the less. It was a distinction not shared by the rest of the family. Leslie and Rita were British by birth and Lew had been sensible enough to become naturalised. My half-hearted attempt to do the same had foundered when the solicitor I consulted disappeared with his clients' money. But apart from the irritation of losing my down payment I cannot say that I was particularly worried. After all, I had a valid passport, or rather a travel document known as a Nansen passport, which enabled me to travel more or less freely throughout Europe. The Nansen passport was brought in by the League of Nations in the early twenties to give refugees a status which stopped short of full national citizenship. With the passing of the years, holding a Nansen passport did not seem to be much different from holding a British passport. I had also to take into account that naturalisation required the applicant to be in a sound financial position – a rarity for me in the pre-war years.

Since naturalisation was not even a starter once war was declared, my only options were either to join the Pioneer Corps which would have had me working with a pick and shovel (not my forte) or to continue as I was. I decided that I could best contribute to the war effort by providing a little light relief from what was then an unrelenting catalogue of bad news.

Of our family, Leslie took the hardest knocks from the war. When he was called up for the RAF in November 1940, he was well on his way to proving that when it came to running an agency, he had the lead on both his elder brothers. After less than a year on his own he had recruited an impressive range of star turns, including Billy Cotton and his band. More to the point, he clearly loved agency work whereas both Lew and I were more inclined to see it as a means to an end.

Leslie's first posting was Hendon, close enough to keep an eye on the business and even to help it on, largely by persuading stars to appear in forces concerts. In this way he acquired George Formby, then at the height of his fame. But Leslie's fortunes took a dip when he was sent off to North Africa. By then he was not only a businessman but a family man as well, with two children, Michael, who forty years later was to become head of Channel 4 and Lynda. Distance and a prolonged absence threatened his business and destroyed his marriage. He suffered too with his health. Having caught typhoid he was on the critical list for several weeks. I don't think he ever fully recovered.

Fortunately for the business, brother Lew was ready to give a hand. Having been invalided out of the army, Lew decided to break up his partnership with Joe Collins and to join Leslie to create a new agency. There was never any question of me going in with them. Lew and I were too much alike to spend long in each other's company. Both outward-going personalities who enjoyed the limelight, we were natural competitors. Leslie, on the other hand, was more the backroom boy who was happiest when he had his head down in the account books or was negotiating on the telephone. It is often said that Leslie was a shy man but he certainly did not suffer any inhibitions when it came to arguing a deal. It was just that he found socialising an unwelcome distraction from his life's purpose which was to achieve better terms for his clients and higher profits for Lew and Leslie Grade. They made a perfect couple. Three would have been a crowd.

Hello America was followed by *Meet The Girls*, another touring production, this one shaped to the comedy of the diminutive Hylda Baker. Now remembered for her television series *Nearest and Dearest* or by an older generation for her invariable reaction to a dim-witted observation from her stooge – 'She knows, you know' – Hylda was a great one for spicing her act with unscripted blue jokes. The audiences took to her Yorkshire humour but the watch committees were not so keen. I hate to think how many times I journeyed the length of the country in my efforts to persuade her to tone down her performance. The young producer wanted a clean reputation for his forthcoming venture into the West End.

There were those who thought me crazy even to consider mounting shows in the heart of London. Logic was on their side. When I started putting together ideas for potential backers, the Battle of Britain was at its height. In the autumn of 1940, when I was sifting plays with the theatrical agent Eric Glass and checking on the availability of actors, some eighteen thousand bombs dropped on London. It was not the most promising setting for a relaxing night on the town.

But the argument had its flip side. For the first time in decades the West End was an open market. Because the established producers were unwilling to commit themselves, the newcomer like myself had a choice of theatres, at low rents. By the end of the war, and without investing a fortune, I controlled no less than seven West End theatres

– the Whitehall, Garrick, St Martin's, Saville, Comedy, Winter Gardens (now the New London) and the Duke of York's.

Raising money for shows to fill the theatres was more of a challenge. I had to persuade potential backers that despite the Blitz there were audiences ready to be entertained. The evidence for this was patchy though it seemed to me that, given the right product, the public would welcome the opportunity to rediscover a brighter side to life. It was not the time for adventurous new writing – even assuming there was any to be tapped – rather, I promoted revivals of old favourites, like *The Admirable Crichton* with Barry K. Barnes and Diana Churchill and of nostalgic musicals such as *Rose Marie*, *No, No, Nanette*, *The Count of Luxembourg*, *The Duchess of Danzig*, and many others.

With the West End theatres and numerous touring shows, I had a lot of money coming in and, invariably, a lot more going out. That I survived was largely thanks to my supporters club led by the Hyams brothers. Sid and Phil Hyams owned a chain of super cinemas, three- to five-thousand seaters in London's inner circle from the Trocadero at the Elephant and Castle to the State at Kilburn. With a rock-solid faith in their own sector of the entertainment industry, fully justified by the queues for all prices, they were ready to take a gamble on live theatre. I cannot claim they made a fortune out of me but they did get their money back with a better than average interest, even if at times they had to wait for it rather longer than they had anticipated.

I started badly with *Jam Today* at the St Martin's. Of the play I have no memory whatsoever but I do recall the female lead – Beatrix Lehmann, a formidable lady who was not given to bearing fools gladly. I was much in awe of her and hardly dared open my mouth in her presence. But it was not she alone who made me jittery. Lost in wonderment that I was actually presenting West End shows, I was exceedingly anxious and more than usually tongue-tied in conversation with all the stars I encountered. As late as 1951, when, with Laurence Olivier, I presented *The Madwoman of Chaillot* at the St James, I still found that what we called the legitimate theatre filled me with trepidation and awe. Countess Aurelia as played by Martita Hunt could transfix me with her lance-like stare. The first words I spoke to her were during a break at the final dress rehearsal. She came down to the stalls, a proudly elegant figure in a full, trailing dress and a wide plumed hat.

'You'll be pleased to know, Miss Hunt,' I offered nervously, 'the box-office is very busy.'

She glared fiercely. 'My dear Mr Delfont, fuck the box-office.' And she whirled past me.

Another illusion gone.

Perhaps she knew more than I suspected. The critics were kind but business was slow. As with all the other shows which failed to live up to expectations, I was disappointed but not devastated. I had found that it cost about three thousand pounds to mount a West End production. If it had enough energy to run a year, the profit could be close to ten thousand with at least as much again from a provincial tour. *The Madwoman of Chaillot* did not do so well as that but it covered its costs and contributed a modest return.

By 1942 I was ready to take on a more ambitious role as a producer. It had long since occurred to me that if I wanted to be in the front line of popular entertainment I would have to tackle a musical. Even in those days the investment – and the risks – were enormous. We were already in the age of the blockbuster musical though the style was deeply rooted in Viennese operetta. (For the first sign of the American invasion we would have to wait for the opening of *Oklahoma* at the Drury Lane in 1947.) Typical of the popular shows in the thirties and early forties were Ivor Novello's *Careless Rapture* and *The Dancing Years* at Drury Lane, Noël Coward's *Bitter Sweet* which the great C. B. Cochran presented at His Majesty's and, beating all records for theatrical excess, *White Horse Inn*. For this extravaganza Sir Oswald Stoll transformed the Coliseum into a Tyrolean village in which one hundred and sixty actors, three orchestras and innumerable yodellers and dancers, not to mention horses, dogs and other farmyard animals, gave their all for six hundred and fifty-one performances. Stoll invested more than sixty thousand pounds in *White Horse Inn* which, allowing for changes in money values, puts it into a higher cost bracket than most contemporary musicals.

I had no immediate hope of rivalling Stoll but I was on the lookout for a show that would need twenty-five or thirty thousand up front to make the production worth while. It was at this point that Richard Tauber burst into my life. Richard never did anything quietly. His personality was his voice, a rich fulsome tenor which carried all before it on a wave of exhilarating sound. He was overweight and suffered a pronounced limp, arthritic hands and a stray eye but on stage he was magic.

Richard's first performance in London was in 1931 when he brought over Franz Lehar's *Land of Smiles*. The encores for 'You Are My Heart's Delight' alone put him into the league of top earners (he was paid one thousand five hundred pounds a week at the Drury Lane) and ensured him a loyal audience for any other shows he might attempt.

My opportunity came when he had finally decided to abandon the uncongenial politics of his native Austria to settle in Britain. I heard from Eric Glass that another Tauber spectacular was on offer but that this time it was Tauber's idea and his music. The story, familiar to all operetta fans, was of a struggling composer whose doting lover helps him to achieve recognition. Its natural setting was old Heidelberg but Richard planted his operetta in eighteenth-century Britain and called it *Old Chelsea*. The big number in the show was 'My Heart and I'.

Utterly convinced that *Old Chelsea* was a winner, I had no difficulty in persuading the Hyams brothers to back my judgement. They put up nearly all the start money to the tune of thirty thousand pounds. Richard Tauber was to star, of course. As the young composer he belied his appearance and his age (he was fifty plus) but it was unthinkable that anyone else should play the role. The female lead was more of a problem.

Eric Glass rang. 'I've got just the girl for you.'

'That's great news,' I said. 'What's her name?'

'Carole Lynne. She's in a revue at the Comedy.'

I nearly dropped the receiver. 'Are you mad? How can I cast a girl from intimate revue opposite Tauber? I need a real star.'

Eric was persistent. 'But I've told you. She's first class. You'll have made a discovery. Anyway, why don't you mention her to Richard? It can't do any harm.'

I said I would think about it. Meanwhile I asked around if anyone else had heard of Miss Lynne. It appeared that her only experience of a full-blooded musical was in an ill-fated Hungarian-style operetta called *Paprika*. A spin-off from *White Horse Inn* which it tried to rival with its named cast of over ninety, an army of 'passers-by, guests, ladies-in-waiting and gypsies' and a peasant choir who 'sang and danced in a world of wheat and wine', the show briefly occupied His Majesty's before disappearing without trace. But Carole Lynne survived. After a season in *The Gate Revue* she went on to three George Black revues, latterly sharing the bill with up-and-coming comedy actors Vic Oliver and Max Wall. I was still not convinced.

Having dismissed Carole Lynne from my mind, I set up auditions at the Stoll, a vast barn of a theatre which was later to make way for the Royalty. It was a long day. Richard was in the centre stalls hunched in his seat listening intently as one by one the young hopefuls paraded before him and one by one went away disappointed. He was more than halfway through the list when he was confronted by an actress who made him sit bolt upright. She sang prettily and looked gorgeous. Richard made his decision.

'This is the girl I want. She will be my Mary Fenton, my star.'

I walked down to the footlights to ask her name.

'Carole Lynne.'

It was hopeless to argue but I remember thinking to myself, I hope she doesn't expect to be paid like a star. Having totted up all the figures I reckoned that putting Carole Lynne up in lights was worth forty pounds a week. I offered twenty, she accepted thirty.

Old Chelsea toured Edinburgh, Birmingham, Norwich and Brighton before its London opening at the Princess, now the Shaftesbury Theatre. Everywhere it had rave reviews with Carole picking up a disproportionate share of the praise. The *Express* dubbed her 'one of London's brightest young stars'. Everybody was singing 'My Heart and I' though no one could match the sheer power of Richard Tauber's delivery. And he did it without microphones, which he regarded as an insult to his talent. At one theatre where there were fixed microphones between the footlights, he rejected assurances that they would not be switched on during his performance.

'My audience will *think* I am projecting my voice artificially.'

He almost spat out the last word. In the end, the only way of mollifying him was to bend the microphones forward so that they were flat against the stage and could not be seen from the front.

We had been running at the Princess for less than two months when the first V1s fell on London. Otherwise known as 'flying bombs' or 'doodlebugs', these latest weapons from the German arsenal were all the more terrifying because they were beyond human control. A government warning was put out on the lines that when 'the engine of a pilotless aircraft stops and the light at the end of the machine goes out it means that an explosion will follow in five to fifteen seconds'. I have good reason to remember the gist of the message because leaflets were delivered to the theatre and I heard someone in the box-office say, 'This means the end of *Old Chelsea*.'

Because the blast of the doodlebug was over a wide area, not concentrated like that of a conventional bomb, direct hits on crowded buildings caused a huge loss of life. In fact it was no more dangerous sitting in a theatre than in front of the fire at home but the media's concentration on numbers – as when Woolworths in Deptford was wiped out killing one hundred and sixty shoppers – made the public wary of venturing far from home. We soldiered on for a few more weeks but audiences were down by half and still falling.

Every evening, Richard went in front of the curtain to reassure those who were bold enough to turn up. 'If there is an air-raid warning, you are quite at liberty to leave the theatre. But I think you will be safer here and come what may we will do our best to entertain you.'

However close the explosion, and we had several in the neighbourhood of the theatre, I don't recall anyone getting out of their seat or anyone on stage losing a note. But this was not enough to keep us in business. *Old Chelsea* closed, the Princess went dark and hopes of making my fortune evaporated.

Fortunately, the provincial theatres were in better shape. To recover I had in mind a revival of a sure-fire favourite, *The Student Prince*, with the lead going to Bruce Trent, a popular young singer on radio and a rising star of the musical theatre. Having settled matters so far it did not take me long to realise that for Kathy, the love of Prince Karl's life, I had to look no further than the cast of *Old Chelsea*. I went to see Carole in her dressing-room.

Perhaps I tried too hard to impress; or maybe I was ill at ease because I was not altogether sure if I was entertaining a beautiful girl or interviewing a likely employee. In any event, Carole gave every sign of wanting to hurry the social preliminaries and to get down to business.

'I like the part,' she said, 'but I'm not sure I want to tour again. Anyway, I don't think I can afford it. I've a flat in London to pay for.'

I had given the matter a little thought. Carole was on thirty pounds a week. Allowing for her favourable notices and undoubted success with audiences, I knew I had to pay her more. I reckoned she was worth sixty pounds. I offered forty.

'I'll have to think about it,' said Carole. 'Speak to my agent.'

I realised that I was in for a tough negotiation, but not quite how tough. Her agent demanded no less than one hundred pounds a week. I argued, of course, hoping that word would get back to Carole that a compromise was in order. But there was no budging her.

A few days later, when I was signing her contract, I realised that I was quite taken with a girl who knew her own mind.

Over the next month I saw a lot of Carole, in rehearsals for *The Student Prince* and during the weekends when Richard Tauber would invite us both to lunch in his favourite Mayfair restaurant. We were there as friends of Richard not as a pair but our host soon caught the whiff of romance, at least from my side of the table. Separated from his wife Diana Napier and desperately in love with a young designer, Esther Moncrieff, Richard was in the mood for mad flights of fancy which had Carole and me living together in perfect harmony.

'Of course, you are ideal for each other,' he assured me more than once. 'You will make a beautiful couple.'

I felt bound to point out that I was merely fond of Carole, not obsessed by her. In any case, Carole showed no sign of wanting to advance the relationship.

'She will,' declared Richard with all the certainty of a dedicated matchmaker. 'You'll see.' But he did have a warning. 'You know she is married.'

As a matter of fact, I did know. Her husband, Derek Farr, was a romantic actor, popular on stage and screen. They had met in rep when Carole was barely eighteen. Derek was her first love. They were engaged for two years while building their careers, his in films, hers in the theatre. Inevitably, they saw very little of each other. Eventually they married. That was in June 1939, just three months before war was declared. Derek was allowed to finish his latest film, *Quiet Wedding*, before being called up. He was posted to Catterick to train for his commission. Carole, meanwhile, was in *Black Velvet*, a big success at the Hippodrome, and had scarcely any chance to see Derek before he was sent abroad. Much later she told me she had never really felt married.

For me, the immediate problem was solved by Carole departing on the tour of *The Student Prince*. We were out of contact for several weeks. Then she came back to London while the show was on rest for a fortnight. She had a flat in Huntley Street just off the Tottenham Court Road and I rang her there to ask if she was free for dinner.

She said that any other time would be fine but on that particular night she was planning to stay home to wash her hair.

The next day I bumped into Sid Hyams.

'Nice girl, Carole Lynne,' he said by way of conversation. 'I saw her last night. She was dining at Manettas restaurant.'

I thought, how could she do this to me? The rush of jealousy made my face hot. I knew then without a shadow of doubt that I was very much in love.

Chapter 6

Falling in love with Carole was one thing; persuading her to fall in love with me was altogether a different proposition. Though alone in London she had plenty to occupy her, notably a career that was beginning to take off in a big way. After a dozen meetings, invariably semi-social with others in the theatre world gossiping away in the background, I felt that I hardly figured in her routine except as an actual or prospective employer. Richard Tauber did his best to put matters on a more personal level and no doubt he spread the word because I was soon receiving invitations which put Carole next to me at sundry dinner tables.

But that was as far as it went, for the moment. Many years on, I was interested to see a newspaper interview with Carole in which she confessed that at first, I was not her type.

'He seemed very odd to me. I'd never met anyone like him. He was dark and arrogant with an austere, forbidding appearance. And he had a deep distrust of most women – I'd say he was a misogynist. It took years to break him down.'

I did say she was a girl who knew her own mind.

Fortunately, unaware of the formidable obstacles I had to over-come, I persevered with my love life while at the same time struggling to keep my career on the move. The premature closure of *Old Chelsea* was a great disappointment but success was near enough for me to want to try another musical – and soon. With the end of the war in sight, the West End was enjoying a revival of interest un-matched since the early thirties. All I needed was the right product.

The natural tendency of the musical theatre was to play safe with revivals like *Show Boat*, *The Vagabond King* and *Desert Song* or to throw money in the direction of box-office stars like Noël Coward and Ivor Novello. I wondered if it was not time for something new. I actually toyed with the idea of creating an entirely original British musical but was overwhelmed by a wave of cynicism. The reaction of Terence Rattigan was typical. He told me that he would never dream of engaging in anything so gross and vulgar. It was then that I started thinking about importing a show from the States. It is hard to imagine now but with travel restrictions and a shortage of technology (no LPs or tapes) we had to rely on hearsay to make an advance judgement on the scores of *Oklahoma* or *Annie Get Your Gun*, to take the biggest shows on Broadway. As it happened, these two were way beyond my means but another Broadway hit, Cole Porter's *Something for the Boys*, did look to be a possibility. It needed about forty thousand to put it on at the Coliseum but with catchy numbers of the quality of 'Hey Good Lookin'' backed by the Cole Porter reputation I didn't think I could go far wrong. It was a beautiful illusion. *Something for the Boys* came and went within a month. On the day I decided to close the show, I was at the matinée. There was an audience of forty. Halfway through the first act I went to the gents to find that a paying customer had beaten me to it. He turned as I came in.

'It's the same for you, is it?' he said with feeling. 'Waste of bloody time.'

Trying to learn from experience, I noted that *Something for the Boys* was 'a badly constructed show pretty well impossible to cast' by which I meant that it was an all-American musical needing an all-American cast – and a star. For my next venture I stayed closer to home with a reworking of the Johann Strauss operetta *Die Fledermaus* to make a new musical called *Oh Rosalinda*. Weighing up the odds, on the plus side we had a proven score which suited audiences' war-weary mood of nostalgia for the good old days. The minus points started with the cost – there was no way I could manage this on my own – and the absence of a lead role for Richard Tauber. In his younger days he had played Count Orlofsky with great style; now age disqualified him. But I did turn to Richard for advice on the casting and on the delicate matter of who should conduct the orchestra.

'Why don't you ask me?' he boomed.

I couldn't believe he was serious. He was qualified certainly – some critics ranked him as fine a conductor as he was a singer. Indeed, the year after *Old Chelsea* he had spent touring with the London Philharmonic. But how would audiences react? They expected to see him up on stage not half buried in the orchestra pit. I shifted tack.

'The conductor is not the star. You can't expect to make a lot of money.'

He looked at me shrewdly. 'How much do you expect to pay your musical director?'

I said, 'No more than sixty pounds a week.'

He gave a wide grin. 'So, I will be proud to conduct the orchestra.'

This was from a performer who was used to earning twenty times as much.

The more I thought about it the more inclined I was to take a gamble – knowing that this time, losing could well have the touch of finality. Richard was a big draw whatever he did. With his outsized personality he was bound to give a lift to the show. The only danger was of him overwhelming what was happening on stage. I did not put it past him to climb out of the pit to join in the choruses.

As co-producer I fastened on to Tom Arnold who had founded a sizeable fortune on pantomime and touring musicals and had the lease on the Palace Theatre on Cambridge Circus. Tom had only one suggestion. *Oh Rosalinda* should become *Gay Rosalinda*. It was done.

We opened at the Palace on 25 February 1945. Count Orlofsky was given a dashing interpretation by Peter Graves who had made his name in Ivor Novello musicals. But, as he was the first to admit, he was no match for Tauber who hammed it up like mad to grab audience attention. On an ordinary night he would limit himself to singing along with the cast at a voice level that was soft for him but which could clearly be heard in the front stalls. At his wickedest, he would vary the tempo to put a singer (usually Peter Graves) off his stride. One night when Peter made a grand entrance, pepped up for a big number, he gave the cue for the music and nothing happened. He looked down and there was Richard slumped in his conductor's chair, pretending to be asleep. Peter tiptoed up to the footlights, leaned over the pit and repeated his cue line very loudly. Richard sprang up, raised his baton and the orchestra played.

It was the sort of joke that could only work in a good-humoured company and in a show like *Gay Rosalinda* where the audience was happiest when it was treated as part of the family.

As the advance bookings promised a longish run (we were on for a year at the Palace with a move to the Princes for the summer and autumn of 1946), I felt sufficiently relaxed to have another try at putting my private life in order. Sheer perseverance paid off though later Carole told me that she was finally won over because I made her laugh. Imagine, keeping an affair going by thinking up at least one good joke a day.

With the female side of my family evacuated out of London, I had moved from Streatham to a penthouse flat in Mansfield Street near Broadcasting House, a short walk from where Carole lived on the Tottenham Court Road. In theory, this should have made for a perfect liaison but absences from London could disrupt the idyll and even when we were together in the city, we came up against forces which could make any relationship intolerable. Like my butler.

This was his own choice of job title. It gave a rather grand idea of his duties which were to caretake for the entire apartment block and to be on hand for special functions, at overtime rates. But he modelled himself on Jeeves and excelled at drinks parties where he hovered solicitously, knowing precisely when to refill the glasses and, more importantly, when to lock away the bottles. His name was Potter.

Potter did not object to girlfriends as long as they came and went. It was when they showed signs of becoming permanent fixtures that he started worrying. And the idea that any of his young gentlemen should marry utterly appalled him.

When I confessed that Carole was more than a passing fancy, he reacted as if I had announced a terminal illness.

'Oh, sir, are you sure?'

I said that I was absolutely certain.

He breathed in sharply. 'In that case, sir, I offer my sincere congratulations.' He turned at the door to deliver his exit line. 'But I beg you to remember. *She* can never do for you what *I* am able to do.'

Disapproval of another sort came my way from my landlord who had been told of certain improprieties. I had invited Carole to dinner, cooked as only Potter knew how when he was trying to impress. We had just settled down to eat when we heard what sounded like a plane in trouble and went out on the balcony to look. What we saw, silhouetted against a red sky, was a sausage-shaped object with flames shooting out the back. This was the first buzz bomb to come our way. As we watched, the engine cut out and the bomb fell. Carole was frightened and, anticipating more raids, instead of going home she stayed on with me long after Potter had departed. The neighbours talked. What was going on in the Delfont apartment, they wanted to know, with young ladies 'popping in and out all night'? I explained to the landlord that it was only one young lady and pleaded the abnormal working hours of stage actors as justification for a flexible social life. He was unexpectedly sympathetic – and helpful. His suggestion for preserving the decencies without causing undue hindrance was for us all to agree to refer to Carole as Mrs Delfont.

This was fine by me but less appealing to Carole who felt as if she was committing bigamy. It was clearly time to sort out a few problems. We both knew we loved one another. Carole was fond of Derek but she did not love him. There was no question of her going back.

Setting up a divorce in those days was not the easiest of matters, particularly when one of the principal characters in the saga was out of the country. The lawyer I picked out of the phone book was not hopeful. Nothing could be done, he said, without the co-operation of Derek Farr and since he was the offended party he had no reason to do us any favours.

A few months passed by.

Carole rang me from Glasgow, the latest stopover on her tour of *The Student Prince*. A worried voice said, 'Derek is home.'

I said, 'Do you mean he's there; in the hotel?'

'Not yet.' Well that was something. 'He'll be in London today, but then he's coming straight up here, on the night train. I don't think I can face him alone.'

'I'll be with you as soon as I can,' I told her. 'Try not to worry. We'll work something out.' I rang off.

The midday express from King's Cross got into Glasgow late that evening. I went straight to the Central Hotel, checked in and rang Carole. I half expected to hear Derek's voice but it was a tired and tearful Carole, just back from the theatre, who answered. I went up to her room.

I tried to calm her down, asking her if she wanted me to talk to Derek when he arrived.

Her reply was emphatic. 'No. I must speak to him first. I just don't know how I'll tell him. It's awful. I don't want to hurt him but whatever I say, I know I will.'

I went back to my own room to pace up and down for an hour or two. Then I sat down and closed my eyes, wondering what it would be like to lose Carole. I knew she was the only girl I would ever love.

Suddenly the telephone rang. Carole was talking.

'Bernie, it was dreadful. He sensed something was wrong. He asked me if there was someone else. I told him there was. I tried to explain how it happened and said I wanted a divorce. He wouldn't believe me. He said it was just infatuation, a natural thing, because we'd been apart for so long. He wants us to get to know each other again.'

Now it was my turn to try to convince Derek that we were serious. I allowed five minutes to collect my thoughts before making the call. He answered immediately. I told him who I was and asked if I could see him in his room. He insisted on coming to me.

I opened the door and we shook hands as he crossed into the room. He was a strongly built man, dressed casually. He made some remark about meeting under unfortunate circumstances. The tension was apparent.

I said, 'I'm sorry, I can't think of any better way of putting this but Carole and I have fallen in love. She wants a divorce.'

He turned away, plainly upset. 'I'll have to think about it.'

I talked on about how we had never meant it to happen, how it distressed us to hurt him. 'But we have to face facts.'

Derek said, 'I told you. I'll think about it.'

I was left wondering if there was any other way I could have handled it. When he had gone, I went to Carole's room. We sat together for a long time, saying very little but pondering the future. Three people had very little sleep that night.

The tug of war with Derek went on for months. The more Carole insisted she loved me, the stronger was his conviction that she would eventually come back to him. I made another visit to the solicitor. Was there nothing we could say to persuade Derek to grant a divorce? Apparently not, but we could *do* something. The only way of showing Derek that Carole would not change her mind was for her to move in with me. Today, young people would not think twice about it, but in the forties, the threat of scandal was real. We feared the gossips. All the same, we were tired of make-believe. I found an apartment that suited us both in South Audley Street. After six weeks Carole was served with a writ. We welcomed its arrival like a win on the football pools. Now we could really start planning.

The press gave the divorce the full treatment: it was only to be expected. Derek was ideally cast as the tragic hero, the war-weary veteran of Tunis and El Alamein who sacrificed his happiness for the greater cause. It was not quite like that, as we all knew, but, outside my own circle, I was the villain, an opinion reinforced by Mr Justice Wallington who was somehow given the impression that in Glasgow

My solo act, *circa* 1936.

Carole in 1947.

Our wedding day, 22 January 1946. *Left to right*: Helen Debroy-Somers (Carole's mother), Leslie, myself, Carole, Richard Tauber, Kathy and Lew.

At a rehearsal of the Royal Command Performance at the Coliseum Theatre, 1958. *Back row, left to right*: Tony Hancock, Arthur Scott, Harry Secombe, Max Bygraves. *Front row, left to right*: the manager, Hetty King, myself, G. H. Elliott.

With Lord Forte at the Talk of the Town, *circa* 1960.

With the children, Susan (*left*) aged thirteen, Jenny aged eleven and David aged seven.

After the Royal Variety Performance, 1963, at the Prince of Wales Theatre.

With George Burns (*left*) and Jack Benny, 1966.

Mrs Winogradsky with her sons at Michael Grade's wedding, 1967.

I had pushed my weight around, demanding to see Derek in my room, and generally given him a hard time. The judge thought such behaviour was 'monstrous', a verdict I would have been the first to endorse, had the accusation been true. It wasn't but since, quite naturally, neither Carole nor I was contesting the divorce, I had no opportunity to argue my side of the case. I was ordered to pay full costs and one thousand two hundred and fifty pounds in damages.

The day after Carole was granted her decree nisi, I set up my most successful double act to date – Bernard Delfont and Carole Lynne, henceforth to be known as the Delfonts. A little while later we were delighted to hear that Derek had married Muriel Pavlow, an exciting young actress he had met in *Quiet Wedding*. Carole and I were married at Caxton Hall, at that time famous for theatrical weddings, on 22 January 1946. Richard Tauber was best man.

The family turned up in force though my mother could not bring herself to appear at a pagan ceremony. It was the same for Lew and Leslie, both of whom married (in Leslie's case, twice) outside the Jewish faith. But there was no ill feeling and the lady who called herself Mrs Delfont or Mrs Grade, depending on the company she was keeping, had to wait until Rita had found the right man for the opportunity to enjoy a full-blown Jewish wedding.

The splicing of the Delfonts had the usual moments of tension as when my best man made a great show of losing the ring. The registrar, who had seen it all before and was wearily reconciled to seeing it all again, remained impassive. It was only when I was fumbling to place the ring on Carole's finger that he came to life. Leaning forward to impart what I assumed to be some words of worldly wisdom, he cheerily remarked, 'I see you're doing shows with Tom Arnold.' He followed up with effusive congratulations, not on my marriage but on the magnificent revival of *Rose Marie* at the Stoll.

The honeymoon was a weekend in Bournemouth. To start off in style I asked for champagne to be waiting for us and – a bit of a letdown this – the only sandwiches available in those days of rationing: spam. Three of us checked in at the Carlton, me, Carole and Carole's miniature Pekinese which was hidden under her coat. This subterfuge was occasioned by a large notice outside the hotel saying NO DOGS ALLOWED. Once in, we thought, they can hardly throw us out. Our faith in the easy-going nature of hotel managers was misplaced. The cork was still in the champagne when the telephone rang. I listened to the fatal words.

91

'It has come to my notice . . . etc . . . etc . . . You'll have to leave.'
'Give me an hour,' I said.

On the way into town I had seen a show-bill promoting Grande and Maxted, a dancing act I had known in my performing days. Having a fair idea where they would be lodging I thought of calling by to ask a favour. The upshot was that Grande and Maxted agreed to be dog-minders for a couple of days. I dumped the animal and returned to the champagne and spam.

The honeymoon had to be a short one because Carole was appearing in *Big Ben*, a musical satire of contemporary politics by A. P. Herbert and Vivian Ellis, in which she had a show-stopping number, 'I Want to See the People Happy'. The producer was Charles B. Cochran, the titan of the English stage whose nerve had held through decades of showmanship on an epic scale. Now into his seventies and in fragile health, Cochran was still in fighting mood, ready to back his own judgement, right or wrong, and to face up to all emergencies. Some weeks into the run of *Big Ben*, one of his leading ladies, Gabrielle Brune, had to leave the show because she was having a baby. Not long afterwards, Carole had to tell Cocky that she too was about to start a family. She offered to stay on until she grew out of her costume.

The harassed producer rang me to vent his feelings. 'There's something very strange going on in this show. Suddenly, all my stars are getting pregnant.'

I sometimes wonder if Cochran's last years would have been easier if he had listened to an American agent who wanted him to mount a musical version of *Pygmalion*. But Cochran dismissed GBS to music as 'a perfectly frightful idea'. He was much happier putting his money into a topical show, particularly one that poked fun at the establishment. I got to know Cochran well during the pre-London run of *Big Ben*. His charm was unfailing. Whatever the crisis – and there was at least one to fray the nerves – everybody ended up believing that if Cochran was happy, there was no right on earth to feel depressed.

Even the Lord Chamberlain succumbed. By an extraordinary failure of memory, which may have had more to do with tactics than with true neglect, a copy of the script did not go to the official censor, who in those unliberated days had the final word on what could or could not be presented on stage. There was much blustering when the error was noticed. By then Cochran had a full production ready to take to the road and there were fears of radical changes – even cancellation. But in Cochran's view the sensitive material – jokes about live politicians and scenes inside Westminster which were technically breaches of parliamentary privilege – was best seen in the context of a live performance. Judged on the printed page, it was too easy to imagine offence where none was intended.

Apparently the Lord Chamberlain agreed because he insisted on only one minor amendment. Dialogue between characters who were recognisably Nancy Astor and Jack Jones, the Labour MP famed for his brewer's girth, ended with Jones declaring, 'I'll lay my stomach against hers any day.' This was changed to: 'I'll bet my stomach against hers any day', a form of words which mollified the censor without destroying the joke. Audiences were used to listening between the lines.

Big Ben was in Manchester when Cochran became ill. He had suffered for years with arthritis of the hip and now he had serious kidney trouble. The doctor ordered him to bed. I was on a flying visit when I was told he wanted to see me.

'If anything happens to me,' he told me, 'I want you to take over the show. Will you do me that favour?'

Favour? What a way of describing such extravagant flattery. I agreed, of course, though in the event I did not have to live up to Cochran's expectations. Too ill to attend the first night at the Adelphi, he was strong enough to direct operations from his flat in St James's Court. A darting memory is of him propped up in bed, loudly bemoaning the medical ban on his favourite cigars while consoling himself with the latest figures from the box-office.

The feel of success, so strong in the first week of *Big Ben*, did not last. It was the sort of show to command an enthusiastic audience for a limited period. After one hundred and seventy-two performances, Cochran accepted defeat or, as he liked to think of it, a tactical retreat. He remained loyal to A. P. Herbert and Vivian Ellis, commissioning them to write a Victorian light opera which was to be Cochran's most successful musical. *Bless the Bride* opened in April 1947 and ran for over two years, to prove that the Americans did not have it all their own way. I was lucky enough to share in the triumph. Cochran sold me the touring rights to *Bless the Bride* on very favourable terms.

At the beginning of 1947 I took full-page advertisements in the *Express* and *Mail*. The message was, 'You're Never Far From a

Bernard Delfont Family Show'. It was true. My name was on fourteen West End and touring productions, not to mention numerous seaside shows. A large part of my strength was the people I had around me. Not long after the war, the agency side of the business was given a boost by the arrival of Keith Devon. Having spent a lot of energy persuading me to set up on my own, Keith had followed his own advice and opened an office off the Charing Cross Road. I lent him a hundred pounds to help him do it. There was no doubt that he had the gift – building up performers of star quality like Bonar Colleano Jnr, and Mantovani and his Orchestra was proof enough – but he felt he could achieve more as part of a larger organisation.

He took the desk opposite Billy Marsh. They made an odd couple, the short and the tall: Billy very much the loner who kept his thoughts to himself; Keith the ebullient socialiser, always ready for a laugh. In their different ways, they were among the shrewdest operators and they were both supreme talent spotters. Talent is seldom the revelation that audiences assume. It does not necessarily shine out in a first performance. More often, it is well hidden and it takes a skilled observer to make the connection, and that's only the beginning of the story.

Talent needs careful husbandry if it is to thrive. When Billy Marsh first saw Frankie Vaughan on stage, the singer finished his act with a none too exciting impersonation of Al Jolson, rendering 'Mammy' on bended knee. Like a dozen identical acts it was destined for the reject bin. But Billy spotted other possibilities. Borrowing a song made famous by Vesta Tilly, he persuaded Frankie into top hat and tails to seduce his audience with 'Give Me the Moonlight'. Now that *was* an act with staying power.

Again to Billy Marsh goes the credit for discovering Norman Wisdom. Or rather, it was Stan Laurel of Laurel and Hardy who first detected Norman's touch of comic genius. Billy had the good sense to follow up with a visit to the Victoria Palace where the unknown comedian was appearing in a charity show. Billy liked his act but admired even more his cheek in wangling himself on to the second half of the bill. He had done so, it turned out, by persuading Vera Lynn to change spots, pointing out that by so doing Vera could get home early.

Norman had been having a rough time, hitch-hiking his way home from Brussels after the failure of a show called *Piccadilly Nights*.

Billy told him his worries were over. 'One day you'll be a star.'

'Never mind that,' said Norman. 'What about Monday week?'

On stage the self-assertive Norman was transformed into the universal victim, the put-upon little man recognised by Stan Laurel as a kindred spirit. But it was not until Billy teamed Norman Wisdom with the magician David Nixon for a summer season at Scarborough that Norman acquired his passport to instant recognition. There was a routine in which David asked for a young boy to come up from the audience to help him with one of his tricks. The volunteer, of course, was Norman in a suit several sizes too small for him. Thereafter, his fans could not imagine him in any other clothes.

It was not more than two years before I was sitting down with Norman to sign a contract guaranteeing him four hundred pounds a week or about as many thousands by today's value.

He looked at it in astonishment. 'I can't believe this,' he said. He bent down to sign then suddenly looked up, the pen still poised. 'Couldn't you make it five hundred?'

Another in the same league as Billy Marsh and Keith Devon, though this time on the production side, was Dickie Hurran. We met at just the right time. I was at the London Casino sorting out a few problems with the American singer, Vivian Blaine, known as the Strawberry Blonde. Did I say a few problems? The list was interminable. The blame rested squarely on her husband who acted as manager but liked to think he was producer and theatre manager rolled into one. When the lighting was changed to suit him there was something wrong with the sound and when that was fixed, somehow the backdrop wasn't quite right.

I was near exhaustion when Keith Devon appeared. He and Dickie Hurran had been having lunch round the corner in Frith Street and had popped in to see how we were getting on. As it was apparent that we were not even at the starting gate, Keith suggested that his friend, who knew a thing or two about staging a show, should lend a hand. In five minutes flat, the lighting, sound and backdrop were entirely to the satisfaction of Miss Blaine and her minder. I was impressed.

I took the trouble to find out a little more about Dickie Hurran. He had served his theatrical apprenticeship as a song and dance man before shifting over to production. One of his jobs before the war had been to put on the entertainments at the Coconut Grove, a night-club off Regent Street, famed for its bottle parties. This was a neat trick for getting round the archaic licensing laws. Confirmed revellers were invited to put in an advance order for, say, a dozen bottles of whisky, which were then set aside for the buyer and his guests to draw on at any time of the night. It was, as I say, a clever idea but it needed careful control if it was not to get out of hand and attract the interest of the police. The entertainments manager had a critical role in creating a floor show that could hold the attention of the customers against the rival attraction of the bottle.

The job I had in mind for Dickie Hurran was entirely different from, but on a par with, the challenge of the Coconut Grove. I wanted him to put some beef into our summer shows. I had started in this business early on in the war when the holiday resorts were deep in depression. Of the established producers few were ready to take their chances on filling seats at the end of the pier and when they did so it was on a tough deal with the theatre owners – sixty per cent of the box-office with a guarantee to the producer. I reversed the rule offering the theatre owners, mostly local councils, forty per cent and a guaranteed minimum. Suddenly, I was a very popular producer indeed, if thought to be a little eccentric. But I knew what I was doing. If times improved I would have a big share of a profitable market; if they worsened then everyone would lose, including those who kept their money in a shoebox.

Having signed up eager theatre owners from Torquay to Southsea, I had to put together at least half a dozen shows in less than six months. For a beginner I did not do too badly, with a break-even on the first season. But the entertainment was not what you would call top class. We worked on narrow margins saving what we could on presentation – it was amazing what you could do with a simple backdrop and an empty stage.

Investment in scenery and costumes was long term. Anything we made we held on to, adapting it from one show to another across the years. Out of season, we packed it all away at the Wimbledon Theatre on which I held the lease and at Dancy Yard behind Lambeth tube station where we shared two large sheds with Jack Hylton. Overseeing the Dancy Yard emporium was a caretaker of the old school called Harry Shuff whose wife, Jenny, was our wardrobe mistress. Harry was a stickler for duty and I valued him highly but he did make one serious mistake. Dickie and I were trying to find a hint of encouragement in the latest box-office figures when Harry turned up looking as if he had been run over by a tram. I asked him what he'd been up to. He was only too ready to tell me.

'Terrible news, Mr Delfont,' he blurted out. 'There's been a fire at Dancy Yard.'

I caught a glance from Dickie. I knew what he was thinking. A good blaze, immediately followed by a handsome insurance cheque were just what we needed to transform our season.

But Harry had not finished his story. 'Don't worry, Mr Delfont. It's all OK. Jack Hylton's scenery and dresses went up but I managed to save all our stuff.'

I don't often swear but this time it was irresistible. 'Harry,' I said, 'why don't you mind your own bloody business?'

When Dickie got into his stride, he spent his summers chasing in and out of London, rehearsing a show for a week in the bar area of a Delfont theatre (the space came rent free), then taking it out to one of the resorts before roaring back to start on the next show. In this way we filled as many as fifteen seaside theatres. In the winter, Dickie abandoned the promenade for the big towns where he presented variety bills and pantomimes.

For want of star names we made heavy use of promising newcomers discovered by the Delfont agency. This had obvious advantages for both parts of the company but it was not a cheap option since neither Billy Marsh nor Keith Devon could get out of the habit of striking the best possible deal for their clients.

There was the occasion when we needed a singer for Weymouth. Keith had just the girl: very pretty, great voice but lacking the presence that would come with stage experience. She was worth fifteen pounds a week, said Keith. 'We can't afford fifteen pounds,' I told him. He shrugged and said that was what he could get her in another holiday show. It looked as if we would have to do without a singer until Dickie decided he could get by with one girl fewer in the chorus. The sacrifice launched the career of Joan Regan. Another graduate of summer show was Ruby Murray. She appeared at Southsea, scored a hit record ('Softly, Softly') and made straight for the Palladium.

To jump ahead a little, by the late forties it was clear that the days of cheap seaside variety were numbered. Holidaymakers with more money to spend demanded a corresponding upgrading of their entertainment with names they could recognise from radio, or, increasingly, from television. I began concentrating on the larger resorts like Scarborough, Eastbourne and Blackpool where I could mount summer spectaculars fronted by performers of the excellence of

Harry Secombe, Peter Sellers, Winifred Atwell, Morecambe and Wise. Peter Sellers charted his progress towards stardom by changing his car ever more frequently until, it seemed to me, he had a new model every week. By the same token, we could all tell when Morecambe and Wise made their breakthrough because thereafter Ernie Wise would talk about little else except the money he was making on the Stock Exchange. But the hunt for new talent was as frantic as ever. I remember seeing Benny Hill in a summer show at Margate. He was stooge then, playing up to the antics of Reg Varney, one of the top acts on my agency list. Reg was as good as ever but I could not take my eyes off Benny Hill who had the gift of all great comedians of attracting laughs just by standing there on stage. It was not long before he was topping the bill in a Bernard Delfont show.

The move towards quality entertainment in seafront theatres was predated in the West End and on the major provincial circuits. For a short time after the war, it was amazing what we could get away with. When I co-presented a revival of *Rose Marie* with Tom Arnold we both went to the first night at the New Theatre in Birmingham. At one point in the show there was a longer than usual scene change and to cover the awkward pause the orchestra started playing the big number, 'Rose Marie, I love you, I'm always dreaming of you . . .' Since this must have been the thousandth time I had heard the tune, I said to Tom, 'Let's take a break. There's a place round the corner we can get a drink and sandwich.' We were gone about twenty minutes. When we returned to our box the curtain was still down and there was the orchestra plodding away, 'Rose Marie, I love you . . .' It was no way to treat an audience but then – and this was the point – no one had left the theatre or even complained.

It was not much different from when Sir Harry Lauder was the darling of the Scottish music hall and I was appearing with him at Her Majesty's, Aberdeen (surely I must be one of the few survivors among his supporting acts). He would sing 'Roamin' in the Gloamin'' or another of his popular numbers before disappearing into the wings to carry out a leisurely costume change. While he was gone the orchestra repeated the tune as often as he needed to perfect his disguise. Then back he would come for another song and another exit, leaving the orchestra to entertain. This would be repeated for up to half an hour, of which at least half Lauder was off stage. But those days were long gone and even after my experience of *Rose*

Marie in Birmingham I could not imagine they would ever return.

At any rate, in the West End, variety could only survive if it was top drawer. Of that, I was certain. As the *Evening News* reported me as saying: 'The truth is that people in the West End don't want variety in the sense the term has always been understood. At suburban music halls they can see ordinary turns at a top price of six shillings. For thirteen shillings and sixpence in the West End they want something different.'

Freely translated, 'something different' meant American imports, the screen stars who had kept Britain entertained throughout the war. Now the public wanted to see them in the flesh and they were ready to pay for the privilege.

The big question for me was whether I could afford to back my judgement. A dispassionate observer would have said that I was trying to do too much. Skilful cross-accounting between various parts of the company disguised a mountain of debts, and this at a time when working in show business was an automatic disqualification for a bank overdraft. I did try the money-lenders once or twice but the interest rates were crippling – thirty per cent or more. And to fall behind with a money-lender was an invitation to bankruptcy. The deposit was a collection of post-dated cheques, up to fifty in my recollection, which were handed in to the bank on the dot. If one bounced, so did the borrower.

There were means of raising cash from the bank for short-term emergencies. One trick was known as the 'crossover'. A group of friends would swap cheques of equal value, say one thousand pounds. Since paying in was recorded faster than paying out, we were all in credit for a few hours. I did say it was short term.

The only reliable source of temporary finance was the generosity of good friends. Top of the list was Al Burnett, one-time comedian ('a bad boy from a good family'), an East Ender who ran smart night-clubs – the Stork Room in Swallow Street and the Pigalle in Piccadilly. In the months ahead Al regularly came to my rescue with a bag of bank-notes skimmed off the previous night's takings. If we were unable to meet up, he would call at my flat in the early hours. There were mornings when I woke up to find the front door mat strewn with fivers.

Susan Jane was born in April 1947. It was a difficult birth, but within a few months Carole and Bruce Trent were off on a tour of the music halls with their selection of popular songs from the shows.

99

They were back in London to play the Lewisham Hippodrome when Carole collapsed after the first house and had to be rushed home.

The doctor could tell immediately what had happened. Carole had suffered a miscarriage. She was ordered to take a complete rest. We all thought this would do the trick but at the end of a week, I began to worry even more. Carole showed no sign of recovery; in fact, she seemed to be getting weaker by the day. I was sitting by her bedside when I heard her whisper one word, 'Schlyer'. This was the name of her gynaecologist. I had to bend towards her to hear the rest. 'Please ring him; he's back from holiday today.'

He came round at once and within minutes was on the telephone booking Carole into a nursing home. It was touch and go. She had to have several blood transfusions before treatment could begin and it was several weeks before we could see that she was on the mend. The doctors warned that there might be difficulties in having another child.

It was easier for me to compensate by throwing myself into work. I told myself I had to get on with my life; we needed the money. Then again, if there was an ideal opportunity to launch into top flight variety this was it. With the Holborn Empire put out of action by the Blitz, the only rival for business was the Palladium where, after the death of George Black, Val Parnell was settling in as head of Moss Empires. Val was notoriously ambitious but my feeling was that he had enough to occupy him with the spectacular revues that were the hallmark of Palladium entertainment. Surely, he would not worry too much about my little scheme.

I had, I thought, one other strong argument for taking the plunge – a seven-year lease on the London Casino. A cabaret restaurant before the war, the Casino had then become a services club until it was reopened by Tom Arnold and Emile Littler as a musical theatre in 1946. It was in a good position just off Cambridge Circus to one side of the Palace Theatre, close by the Soho restaurants.

I began putting out feelers to the US, hardly daring to think of the money I needed to attract stars with international appeal. It soon became clear that I would not get much for less than a thousand pounds a week. (Multiply by at least twenty for some idea of what that means in today's terms.) Even at this level the prospects were limited to performers who were past their Hollywood best. Not that this mattered very much to the British public who, inevitably, were some way behind American fashion. For them, the likes of Chico Marx or Laurel and Hardy came as fresh as green grass.

The fame of Laurel and Hardy rested almost entirely on their Hal Roach shorts – every one a classic of screen comedy. But so tied were they to their cinema reputation, few people remembered that they started their careers in variety and that Stan, in particular, had no greater love than live theatre. Add the knowledge that Stan was British-born, the son of an actor-manager and we had the basis of a deal well before we got to talk about money. What I did not realise when I made my approach was that Laurel and Hardy had had enough of films. Disillusionment had set in after the agony of working for the big studios where they were forced to rework tired comic formulas. They were positively eager to appear at the London Casino.

Booked first class on the *Queen Mary*, they docked at Southampton and came on to London by train. When they arrived at Waterloo it was cold and pouring with rain. What a contrast to California, in everything that is except the warmth of the reception. Thousands of fans jammed the station forecourt. Stan and Ollie had no idea there would be such a welcome; and nor had I. But it took me no time at all to realise that I was on to a resounding hit. I increased the publicity budget and topped up the price of the best stalls.

Then I made a mistake. I invited Val Parnell to Newcastle where Laurel and Hardy were booked on the start of a brief pre-London tour. Word had come back to me that Val had no faith at all in my ambitions for the Casino. For him, offering twice or three times the going rate for the top of the bill was a recipe for disaster. Now with Laurel and Hardy I had proved him wrong and I was not afraid of telling him so.

'There you are,' I boasted as the customers thronged into the Theatre Royal. 'Didn't I say I could afford to pay a thousand a week?'

Val went away in thoughtful mood.

After a triumphal first night at Newcastle, I went back to the Station Hotel with Stan, Ollie and Stan's wife Ida. We were in the mood to celebrate but in the year of the big freeze with all fuel on strict ration, the euphoria soon passed. Instead, we concentrated on keeping warm. Wrapped in our overcoats, huddled round a small fire, the scene was reminiscent of one of the early Laurel and Hardy movies when the jokes turned on the predicaments of genteel poverty. Any moment now, I thought, we'll be breaking up the furniture for firewood. Instead, I saw Stan assuming his mask of utter dejection, pluck the last piece of coal from the bucket and place it delicately in

101

the middle of the grate. As if pronouncing a valediction, he sighed, 'There'll always be an England', and we all chorused back, 'Another fine mess you've got us into.'

Back in London, with the sold out notices posted outside the Casino, I had a message from Val Parnell. He wanted to see me. It wasn't difficult to guess what was bothering him.

He was on the attack before I could sit down. 'You must stop this nonsense,' he ordered. 'You're hurting the Palladium and I won't have that.'

I ventured the thought that the West End was big enough for both of us.

'Not while you're putting on variety at the Casino. I'm giving you fair warning. If you go on, I'll break you.'

The disbelief must have shown on my face.

'You think I don't mean it? Well, just remember what I've said next time you try booking one of your acts for Moss Empires. I'll put a ban on the Delfont agency. How long do you think you'll last then?'

The straight answer was not very long at all but I had no intention of conceding. 'Val,' I said, 'I can only tell you that I've invested too much in the Casino to stop now. But we might make a deal if you're willing to pay. What do you say to twenty thousand?'

It was the first time I had seen him speechless. But only for a moment. 'Get out of here,' he shouted. 'Right now; get out.'

I didn't stay for a third invitation. As I walked away from the Palladium a much-told story of Val Parnell came to mind. His secretary announced a visitor.

'Who is it?' demanded Val.

'Someone who wants to shoot you, sir.'

'Tell him to join the queue.'

I was banned from Moss Empires. Then Val did something far worse. He went into direct competition by hiring the most popular American acts at fees I could not begin to match. I first got wind of the change of policy at the Palladium when I spoke to Lew and Leslie who I knew had strong contacts with American show business. I mentioned a few names.

Lew shook his head. 'There's not a chance of booking them. Val Parnell comes first.'

I pleaded family loyalty, I pleaded wife and daughter, I pleaded lots of things but Lew was adamant. I couldn't blame him. The interests of the Grade Agency dictated a good working relationship with Val Parnell who had not only the Palladium at his command but all the best provincial theatres. Still, I can't say that I was not hurt.

I had one or two clear victories over the competition, however. Chico Marx was a real coup. He played to near capacity at the Casino and when he finished there and I found that he had three weeks to spare, I persuaded him to follow up with some provincial dates. But because I was banned from Moss Empires I had to book him for the second string of theatres. I am not sure the poor man knew what he was letting himself in for. His itinerary was Hull, Dudley and Coventry. When he returned home he sent me a cable: 'Eternal gratitude for sending me to Hell, Deadley and Cemetery.'

The Casino was fading some time before Val launched his variety programme. Our latest American import was the Inkspots but though they sang to packed houses we had to drop prices to bring in the youngsters which meant that we barely broke even. There was a moment of hope when Val opened with Mickey Rooney, who was a fair disaster, completing only three weeks of his four-week engagement. But he followed up with Danny Kaye. Here was a young comedian, a true original, who could hold an audience for forty-five minutes. I knew when I was beaten.

I did try to keep going with British acts. Norman Wisdom, then at the outset of his career, did well, stealing the show from Alan Jones, now best known as the father of Jack Jones. Alan was a great singer in his time but when I booked him he was too much in love with the bottle to perform at his best. The catalogue of his misbehaviour stretched from Blackpool, where he failed to turn up at the theatre for two days and was sent home on the third, to Chatham, where he locked himself in his dressing-room. In fairness, when we tried him again three years later he was in much better form, apologising profusely to me for his past failings.

Another British success story was Winifred Atwell who came to me quite by accident. There was a big charity concert at which Carole was due to appear. But at the last moment she fell ill and, stuck for a replacement, I turned to the agency. Keith Devon said he had a coloured girl, a pianist who had the makings of a star. The applause that night for Winifred Atwell proved him right and I immediately booked her for two weeks at the Casino. The trouble was, there were simply not enough Norman Wisdoms and Winifred Atwells.

103

One of my great regrets was giving up any thought of ever again presenting Richard Tauber. His health would not allow it. After the success of *Gay Rosalinda*, he followed up by conducting *The Birdseller*, also at the Palace. By the first night, he was breathing so hard he couldn't climb the stairs to his dressing-room on the first floor. He had to make do with the artistes' quick-change room on the prompt side of the stage. In July 1947, an X-ray showed that he had lung cancer. I went to see him in hospital. He was fast losing weight and though he was told he had an abscess of the lung, he must have guessed the truth. A fortnight later he spoke to me on the telephone. I heard a throaty voice struggling to speak.

'I will never sing again, Bernard. This is the end of me.'

He died on the eighth day of 1948. At a memorial concert at the Albert Hall, seven thousand fans stood shoulder to shoulder to sing 'You Are My Heart's Delight'.

At least I can say that variety at the London Casino ended on a high note, and with an American act. Ralph Slater was billed as 'the world's fastest hypnotist' which was fine if he could live up to his claim. But I did have a worry about costs.

'How many fares have I got to pay for?' I asked his agent. I expected to hear that at least half a dozen stooges had to accompany him but instead I was told, 'There's only him, you only have to pay one fare.'

Confident that stage hypnotism was no more than a simple trick, I assumed that Ralph Slater would be recruiting his stooges once he arrived, but when we met he assured me that he worked alone. I kept a closed mind on the subject expecting to be let in on the secret before the first night.

But then he wanted to hold a press conference. This worried me. All I needed was a column in the *Express* or *Mail* revealing that my star turn was a con artist. I tried to dissuade him and when he insisted and I saw the list of notables he had invited, I took the coward's way out, pleading a full diary as an excuse for not attending what I was pretty certain would turn out to be a theatrical wake.

The press conference was well under way when I had a telephone call from the theatre.

'You should get over here. You've never seen anything like it.'

I hurried to the Casino to find an audience of hardened reporters in total rapture. On stage a dozen of their colleagues were performing weird contortions on the orders of Ralph Slater. An eminent reviewer was hunched like a begging dog, panting to be given a bone.

I was convinced and so was everyone else. Ralph Slater was the only performer I have encountered to get rave notices before the first night. He was a sell-out.

And that, for the Casino, was that. Except to postscript its transformation into the Prince Edward. Once more under the Delfont banner, the theatre has enjoyed a succession of long-running musicals like *Evita*, *Chess* and *Anything Goes*.

I did not dwell on the failure of the Casino. I had long before learned that anyone who wasted time worrying about flops or gloating over triumphs did not deserve to be in show business. And I took some comfort from the knowledge that there was still an audience for music hall. The problem for all producers, not just me, was in finding the talent to satisfy demand. The public was not to be fobbed off.

There is a story about the singer Phylis Robbins who made her name on radio with Henry Hall and his Orchestra. Her big hit was a catchy sentimental number, 'How Much is That Doggy in the Window?'. Her chance as a live entertainer came when Florence Leddington, the booker for the Syndicate Halls, was short of a top of the bill for a week at the Metropolitan, Edgware Road. Florence rang Phylis's agent who reacted cautiously. Phylis was not a music hall act; she did not have the build-up to sustain a full ten minutes.

Florence was not to be put off. 'All she has to do is to choose a couple of songs. As long as she finishes with "How Much is That Doggy", she'll do fine.'

Phylis was booked.

The first couple of nights she got by but by midweek the audience was restless. To the rear of the theatre was a long bar where customers could drink during the show. This is where the trouble started. She was midway through 'Red Sails in the Sunset' when she faltered.

A loud voice echoed across the auditorium. 'Give us the dog, Phyl, and piss off.'

It was tough on Phylis but whoever said show business was easy?

Chapter 7

There wasn't much left after the Casino. What money I could raise, I raised, for example, by selling off my half of the Garrick Theatre to Jack Buchanan who was keen to take over the management. This was a sad retreat on my ambitions to produce more mainstream theatre, though I distinguished myself at the Garrick by co-presenting two plays with Laurence Olivier. The second of these, an American import called *Born Yesterday*, was a great success and launched the career of Yolande Donlan.

I did hold on to the Saville, expecting a hit with *Roundabout*, a musical comedy with Bobby Howes and the lovely Pat Kirkwood. Instead it fell straight through the floor with the first night audience clapping politely from the stalls and booing loudly from the gallery. It did not help that the show was clumsily directed but the problem was compounded by Bobby Howes, who resented the popularity of Marilyn Hightower, a red-headed ballerina who stole what there was to steal of the show. At the curtain call, he insisted on a solo bow, ignoring encores for Marilyn who very properly stayed in the wings. When the audience resorted to a clearer indication of its preference, he stupidly began to exchange insults which caused the stage manager to bring down the curtain and to keep it down. Unfortunately for Bobby Howes, it was a fixed curtain so the only way he could get off was to crawl under the tassels on his hands and knees.

I tried to comfort myself with the thought that this must be my lowest point. I was wrong. With the Saville I still had some way to go. The next disaster was a summons for non-payment of rates. And the disaster after that was a phone call from a young and eager reporter on the *Express*. He had a question for me.

'Is the rumour true, Mr Delfont? Is the council taking you to court?'

It seemed pointless to argue. 'Yes, I'm afraid it's true.'

I should not have been surprised when the next morning I opened my newspaper to see the headline, 'Delfont Sued For Rates'. But I was taken aback. I had no idea that my small sin of omission would command such attention. The journalist who gave me such unwelcome prominence was David Lewin, soon to become one of the leading show business writers in Fleet Street. Now an old friend, he confesses that our first exchange caused him as much surprise as it did me, but for a different reason. He expected me to make excuses or to bluff a denial or even to threaten proceedings if anything appeared in print. He was not used to the straight answer.

In return he did me a favour. Or rather, he tried to do me a favour. He told me about a French singer, Yves Montand, who was enrapturing Parisian night life. Wasn't it time that London shared the excitement? I went over to Paris to see for myself what all the fuss was about. After one performance, I was sold. Not yet thirty, Yves Montand was a rarity whose appeal spanned the ages. The youngsters adored him, so too did their parents and, for all I knew, their grandparents as well. An idea began to form. I would combine the appeal of the music hall with the night-club to create a form of intimate variety. The Saville was available, so too was Dickie Hurran who was eager to direct his first West End show. A deal was struck with Yves Montand.

The first night was as near perfect as any opening I can recall. The audience was in ecstasy, Yves Montand was exhausted by encores and the critics departed wreathed in smiles to compose notices of undiluted praise. And then – nothing. The box-office slumbered. London was not ready for Yves Montand which was a sad reflection on London and an even sadder reflection on my commercial credibility.

My need for a money-spinner was now greater than ever. Seeking inspiration, I looked back over my list of successes. A popular touring production caught my eye, the *Bouwmeester Continental Revue Spectacle*, better known here as *Ta-Ra-Rah-Boom-De-Ay*, the show that lifted Frankie Howerd from the long-running radio series *Variety Bandbox* into live entertainment. On his home ground Bouwmeester's revue spectacle was billed as the *Dutch Folies Bergère*, a not altogether accurate description but one which he encouraged. No doubt he would have preferred the real thing – to produce the *Folies Bergère*, but to do that he had to overcome the objections of a temperamental Frenchman, Paul Derval, the begetter of the modern

Folies who watched over his creation with the possessiveness of a mother hen.

I knew just how difficult it was to persuade Derval to loosen his grip on the *Folies* because I had already tried, and failed. But I was now a more seasoned producer with experience of massaging giant-sized egos. Maybe it was time for me to try again. I started with at least one advantage. I knew what not to do. The wrong approach was to suggest that anyone else could possibly rise to the same level of achievement as Paul Derval. A succession of producers had found out the hard way that he did not enjoy comparison with his rivals, least of all with Florenz Ziegfeld whose *Follies* were the success story of Broadway in the twenties and thirties. Ziegfeld, according to Derval, was like all American showmen, bold and brassy, lacking that essence of sophistication that raised the *Folies Bergère* to the level of high art.

The dismissive tone was unfair on Ziegfeld whose song and dance extravaganzas did much to shape the great American musical while, incidentally, giving us some of the most haunting Broadway tunes of the pre-war years. When, today, I hear someone humming 'A Pretty Girl is Like a Melody', I wonder if they know they are paying tribute to the Ziegfeld *Follies* of 1919 and all the subsequent *Follies* which shared the number as their theme song.

But if Derval's claim for the *Folies Bergère* could sound pretentious, particularly to those who were used to putting on bigger shows in bigger theatres, it was true to say that he offered a rare combination of the exotic and the spectacular. Put at its simplest, the *Folies* consisted of a series of tableaux, as many as sixty in a show of over three hours. These might be sumptuously costumed like the Russian Cossack Festival or Waltzes of Old Vienna or hardly dressed at all like Venus Arising or the Judgement of Paris. Of course, the female nudes were the chief attraction but the crowds would not have come in if there had been a hint of salaciousness. The genius of Derval was to take the *Folies* to the limits of propriety and to hold it there, never once transgressing into vulgarity. I suppose this is what he meant by his 'art' though I would put it more prosaically by giving credit to a talent for appearing to be daring without actually causing offence. The *Folies Bergère* was the prime example of a show that was naughty but nice.

Knowing how difficult it was to pull off this trick, I was happy enough to accept Derval's first and vital condition for any deal – that he and his team should be consulted on every detail of the London production.

A year or two earlier, Val Parnell had balked at terms which seemed to take away his right to produce. 'I'm not going to have Derval decide how I spend my own money,' he told Alec Shanks, one of the regular *Folies Bergère* designers who had acted as intermediary.

When he heard that I was taking an interest, Val voiced his opinion in his usual forthright manner. 'You must be mad. You'll have that Frenchman leaning over your shoulder all the time. What does he know about English audiences?'

Normally, I would not have been tempted to argue with a man who, until recently, had looked on me as a sworn enemy. But if I was to go ahead with the *Folies Bergère* I needed a suitable theatre – not too large, central and with a name for top-flight entertainment – and Moss Empires had the answer. The Hippodrome was just off Leicester Square, it was about the same size as the home of the *Folies Bergère* in Paris and it was in need of a show. Of course, Val was not one to let out a theatre to any producer who turned up with the rent. He had to be convinced that the product was up to his exacting standards. Given his opinion of Paul Derval, it must have seemed that I was on to a loser. He was not renowned for changing his mind.

But I had a trick in reserve. His name was Michel Gyarmathy, a magnificently gifted costume and set designer who began to make his reputation with the *Folies* just before the war. He arrived from Budapest at a time when the *Folies* was paying for star names to boost the appeal of what, for many, had become formula productions. Gyarmathy brought style back to the *Folies* with spectacular tableaux that defied the proportions of a stage only twenty feet deep. He did it by relying on height, giving extra depth to his sets by raising the up-stage levels to a near vertical gradient. It was said that the idea occurred to him in his student days when he learned stagecraft from a seat in the gallery.

It might be expected that, as a Jew, Michel Gyarmathy's career would have come to an abrupt halt with the Nazis' entry into Paris. Not a bit of it. The *Folies Bergère* was enormously popular with the occupying forces, so much so that when Paul Derval told the Gestapo that without Michel there could be no *Folies*, they proved uncharacteristically eager to bend the rules. The arrangement was for Michel to have his own apartment at the theatre, built under the stage. And that is where he remained throughout the war except for a nightly excursion to a café on the Champs Elysées where he would sit for half an hour drinking his coffee, watching the traffic go by. Last year, when Dickie Hurran was in Paris, he called by on the off-chance of seeing Michel. When there was no answer at his flat, Dickie took a walk. There was Michel, at the same café, at the same table, taking in the Paris scene that he had enjoyed for over forty-five years.

Back in 1949 I had the advantage over Val Parnell of knowing something of the work of Michel Gyarmathy. Here, I argued, was a designer of genius who had the same international potential as the leaders of the great fashion houses. Val was not convinced. If Gyarmathy came to London it could only be under the tutelage of Paul Derval and that, for Val, meant handing over control to a foreigner he had already decided not to like. Meanwhile, I had come to a provisional agreement with the Frenchman to present the *Folies Bergère* in London. He assumed that I had a suitable theatre lined up. I decided to take a chance on showing him the Hippodrome while fervently hoping that Val would have a change of heart.

All I can say is that he left it late enough. Val rang me less than forty-eight hours before Derval was due to arrive to inspect his London venue.

'If you go alone on this, you're asking for trouble,' he bellowed. 'We'll work together. If I like the show you can have the Hippodrome.'

From which I concluded that my attempt at the Casino to nudge him off his pedestal had earned me a certain respect.

I still had a long way to go. The most I had from Val was a promise to let me know if he decided that the *Folies* was a production worthy of his patronage. He would not make up his mind, he said, until the out-of-town run, scheduled to open in Birmingham in less than a month. By then, of course, I would be committed to spending a great deal of money and, assuming the worst with Val giving me the thumbs down, far more than I could afford. I tried to put this unpleasant thought out of my head by concentrating on more immediate problems such as the dock strike at Portsmouth which held up the delivery of scenery and dresses for several weeks. When, at last, we were able to open up the crates it was like catching the full force of Old Macdonald's farm, not at all the aroma that a paying audience would expect on their night out.

Dickie Hurran, who was directing the show, suggested that if we left the crates open for a few days the smell would dilute sufficiently for strong scenery removers to attempt the unpacking. This made sense but to be on the safe side I hired watchmen to protect my investment. I shouldn't have worried. When, after a decent interval, we returned to check the damage I did not need to be told that no one had approached the containers or, if they had, they had soon backed off again.

With time pressing I gave the go-ahead on remaking most of the costumes. A brave decision? Not really. It was either that or calling the whole thing off.

The good news was the response to the auditions – over two thousand girls for a company of a hundred. We were looking for style and charm and beauty – and we found all three in abundance. Dickie Hurran cast a professional eye over the line-up. 'Thank you, dear. Very good. Next,' was his constant refrain for three days. I was surprised at the general lack of inhibition. Young ladies who chose to be chorus girls were expected to reveal a lot but not all – or nearly all. (Essential modesty was protected by the cache-sexe, a theatrical version of the fig leaf.)

Yet here they were, queuing for the privilege to be the first British *filles des Folies*. I had no doubt that Paul Derval would be proud of them. I was reminded of my unshakeable confidence a few years later when I paid one of my many visits to the Paris Lido. The cabaret at the Lido was simply breathtaking with one of the best chorus lines in the business. When I congratulated Pierre Gueran, who masterminded the show, he asked if I would go backstage to meet some of the girls. I was only too happy to oblige, thinking to myself, if only they would work in some of my shows, what a difference they would make.

I was in for a surprise. All the girls were British.

'But why didn't you work for me?' I wanted to know.

'We tried,' they said. 'But we failed the audition.'

I went away duly chastened. It just showed what the spirit of Paris could do for you.

As soon as our *Folies Bergère* went into rehearsal we had a visit from the Lord Chamberlain who wanted to check that we were keeping within the bounds of good taste. Nudes were permissible but only in a context that was judged to be respectable. The analogy that comes to mind is a naked woman in an old master painting because, like Venus preserved in oils, our nudes had to remain absolutely motionless. The assumption, I suppose, was that unclothed beauties

111

on the move were more likely to excite the passions of a male audience, though the opposite was held true in the States where the nudes were not allowed to stand still. None of it made very much sense but as a commercial producer I had to follow the conventions.

Negotiations with the Lord Chamberlain's office were amicable to a fault but there was evidently a worry that the arrival of the *Folies* was the start of a wholesale importation of sinful Paris. I had to promise not to make too much of the girls in my promotion and to try for a balance between the scenes featuring nudes and those where all the participants were fully clothed. This set us off on a frantic hunt for comedy talent, names that would add lustre to the show without dominating it by taking superior billing to the *Folies*.

To Dickie Hurran goes the credit for bringing on a wild-eyed young comic with an Einstein shock of hair who could keep an audience in fits with impersonations that relied less on his voice than on eccentric props. At the audition, Michael Bentine used a folded inner tube to give an entirely convincing demonstration of Al Jolson singing 'Mammy'.

Another find was Tommy Cooper, one of the great originals, a clown more than a comedian who earned his laughs by *not* being able to perform the simplest conjuring tricks. Much of the humour was in anticipating how things would go wrong, an effect that could be more difficult to achieve than making them go right. I first saw Tommy Cooper in a club in Cork Street. Dickie Hurran urged me to go along for what he promised would be a revelation. It was, but not quite in the sense he anticipated. Poor Tommy worked his heart out for a totally unresponsive audience. Apart from Dickie and myself giving moral support there was not a single laugh. If anything, the gloom deepened as the act wore on and Tommy wore himself out. Afterwards, I talked to the manager who agreed it had not been a good night.

'But then,' he added, 'what can you expect? We were sold out to German tourists.'

Evidently, the foreigners went away with a poor view of British speciality acts if, as they gathered, Tommy Cooper was among the best conjurers we could find in the West End. Fortunately, the *Folies Bergère* audiences were more responsive to his brand of fooling.

Having contended with the Lord Chamberlain we next had to persuade the Birmingham Watch Committee that we would be on our best behaviour. Each town had its official guardians of morality with their own, often idiosyncratic, interpretations of decency. The Birmingham committee – all men, I couldn't help noticing – seemed to enjoy the rehearsals; they stayed long enough, anyway. But one after another they took me aside to confess their great worry, that come the first night one of the girls would actually move.

'It doesn't have to be deliberate, you know, Mr Delfont,' warned the chairman. 'It only takes one little mistake and we're in trouble.'

He was too polite to say so but what he really meant was that it only needed one little mistake for *me* to be in trouble.

I passed on my concern to Dickie Hurran. 'If any of those nudes so much as moves a finger, I'm out of business. And one of them's got a cold. What do we do if she sneezes?'

Dickie assured me that she was already halfway to recovery. Running through the programme, the highest risk was a tableau called Lions at Bay in which sundry girls were frozen in various representations of terror while a fearless muscle-man held off the attentions of two marauding lions. Well, 'marauding' may be pitching it too highly since the lions were very elderly and almost toothless. According to Dickie, they barely had the strength to move. But he flatly refused to enlighten the girls who, he reasoned, would perform more realistically if they believed the danger to be real. I couldn't help feeling they were just as likely to panic if one of the decrepit man-eaters gave so much as a hint of energy. But I let the director have his way.

The first night presented me with a ticklish decision: how best to divide my time. There was the entire Birmingham Watch Committee occupying the box with the best view of the stage. I could hardly leave them to their own devices. But there was Val Parnell too, pacing back and forth at the rear of the stalls, barking off questions whenever he caught sight of me.

'Who's this Tommy Cooper? Is he any good?'

'Yes, Val. He's first class.'

'Well I've never heard of him.'

It was not the only signal I had that evening that Val had made up his mind before the curtain went up.

Then I had to contend with Paul Derval and Michel Gyarmathy. To be fair, Michel was always the professional. When he thought something was wrong, he said so but always followed up with a solution. He and Dickie Hurran ran a mutual admiration society which operated quite happily without much interference from me.

113

Paul Derval was more of a problem in that any offence, real or imagined, against his concept of the *Folies Bergère* was thrown in my direction.

All I had to offer in return was a few soothing words, the same formula as I used for Val Parnell and the Watch Committee while trying to keep the three interests apart. There was no virtue in allowing them to share their worries.

All things considered, the show went well; a few rough edges but no one had yet produced a faultless out-of-town run. The audience was friendly. At the half, the bars were humming with good humour. Sadly, the euphoric mood did not extend to Val Parnell. 'It's not right,' he told me. 'It won't do.'

I guessed that he had taken against the costumes. In the rush to duplicate the rejects from Paris, I had overstretched the skills of our wardrobe mistress. There was a hint of making-do which I could not disguise.

'But we can work on it,' I promised Val.

He shook his head. 'It won't make any difference. It's not good enough for the Hippodrome and I'm not taking it.'

He didn't even say he was sorry. I had to concentrate very hard on keeping calm. My career and the livelihoods of some hundred and fifty performers and stage-hands were on the line.

Admitting that the show had its faults, I could not believe that Val would turn it down flat unless, of course, he was out to ruin me in retaliation for the Casino episode. But it was more likely, I decided, that he was testing me, seeing just how far I would go without him. Very well, if that was the game, I was prepared to raise the stakes.

I let the rumour circulate that whatever happened the *Folies* would be coming into the West End. After all, I had my own theatre, the Saville, I could make available. In reality this was impossible as the stage was far too small and the atmosphere somehow wrong for this type of show. But Val didn't know that. I calculated that he would soon come round to the possibility that he had made a mistake.

After a few days, he rang me again. 'I hear you're doing the *Folies* at the Saville.'

I jollied him along. 'We've made a lot of improvements. Birmingham was just a try-out. We've new costumes, scenery, the lot. It'll be a first-class show.'

'Come round to my office,' said Val. 'I want to talk.'

It was the turning point. We opened at the Hippodrome to fabulous reviews and an advance booking that suggested a run of at least a year. In the event we scored seventeen months before changing over to *Encore des Folies* which ran for a year and then to the *Folies Bergère Revue* which took us up to and beyond two thousand performances. For the *Encore* we moved from the Hippodrome across the road to the Prince of Wales. For years, the theatre had been the second home of Sid Field, a much loved Birmingham-born comedian who did his best work in revue. But when Sid died at the tragically early age of forty-six, Val was at a loss to know what to do with the Prince of Wales. It was his idea that the *Folies* should move in there. At first, I was not much taken with his plan. But with Val arguing that it was easier to get shows for the Hippodrome than for the Prince of Wales, I agreed on condition that I could hold on as long as the *Folies* did good business.

What worried me about the Prince of Wales was its small stage but after Dickie Hurran and Michel Gyarmathy had worked their miracles, I soon came to appreciate the warm, club-like atmosphere of the theatre. With the circle front only twenty-one feet from the orchestra, even those in the cheaper seats felt themselves part of the action.

The success of the *Folies* encouraged me to spend liberally on the sequels. The *Encore* absorbed over eighty thousand pounds, something of a record for this type of West End show. I found myself paying out for the most extraordinary props, including the accessories for a Moroccan street market and the interior embellishments of an opera house preparing for the opening night of Verdi's *La Traviata*. Having said yes to all this I was then asked to foot the bill for a bathing pool.

'Only a small one,' Dickie assured me.

Whenever a journalist came within my sights, I peppered him with statistics. We made twelve hundred costumes for *Encore des Folies*. For these we needed a thousand yards of gold braid and a quarter of a billion sequins, not to mention feathered headdresses, white fox furs and enough jewellery to stock a fair-sized emporium.

We brought in some fine acts – Chaz Chase, the little man with baggy pants who ate everything he could lay hands on including his own shirt front, Eddie Vitch, the drunk who threw himself out of bars and a French leading lady, Lilo, a gorgeous blonde who was as cute as a button.

Lilo had only a few words of English which mattered hardly at all until Tommy Cooper joined the cast. There was a part of the show where male volunteers from the audience came up on stage to try their luck on riding the 'bucking horse', a sort of rocking-horse but more unpredictable in its movements. As the hostess for this game, Lilo was taught a few simple phrases to explain to her victims what they had to do and to encourage them in their endeavours. A little nervous at having to express herself in unfamiliar words, she was appreciatively attentive when Tommy Cooper offered to help with her pronunciation. He started by teaching her how to say 'bucking horse' by replacing the first letter with one a little further on in the alphabet. Lilo responded enthusiastically, welcoming her contestants with a big smile and a cheerful invitation to climb up on the 'bucking horse', except that it didn't sound quite like that. Acting further on Tommy's advice she bombarded the riders with observations on their equestrian talents which were nothing short of obscene.

Her slowness in picking up English was no impediment to Lilo's career. She had not been with the show long before she told Dickie Hurran she had received another offer.

'A man called Cole Porter wants me to go to New York. Have you heard of him?'

Lilo was off to Broadway to play the lead in *Can Can*.

We were always on the lookout for new acts with a touch of novelty about them. How could I then resist seeing a tassel tosser at work? Baby Scruggs was American, black and statuesque in the way that the Ancient Greeks appreciated their statues. She wore three tassels, two hooked to a minuscule brassière and one attached to her bottom. When the music started she threw herself into the most amazing gyrations which caused all three tassels to revolve simultaneously, making her look like a catherine wheel with sex appeal. At the rehearsal, an unexpected element was introduced by the performer's mother standing in the wings, screeching encouragement.

'Come on, Baby! Give it to 'em, Baby!'

I thought the act was embarrassingly awful. Dickie Hurran agreed. We couldn't take the chance on her opening the show.

'There's no way round it,' I said. 'We'll have to pay her the eight weeks' guarantee and send her back to America.'

On the way out of the theatre, we passed the box-office. The manager was smiling broadly. He could hardly contain himself. 'What an act,' he enthused. 'Isn't she great? I've never seen an act like it.'

I backtracked on the conversation to make quite sure that we were talking about the same performance.

The box-office manager stuck to his guns. 'She'll be terrific.'

Dickie glanced at me and shrugged. A few minutes later we made Baby Scruggs the happiest tassel tosser in the business. Fortunately for us, the audiences agreed with the box-office manager. She was a sensation.

Having made the breakthrough with the *Folies*, I kept up its popularity by putting in stars like Norman Wisdom, Benny Hill, Frankie Howerd and Winifred Atwell. My next move was to see if I could repeat the trick in Australia where theatre owners were clamouring for our business. The idea was for Dickie to go along with the show. But first there was a small domestic matter to sort out. His wife, Pam, was three months pregnant; Dickie would be away for at least six months.

There was only one solution.

'Take Pam with you. She'll enjoy the break.'

Dickie was not too sure, agreeing only that Pam would consult her gynaecologist.

A day or two later he came into the office wearing a huge smile. 'The doctor says it's fine; as long as we go by boat.'

I was delighted. 'You can do better than that,' I said. 'Book first class.'

They sailed on the *Dominion Monarch* and were one month at sea. Dickie still remembers it as the holiday of a lifetime, though it ended with an unpleasant surprise. He was leaning on the rail, admiring the view of Sydney harbour bridge. Beside him was Tommy Trinder, who was touring his own show. As they neared the quay, Tommy spotted some familiar-looking packing cases.

'Aren't they your props?' he asked Dickie.

'Can't be,' said Dickie. 'They were unloaded a month ago.'

But then he looked more carefully and they *were* our packing cases. They had been stranded by a dock strike. It took several days of patient negotiation and the allocation of bundles of complimentary tickets to get the props released and delivered to the theatre.

Thereafter, the biggest problem was trying to persuade the Australian stage-hands to take their job seriously. There was a tendency for them to regard the stationary nude (the decency rule applied as strongly as in Britain) as a challenge to their sporting instincts. Bets were taken on who would be the first to cause one of the girls to lose her poise. Dickie caught on to the game just in time. Patrolling the wings he found a stage-hand blowing gently over the surface of a box of snuff.

Back home I was counting the blessings the *Folies Bergère* had brought me, not to mention two other long-running West End productions and a few well-patronised touring shows. The speedy recovery from near-bankruptcy meant that I could at last afford to give Carole a really decent home. We were living in a flat off Avenue Road – you could rent flats then – and I knew Carole wanted to move into more spacious accommodation. Having launched into house hunting with her customary energy she discovered, much to her joy, that she was pregnant again.

But after seeing her gynaecologist, the same Mr Schlyer who had been such a support at the time of Susan's birth, she was not so happy. He told her that if she really wanted to keep the baby she would have to rest completely – so no more chasing after estate agents. Even so, after a few scares, she had to stay in bed completely for the last three months.

We were very lucky to have a sweet Austrian girl to help with Susan, now a lively eighteen months, a devoted housekeeper and, for moral support, a boxer, a Peke and a ginger cat! Carole organised us all from her bed. No one was happier than I when Mr Schlyer announced that he would operate the next week. Thus Jennifer Lucy was lifted into the world on 9 July 1949, a beautiful little girl who, in contrast to Susan, did not have to fight to be born.

After a few months, Carole went back to work, playing Cinderella at the Casino with Arthur Askey as Buttons. Her career was in full bloom as I was reminded the other day when Carole was asked for her autograph as one of the stars of *The Ghost Train*, now one of the classic film comedies of the early forties. But it was not long before the strain began to tell.

Carole's last show was a revue called *Touch and Go* which I presented at the Prince of Wales. Among her co-stars was Sid James who was making his West End début. Though well received and attracting good business, Carole had to leave the show well before the end of the run. Trying to meet the demands of being a good mother and working every night – plus matinées – was causing her blackouts (an artiste's nightmare) and to forget her lines. The doctor said she was on the verge of a nervous breakdown and must rest.

She did her best but when Val Parnell was let down by his principal

girl at the Palladium and asked Carole to take over, she felt bound
to come to the rescue. After a week's rehearsal, she opened with
Jewel and Warris and Adèle Dixon as principal boy. This was to be
her last show – although she didn't realise it at the time. Not feeling
too well, she went back to her gynaecologist who told her she was
again pregnant but he did not hold out much hope of her being able
to carry another child to full term. We still did not have our house
but we did have a little cottage by the sea at Middleton in Sussex.
So she went down there to live quietly. Our two daughters, now three
and a half and nearly six, started at the village school and I commuted
up and down to London.

Incidentally, this cottage was to prove very useful to Laurence
Olivier and Joan Plowright when they were first together. A mutual
friend asked if they could stay there to avoid the attentions of the
press who wanted to follow up on the break-up of Olivier's marriage
to Vivien Leigh.

After a few weeks in Middleton things began to go wrong for
Carole. She spoke to Mr Schlyer who said she must come up and
stay in London to be near him in case of an emergency. We rented
a flat near Montague Square and tried to carry on with our lives.
Carole was nearly into her seventh month when she started haemor-
rhaging. I think someone, somewhere, was looking after her because
Mr Schlyer had been in just minutes earlier. He was hurriedly called
back and Carole was rushed up to the operating theatre where little
David was born. Any delay, it was said, might have made it too late
for both of them.

Of course, Carole was very poorly and David was like a tiny doll
– about two and a half or three pounds in weight. He was immediately
put into an incubator but in those days they were not so sophisticated
and the nursing was all-important. It was several days before Carole
could be taken in a chair to see him. She could not believe a baby
could be so small.

She had to stay in the clinic for four weeks and we had to leave
David there until his weight was about five and a half pounds.
But he had the most wonderful nursing, particularly from Nurse
Fazackerly. We will never forget her love and care for him and will
for ever be grateful to her.

David was very small until he was about fifteen years old. Now he
is over six feet tall, a devoted father with a lovely wife, Sarah. He is
a talented silversmith, although he doesn't do much of that now, a

musician and composer, although only for himself and a self-trained renovator of old Devonshire cottages. According to Sarah, those who work with him are driven mad because he is such a perfectionist.

After David was born, I bought a splendid house in Hampstead where my growing family could live comfortably. Carole said she never knew how I could afford this, nor how I managed to pay for all the time she and David had spent in the clinic. I don't know either but somehow I managed.

My relationship with Val Parnell had changed radically after the *Folies*. He was still the tough bargainer but at least he was keen to do business. That said, I did have a few strong cards to play. One of them was Norman Wisdom, then at the height of his very considerable comic powers. After Norman's first film, *Trouble in Store*, Val wanted him for the Palladium. That was fine by me except that I was determined to present the show with Dickie Hurran directing. It was a condition at which Val balked until Norman made it clear that I would have to present the show or he would not appear at all. Val conceded as gracefully as he knew how. It was the start of a long association with Val and the Palladium, lasting all of fifteen years and taking in shows like *Rocking the Town* with Harry Secombe, Alma Cogan and Winifred Atwell, *We're Having a Ball* and *Swinging Down the Lane* with Max Bygraves, and *Large as Life* with Harry Secombe, Eric Sykes and Harry Worth.

So close did I get to Val that I even became involved in his personal affairs to the extent of trying to help him *not* to get married. Val was smitten with a young actress he first saw playing Buttons in panto-mime at the Manchester Palace. This did Aileen Cochrane's career no harm at all as her agent, who happened to be Keith Devon, was the first to admit. She went on to play the top Moss Empire theatres and to appear in many television variety shows. But for Val the first flush of romance soon passed, leaving him in a panic that the affair was getting out of hand. One day at lunch, he confessed his big fear.

'It's not long since I was divorced. I don't need this sort of commitment. Bernie, why don't you talk to her. Tell her how difficult I can be; tell her I'm not the man for her.'

I agreed to have a fatherly chat with Aileen. After all, who better to give the lowdown on Val's character?

I must have laid it on pretty thickly because by the time I had finished Aileen was in tears.

'You're right,' she sobbed. 'I've made a big mistake. I'll call it off.'

Val thanked me profusely. 'I'll never forget it.'

Two weeks later they were married and remained happily together until Val's death in 1972. It makes me wonder what would have happened if I had given Val a glowing testimonial.

As the relationship with Val Parnell changed for the better, so my relationship with Paul Derval changed for the worse. My French partner was increasingly unhappy with our success in London which he somehow imagined as a threat to his supremacy. He was ever picking fault with the shows and when he could not think of anything else to complain about he pressed hard for a bigger share of the profits. When, inevitably, his demands went beyond any reasonable proposition, I decided to call it a day. Our association ended after almost ten years, though I continued to present shows that leaned heavily on the magic of the *Folies*.

Shored up by the revenue from a few successful runs, I felt bold enough to attempt more serious theatre. As ever it was a case of lose some, win some. My biggest disappointment, all the greater for being totally unexpected, was the *First Drama Quartet* with its line-up of theatrical stalwarts and film stars – Charles Laughton, Sir Cedric Hardwicke, Agnes Moorehead and Charles Boyer. The presentation of the *Quartet* could not have been simpler. Appearing against a backdrop of black curtains, they each had a high stool and a lectern. After a brief introduction from Charles Laughton, they launched into a reading of Don Juan in Hell from Bernard Shaw's *Man and Superman*. The effect was totally compelling and during a limited season in New York, the production had been a sell-out. There was absolutely no reason I could think of why their triumph should not be repeated in London.

I had reckoned without John Clements who was directing and appearing in *Man and Superman* at the Princes. Following convention, Clements had excluded the lengthy and complex Don Juan scene from his production but as soon as he heard that the *Drama Quartet* was booked for a London season then he countered by announcing that every Saturday at the Princes, *Man and Superman* would be given in its entirety. Since Clements had an exclusive contract, this meant that I was prevented from bringing the *Drama Quartet* into the West End. When Charles Laughton heard the news, he telephoned Clements from Hollywood. But Clements refused to budge.

I had no choice but to take to the provinces. At first it looked as

121

if my unavoidable speculation would pay off. Wherever they appeared the quartet were met by crowds of admirers. Unfortunately the crowds who blocked the traffic and caused the press photographers to work overtime were not inclined to carry their enthusiasm so far as to pay twenty-five shillings a ticket. Apart from Edinburgh and Bristol, the *Quartet* played to small if devoted audiences. When they were in Manchester, I had a message from Charles Laughton. 'My compliments to Mr Delfont. Should we not forget the theatre and perform our little show in the street?'

When I totted up the figures, my loss came to twelve thousand pounds, a sizeable fortune in 1951. Still, I was proud of the theatrical achievement and grateful to the *Folies* for making it possible.

Chapter 8

I cannot be sure when I first had the idea for the Talk of the Town. It could have been as early as pre-war when I first encountered the theatre restaurants of Paris and Berlin. At that time the only equivalent in London was at the Casino, just after it had changed its name from the Prince Edward, almost a decade before I moved in to rival the Palladium. The enterprise failed, in my view, not because there was anything wrong with the concept but because it was poorly promoted. A show with dinner package was introduced to try to avoid entertainments tax. Since the tax was payable only on performance tickets, the Casino sold tickets for the meal implying that the show was thrown in for free. Of course, there was a fight with the Inland Revenue in which the tax inspector emerged as the victor. That was enough to put a stop to the Casino as a theatre restaurant and it was enough to deter others from treading the same path. But thinking about it much later I felt certain there was a way of handling the figures which would make economic sense.

The proof of the pudding was an Al Burnett enterprise, a club on Piccadilly known as the Pigalle. Al wanted to broaden the attraction of the Pigalle beyond the usual night-club clientèle to take in more of a family audience. He asked me to help him book some suitable acts. It was a small step from there to incorporating a show into a full evening's entertainment from dancing at eight and to a midnight supper. To present the cabaret I brought in Robert Nesbitt who was a top director of glamorous stage spectaculars. Unlike most of us, Robert had come into show business from a well-to-do family and an Oxford education, which is maybe the reason why he has always been known as Robert, not Bob. Starting his career in advertising, he had discovered a talent for writing sketches and lyrics. His part-time hobby soon became a full-time occupation starting with pantomime with Evelyn Laye. His breakthrough was to present the George Black revue, *Black and Blue*, in which Carole appeared and its sequel, *Black Velvet*.

The first show Robert directed for me was *Rocking the Town* at the Palladium. Harry Secombe and Alma Cogan shared the top billing. Alma is not much remembered now, except by those of a certain age. She died tragically early, of cancer, at the height of her fame. The public warmed to her boisterous energy and 'sock it to 'em' style of singing which cut right across the traditional gentility of the romantic melody. She was the perfect match for Harry Secombe, another of those performers who only have to walk on stage to assume the personality equal to a dozen routine acts. At the Palladium they thrived on each other's talents but it did not take an experienced critic to see that such strong performers might just as easily have clashed horribly. The distance between triumph and disaster was measured by the angular frame of Robert Nesbitt.

He was totally unflappable and infinitely polite. At rehearsals, his instructions were couched as proposals to be put to the vote: 'Might I suggest . . . ? Do you think it would be a good idea . . . ? How would it be if we tried it this way?' He always got his way. The only sign, more a hint, of impatience was when a technicality threatened the realisation of his vision. It was then that his urbane tones could be heard from the centre stalls: 'Really, there must be a little man somewhere who can take care of this sort of thing?' at which point there usually appeared a six-foot-three scene shifter or lighting engineer to do his bidding. The Pigalle demanded an intimate show – the total seating was for no more than three hundred – but with exciting names to act as a draw. Among those I booked were Sammy Davis Jnr and Tony Bennett, both making their first appearances in this country.

The formidable task for Robert Nesbitt was to weave together a show which measured up to the qualities of the star performer without threatening to overwhelm. In many ways the trick is more difficult to pull off than, say, directing a straight play where at least the structure of the piece is evident from the first read through. The director of variety is closer to the film director who creates as he goes along and is always ready to change direction if it looks as if there is something new and interesting to explore. Robert lived up to his reputation and more. The Pigalle was a sell-out, Al Burnett was delighted and I started thinking of how to repeat the exercise but on a much bigger scale.

The first problem was to find a suitable venue. There were several buildings on offer but they were either the wrong size or in the wrong position. Then I heard a whisper that the Hippodrome might be available. It would have been hard to imagine a site with more potential. Built by Edward Moss, founder of Moss Empires, the theatre was just off Leicester Square on the corner with Charing Cross Road. It had crowds coming at it from all directions and with the highly decorative red brick façade, no one could resist giving it a second glance.

But I did not get too excited. The Hippodrome was still part of Moss who held quite a few years on the lease. I could not imagine why Val Parnell or his chairman, Prince Littler, should want to get rid of it. I made a tentative approach to Prince Littler and was received with greater enthusiasm than I expected. It seemed that the Hippodrome was badly in need of renovation, so much so, in fact, that the reopening of the theatre was conditional on extensive structural repairs. Prince Littler was not at all sure that it was worth the expense. Competition from television was hotting up – the ITV network was providing the public with the novelty of a second channel – and though Prince swore allegiance to live variety we all knew that he was heavily involved with brother Lew, among others, in one of the new television contractors. It was at about this time that he became chairman of Associated Television (ATV), which held the weekend franchise for London and the weekday franchise for the Midlands. It was not the easiest job in the world. I could well understand that the Hippodrome was an unwelcome distraction.

My attitude was entirely different. I was not then involved in television, I was in need of a theatre and the fact that the roof was falling in did not bother me at all since the alterations I had in mind to convert the auditorium into a luxury restaurant entailed a wholesale reconstruction of the interior. I negotiated a twenty-one-year lease on terms which related the bulk of the payment to the number of people I could attract into the place.

So far, so good. What Prince Littler did not know was that I had only the first half of the formula for success. I was in possession of a great idea but without the money to back it. I asked Robert Nesbitt how much I would need.

'At least three hundred and fifty thousand pounds. Maybe more. In America they'd be throwing in four times as much.'

I was forgetting Robert's experience in Las Vegas where he had been responsible for building the Dunes. It had taught him that you can't buy spectacle on the cheap. But where could I raise that sort of money? The banks were not in the least interested – prudent investment stopped well short of show business. My only sympathetic contact in high finance was a bank manager introduced to me by Maxwell Joseph. I asked for twenty thousand pounds.

'My lending limit is a thousand,' he told me. 'But if you could come up with twenty companies I could let you have a thousand on each.'

It was a start.

My friends were similarly generous to their limits. There were plenty who could afford to throw in a few thousand but despite all their goodwill I could not make the figures add up to the magic sum. To get the measure of the problem, just think of going out today to raise five or six million. That was what I was up against.

I decided to advertise, but subtly. Instead of buying press space to announce that Bernard Delfont could do with some money, I put out a story about an exciting new concept in live entertainment to be known as the Talk of the Town. I laid it on a bit thick, implying that the Talk of the Town was the investment opportunity of a lifetime but not for one moment suggesting that I could not manage on my own. To my delight I made the front page of the London *Evening News* complete with a large picture of the Hippodrome. I sat back to wait for the telephone to ring.

The next day I had a call from Charles Forte (now Lord Forte). I had been on nodding terms with Charles from the days when I lunched at his Jermyn Street restaurant. He sent over the occasional drink for a regular customer and when business was slack we chatted about this and that. That was when he was groping for the bottom rung. Now he was halfway up the ladder. His latest coup was to buy the Café Royal on Piccadilly, a restaurant that was high on prestige but low on clientèle.

The grand scheme was to revive the fortunes of the whole Piccadilly area which had never quite lost its air of post-war austerity. There was much talk of rebuilding the Circus but one plan after another was junked as too radical or not radical enough. Behind the neon lights famous buildings like the Pavilion Cinema and the Criterion Theatre decayed under a thick layer of pigeon droppings. Charles Forte thought it was about time to reverse the trend. The Hippodrome or, as I had now rechristened it, the Talk of the Town, was not strictly

Piccadilly but it was close enough to the Café Royal to spark off an interest in Charles. He asked me what I planned to do about the catering for my theatre restaurant.

I was suitably bullish. 'It's all taken care of – we'll be doing it ourselves.'

He suggested we got together for a talk. I feigned reluctance but gave in without too much of a struggle.

For what happened next I will be everlastingly grateful to Charles Forte. I am still not sure if, at that first meeting, he realised how far I was short of my financial target. But even if he guessed that my bravado was counterfeit, my enthusiasm for the idea must have carried over to him because by the time we parted he had not only taken on the management of all the catering at the Talk of the Town but offered to put up the capital for the entire project. The deal gave me 30 per cent of the profits. The twenty thousand I had borrowed from the bank I found useful for other projects.

For Robert Nesbitt, who had already made hundreds of drawings of how he wanted the Talk of the Town to look, the news that we were financially clear was like the crack of a starter's gun. He was off. To create the essential intimacy of a restaurant in a theatrical environment, he and architect George Pine shut off the gallery with a false ceiling. The dress circle became a mezzanine dining area with a broad staircase on each side leading down to the dance floor and the main part of the restaurant. The stage was reconstructed to allow for such technical wizardry as a lift sunk into a twenty-foot wall capable of introducing into the action a prop as weighty as a vintage Rolls-Royce.

We could seat up to eight hundred which meant that I was able to hold the price of a ticket to two guineas, a bargain even in those days for a three-course dinner and two shows. The first show, at nine o'clock, was usually a dance spectacular in the style of the *Folies Bergère*, complete in itself but also a warm-up for the star of the evening who came on at eleven. Following my own lead at the Casino I went immediately for the big names, opening with Eartha Kitt (hence the need for the centre-stage Rolls-Royce). It was the start of one of the most successful theatrical enterprises of the century. We lasted for twenty-four years with a string of top acts – Judy Garland, Tom Jones, Ethel Merman, Sophie Tucker, Diana Ross, Sammy Davis Jnr, the Supremes, Liza Minelli, Cliff Richard, Lena Horne, Shirley Bassey, Pearl Bailey and on and on and on. From this list you can see that vocal artists had the strongest appeal. Generally speaking, comedians did not do well, though I was always prepared to have a go with an outstanding talent. We were particularly unlucky with Jackie Mason who was billed as an outstanding newcomer but was defeated by summer audiences dominated by Japanese tourists. Nowadays, I'm glad to say, his Jewish humour is a sell-out on Broadway and in the West End.

We had our problems. I knew Ethel Merman had a loud voice, to put it mildly, but when on her first night at the Talk of the Town she came on without a microphone and filled the place with every note, it was unreal. But hearing is believing, or so I thought. A few days later I had a call from the police. Would I please do something fast about Miss Merman. Her use of a revolutionary wire mike, invisible to the audience, contravened the laws on the use of public airwaves. It seemed that she had tuned in to the ambulance emergency service. Patients on their way to hospital were liable to be treated to Ethel Merman giving a spirited rendering of 'Everything's Coming up Roses'.

I had hopes of bringing over Frank Sinatra but somehow we never succeeded in matching dates. I had to make do with meeting him at the Caesar's Palace Hotel in Las Vegas where he was the star attraction when Carole and I were passing through on holiday. After his performance we were invited backstage for drinks. We had been chatting for a while when there was a knock on the door. A young man poked his head into the room.

'Your table is ready, Mr Sinatra.'

Frank made his apologies to us and departed for a session at the roulette wheel. It seemed that when the punters heard that Frank Sinatra was playing the tables they immediately poured in from the streets. He was as big an attraction on the floor as a gambler as on stage as a singer. I wonder if Caesar's Palace covered his losses?

There was one great tragedy at the Talk of the Town and that was Judy Garland. After her much publicised American comeback, I booked her for three weeks. The first night was a sensation. Devoted fans packed the auditorium and roared their approval like a football crowd at the Cup Final. It was no matter to them that she was a little unsteady on her feet. After the show, I went round to her dressing-room to offer my congratulations. But I could not find Judy Garland, or rather I could not find the Judy Garland I knew. Instead, I discovered a shrivelled old lady crouched in front of her mirror.

Could this be the same woman I had seen on stage? The shock of reality was almost too much for me. I mumbled a few words and backed away, leaving her to contemplate the image of a woman who had little more to give.

Each night I expected her to pull out of the show and each night she insisted on going on even though her performance was fading fast. By the end of the first week, the audience was no longer on her side. Instead of rapturous applause she heard the shuffles of embarrassment when her voice cracked or she forgot her lines and on the night when she was up to half an hour late for her opening, the slow handclap with an accompaniment of boos and jeers. We were less than halfway through her run when I delivered an ultimatum. I knew it would hurt her but I could not think of any other way of staving off a catastrophe.

'I'm sorry, Judy. I can't let you go on unless you let me have a doctor's certificate to say you are fit.'

When I opened the paper the following morning it was to find the headline 'Delfont Bans Judy Garland'. Then the telephone started ringing. I was wrecking Judy's career, I was breaking her contract, I was causing untold distress and hardship – the accusations of bad faith rolled over me but I refused to budge. I knew I was dealing with a desperately sick woman, brought low by twenty years of drink and drugs.

Then, as Billy Marsh was trying to book a suitably high-profile replacement, I was handed a piece of paper that forced me to stick to my existing programme. To my utter amazement, someone had found a doctor who was prepared to state, unequivocally, that Judy Garland was fit to perform. I had no choice but to let her work out the rest of her engagement. Every night was agony, for Judy and for the Talk of the Town. Not knowing what she was going through but suspecting a deliberate affront caused by having a few drinks over the top, her one-time fans showed their resentment. There were times when whatever was left from the pre-show meal ended up on the stage.

The Talk of the Town was the last appearance for Judy Garland. It was just a short time afterwards that she died from an overdose of sleeping tablets. She was found in her London apartment by her fifth husband, the disco manager Mickey Deans.

The Judy Garland experience was a sad reminder to me of the time when I wanted to introduce Edith Piaf to British audiences. I went over to Paris to see her perform. On stage she was magnetic, every inch the supreme professional, in total command of her audience. But when, at the end of a triumphant show, I went backstage there was another Edith Piaf waiting for me: a wreck of a woman ravaged by emotional and physical pain. The need to perform, to keep going at all costs, can clearly split the physique as well as the personality. I can't explain it but the performer you see bathed in lights can be hugely different from the real-life person under the make-up.

The Talk of the Town had its tenth birthday in 1969. The format had changed only slightly over the years – the biggest change was moving from two shows a night to just one with all the razzmatazz concentrated on a single star. I was keen to extend the idea; there was even talk at one time of my joining up with Albert Finney to create a string of theatre restaurants presenting not variety but straight plays and musicals. Sadly, the figures did not add up. It was the same story, though in an entirely different context, when I tried to entice Blackpool holidaymakers to a meal and a show at the Winter Gardens ballroom. There were simply not enough takers to balance the budget. Meanwhile, in London, we were pulling them in with another fifteen profitable years to go. I came to the conclusion that the Talk of the Town was unique.

I never forgot that I owed it all to Charles Forte. I went some way in repaying the favour by setting up a deal which brought him three prestigious hotels, the Plaza Athénée, the George V and the Tremoille, all in Paris. But that was only a beginning. When his company went public, he asked me to join the board. I readily agreed, exchanging my shares in the Talk of the Town for shares in Trust House Forte. The relationship continues to this day though my first phase with Charles Forte ended when I joined EMI.

The Talk of the Town closed in 1982. I would have liked nothing better than to have kept it going indefinitely but when the lease came up for renewal and the Cranbourn Estate wanted to increase the rent from an average fifteen thousand pounds a year to two hundred thousand pounds, I knew I was in trouble. Rising costs had already damaged ticket prices: from a two guinea entrance in the early sixties we were now up to twenty-four pounds. The latest jump in overheads would put us into the fifty pounds bracket, far too much for a family of middling income who wanted a good night's entertainment without feeling as if they had to take out a second mortgage. The other, and decisive problem, was the shortage of top stars who were willing to do a week or two at the Talk of the Town (we had long since given up ten- or twelve-week bookings) at rates we could afford. If London was on their circuit they were just as likely to appear for a couple of nights at Wembley or some other arena where they could attract audiences of several thousand with earnings to match. I had to face the fact that the Talk of the Town had had its innings, at least as a theatre restaurant; a very respectable twenty-four years. In show business there are few centuries.

But I am running ahead of myself. Back in 1958, with the launch of the Talk of the Town and a string of successful co-productions with Val Parnell at the Palladium, I decided to embark on another full-scale West End musical. I had the property, an adaptation of *Charley's Aunt* called *Where's Charley?* and Norman Wisdom, who was not at the peak of his career. In fact it was Norman who sold me the idea of *Where's Charley?* Seven years earlier, after seeing the Broadway production, Norman had convinced Frank Loesser, who wrote the music and lyrics, that he was the only performer capable of bringing the show to London. Since then he had been kept busy with variety at the Palladium and the Prince of Wales and with films for the Rank Organisation but now we both felt that it was time for a change of gear. *Where's Charley?* was waiting for us; so too, by happy coincidence, was the Palace Theatre. We had a deal.

Norman was always the perfectionist. He rehearsed longer and harder than any other actor I had ever encountered. But he was also a stubborn man. Once he had fixed on a way of doing something, it was hard to shift him. It was like that with the drums.

Norman took great pride in his drum routine. The little man in the tight suit, for whom just about everything went wrong, would surprise his audience and, apparently, himself with a virtuoso display which silenced the rest of the orchestra. It was fine for a variety show but not, as I tried to point out to him, for a scripted musical.

'It'll interrupt the action. Anyway, it's totally out of character.'

He wouldn't listen. For the tour of *Where's Charley?* out came the drums. And, I have to say, the audience loved it. 'But it's different in the West End,' I tried to explain. 'The critics will be looking to you to act the role, not to switch into a variety routine whenever you feel like it.'

I was getting nowhere. To accommodate Norman's drums at the Palace, the set of *Where's Charley?* was adapted to allow for a staircase from the stage to the orchestra pit where Norman could perform on a raised platform. I spent the money reluctantly, while still pleading with him to change his mind. No way. As the first night approached, I softened.

'All right, Norman. I know you can stop the show with the drum routine. But do me a favour. Cut it out on opening night. Then you go back to it for the rest of the run.'

He was suspicious. 'You really mean it?'

I said, 'Well, after all, I have gone to all the trouble and expense of building the staircase. Would I have done that if I didn't mean it?'

Norman considered the proposition and came down in my favour. 'OK. So I cut the drum routine on the first night but I get to do it every other night.'

He went away a happy man to prepare for what turned out to be a triumphant first night. Fleet Street was unanimous. Norman Wisdom had joined the greats of musical theatre. He was over the moon.

'And tomorrow,' he enthused, 'I get to play the drums.'

I fixed him with a stern eye. 'I'm afraid not, Norman. Not in this show. You've proved you can do without them.'

It took a little time to sink in. 'You lied to me.'

There was no denying it. 'Norman,' I said, 'it was for your own good.'

We remained the best of friends.

Times were great. *Where's Charley?* had a big advance booking, the Talk of the Town was doing well, I controlled several West End theatres, through Billy Marsh and Keith Devon I ran a successful agency and at least a dozen touring shows and a couple of West End hits appeared under my name. We could afford to live in the best part of Hampstead. I had just turned fifty. I felt on top of the world.

That was when I had a heart attack.

Chapter 9

I had just spent three days investigating the property market in Majorca. This unlikely excursion was at the behest of Norman Wisdom who wanted to invest some of his newly acquired wealth on a villa in the sun. It seemed not a bad idea to me but I was a little surprised when he asked me to go along as friend and adviser. Contrary to stage appearances, Norman was quite capable of looking after himself. But then, I thought, why not? I was as close to Norman as only a producer and agent can be, I had a powerful financial as well as personal interest in his welfare and, anyway, I was due for a break.

It was quite an experience. Norman was possessed of frenetic energy which took him back and forth across the island, armed with bundles of estate agents' literature, eagerly scrutinising the relative qualities of this or that des res. His first requirement was a good view: a balcony from which he could enjoy the panorama of mountains and sea. If he could not get a villa at the top of a hill, then it had to be the highest penthouse in the apartment block. My days were occupied walking up hills and up stairs. In the evenings we played table tennis. I told myself that after so long behind a desk, the exercise was doing me good.

On the plane home, I started getting pains in my chest and in my wrists. I did not want to make a fuss but it was obvious from the difficulty I had breathing that I was not at my best. The stewardess told me I was running a temperature and brought me a damp towel to put on my forehead. Norman thought it was something I had eaten which, thinking back over some of the rich and over-sauced meals we had shared, seemed to me the likeliest explanation. But food poisoning was never like this. When we landed at Heathrow, I was in such a bad way I had to be taken through customs in a wheelchair. I was driven home and went straight to bed.

Carole immediately rang Joe Freeman, my sister Rita's husband, who also happened to be our GP. He gave me an examination, told me to lie still (I had no intention of moving) and immediately contacted a top heart specialist. The second opinion arrived with his nurse who, no sooner had she entered my room, suffered an acute nose-bleed.

This was developing into a farce. Though I was still in pain I could barely stop myself laughing. Forgetting about me the doctor turned his full attention to the young lady standing at the foot of my bed with a rosy handkerchief clasped to her face.

'Would you mind giving a hand?'

I said, 'No, of course not. But in the circumstances . . .'

But this doctor knew how to make best use of limited resources. 'If she stands beside you and bends right back with her head in your hands, like so.' He manoeuvred his latest patient into position, making her look as if she was ready to do a backward somersault on to my chest. 'And I stand in front of her, like so.' He followed the ungainly curve of her body and dabbed at her nose with a swab of cotton wool. 'Now all we have to do is to hold it there for just a few minutes and she'll be as right as rain.'

His remedy was effective but I hate to think what an uninformed observer would have made of our *ménage à trois*.

When I was again the focus of attention it was to be told that I had severe angina. A complete rest was ordered. I fretted at the waste of time but the seriousness of my illness was borne in on me when the thrombosis spread to my legs. For weeks I couldn't move. That has to be the worst of it, I thought. But there was still some way to go, as I discovered when the doctors stuck needles in my back to draw fluid off my lungs. I was on my back for over four months.

All this time Billy Marsh was in charge of the business and a wonderful job he did too; so good in fact, that when I did begin to pull round I was not entirely averse to suggestions that I should get right away for two or three months. But I had no intention of losing track of events. We settled on a compromise. I would go to Monte Carlo, far enough away from the office to be clear of distractions but close enough for weekend visiting. And if I felt well enough, with the casinos open from early morning there was no risk I would get bored.

I am not sure how I afforded this luxurious recuperation but money problems were not at the root of my stress. Ever since the age of forty I have had an unshakeable faith in my ability to match up to my expenditure. It is true, I have been blessed with extraordinary luck. Carole likes to tell the story of a costly but disastrous holiday in Torremolinos which I attempted to retrieve by suggesting we packed our bags and made for Paris. Carole was unenthusiastic. It was a cold spring and she had none of the right clothes. Praying for a change in the weather, I persuaded her to go along with my idea. But as the train crossed the border into France I knew she had been right. It was a case of out of the fridge and into the freezer. We stopped briefly at the border. Stretching my legs along the platform I saw a line-up of Citroën taxis, their owners waiting languidly for the next fare. I went up to the driver at the head of the queue.

'Are you available?'

'Yes. Where to?'

'Cannes.'

He gaped for a moment as well he might have since I was asking him to set off on a twelve-hour journey. But he didn't take long to make up his mind.

'Give me ten minutes to call home. I'll need my shaving kit.'

I went back to the train to collect Carole. I won't even attempt to recount the verbal mauling she gave me but it climaxed with a side-swipe of irrefutable logic: 'We barely have enough money to pay the taxi; how can we afford a holiday in Cannes?'

I gave the problem some thought on the journey south. I had a distant relative called Charles Winograd who had an interest in the Casino. Knowing that he stayed at the Majestic, we made straight for the hotel. Luckily, Charles was in residence. I tapped him for a modest loan, installed Carole in our room and left for the gaming tables. In two hours I built up a pile of chips sufficient to repay Charles and to cover the holiday. Once I was into profit – I quit. I believe in pushing my luck but not in giving it an almighty shove.

My convalescence in Monte Carlo was heavier on the pocket though not for the obvious reasons. Window-shopping with Carole on her last visit before my return home, we stopped by Cartier where her eye was caught by a diamond brooch. I was so grateful for her unfailing support over the bad time, I felt I had to get it for her. She refused absolutely. How ridiculous to throw away money on luxuries. But even when I found it cost five thousand pounds, I still had to get it for her. I had every intention of declaring the brooch when we came through customs, but at Heathrow I was whisked aside by the press to talk about the new Royalty Theatre which was due to open in a few days with one of my productions. It was not until we were safely home and I felt the brooch in my pocket that it dawned on me how Fleet Street had inadvertently helped me to avoid paying customs a cool three thousand.

So far so good except that a few days later I came back to find the house swarming with police. We had been burgled. Much of Carole's jewellery had gone, including my gift from Monte Carlo. A young detective asked her to list the missing items. When it came to the diamond brooch, Carole was distraught. She described her most treasured possession in loving detail, explaining when and how it was bought and at what cost to her devoted husband. The detective was sympathetic.

I turned my gaze on Carole and willed her to change her story.

'It's like this,' I said. 'The jewel is a fake; not worth more than a few pounds.'

Carole exploded. 'Of course it wasn't a fake. How can you say that?'

I summoned up all my telepathic powers. 'The jewel was a fake.'

'No it wasn't.'

'Yes it was.'

We were interrupted by a weary policeman. 'I think it would be best all round, sir, if we simply forgot this conversation.'

Carole and I nodded. She said goodbye to her diamond brooch, I said goodbye to five thousand pounds.

My other Monte Carlo-related loss had to do with the Royalty Theatre. Just before I became ill I made a deal with the property developer and takeover king Charles Clore (later Sir Charles Clore). He had bought a site towards the bottom of Kingsway, close to Aldwych. He wanted to demolish the buildings to make way for a new office block but to do this meant sacrificing the Stoll Theatre, a massive two thousand four hundred-seater which had outlived its time.

Planning permission was conditional on Charles making room for a new theatre half the size of the Stoll which he decided to call the Royalty. He offered me the lease. I was delighted and signed up immediately. I had put on *Rose Marie* and one or two other shows at the Stoll and knew that the site had potential. It was on the edge of the West End but close enough to the Strand to be part of a recognisable theatre circuit.

136

The architect's plans showed a luxurious auditorium below ground level without a single awkward sight-line – such a change from the Stoll which offered grandeur at the expense of comfort. Here, I thought, was the opportunity to try modern shows in modern conditions, unprecedented in London before the opening of the National in 1976.

But then I suffered my enforced absence from the West End. At a distance, I agreed to the opening production of the Friedrich Dürrenmatt play, *The Visit*, directed by Peter Brook and starring Alfred Lunt and his wife Lynn Fontaine, on one of their rare appearances in London. All the signs were favourable.

I timed my return to coincide with the first night of *The Visit*: I would not have missed it for the world. But while the notices for the play and the theatre were generally favourable, I had made a fatal mistake in not checking the ground plans more carefully. In my innocence I had assumed that the Royalty entrance would be on Kingsway, the main thoroughfare, where the front of house lights could be seen from Aldwych to the south and from Holborn Station to the north. Instead, it was tucked round the corner in Portugal Street. From the promoter's point of view this was about as effective as trying to sell a new product in a supermarket by packaging it in plain paper. Passers-by barely noticed the Royalty, so why should they have bothered about what was showing there? In any event, that was the view of all the leading producers. Times change: nowadays if you have a hit show it will play well in any theatre.

The Visit carried its short season on the rarity appeal of the Lunts appearing together in London. To keep up the momentum I knew I had to follow with another star name. I thought I had found it when Jack Hawkins, one of the strongest box-office draws in British cinema and theatre, agreed to do a play but our plans fell apart when the deepening croak in Jack's voice was diagnosed as throat cancer. Other stars were reluctant to stake their reputations against the uncertain appeal of a new theatre. It was the same with producers who had shows waiting to come in to the West End. Given the choice, they made a beeline for Shaftesbury Avenue. And who could blame them?

I struggled on through several unsuccessful plays – all the more frustrating because the failures were invariably associated with good notices – until forced to conclude that the Royalty was an unjustifiable drain on resources. If the right product had been available (as it was years later when I put Andrew Lloyd Webber's production of *Cats* into the New London, another off-the-beaten-track theatre apparently doomed to failure) it would have been a different story. But in the early sixties, there were too many theatres chasing too few quality shows. I passed on the lease to Metro-Goldwyn-Mayer who converted the Royalty into a cinema. Later, it was taken over by Rediffusion Television as a variety studio. To this day there are attempts to revive the theatrical fortunes of the Royalty. No one has succeeded so far but in this business, nothing is certain.

On other fronts, the opening of the decade brought good news including an elevation in my status as a public figure: 1960 was the year I was declared legitimate.

My long-delayed bid for naturalisation was supported by theatrical luminaries Sir Alan Herbert, Tom Arnold and Val Parnell, who were happy to do me a favour but were surprised when they heard what it was. Their reaction should have prepared me for the press headlines but it was my turn to be surprised when I picked up the *Express* one morning to find that I had a 'dark secret'. Rather more kindly another paper described me as 'Britain's most successful stateless person'. What I would have become if my application had been turned down hardly bears thinking about. Fortunately for me, no objections were heard and I was granted the right to walk the streets as a free man.

Shortly afterwards I was sent a brand-new passport made out to Bernard Delfont, formerly known as Barnet Winogradsky. Fourteen years later when I became Sir Bernard, the citation stuck to the formula reminding me that I was formerly etc. Only when I joined the peerage was any mention of Winogradsky dropped from the official document. At last, I thought, I am a Delfont through and through. At which point my children demanded to know what was wrong with Winogradsky. I had great difficulty in persuading them that in my young days, any name ending in 'sky' was automatically suspect. Now, judging by the stars I see up in lights, it is a guarantee of fame and fortune.

The early sixties were also significant for me as marking my return to reasonable health. I still made regular trips to the doctor and did my best to follow his advice though I drew the line at his suggestion that I should take outdoor exercise. Fresh air is all very well but I prefer to enjoy it standing still. I did cut down on food and drink. No more wine or champagne; I limited myself to whisky and soda, just two long drinks before a light dinner. My surviving weaknesses were ice-cream and cigars. The supply of ice-cream was strictly controlled by Carole but she gave up on the Havanas.

Incidentally, the popular assumption about my liking for a good cigar is wrong. I do not see it as an image-maker for the big producer, I smoke cigars because I enjoy cigars; that's all there is to it. I am now down to about five a day. No doubt my doctor would like to make it less. But there is something I have noticed about doctors: however much or little you say you're drinking and smoking they always want you to cut back. So now, when I go for a check-up, I adopt a simple rule which keeps everyone happy. When asked how many cigars I smoke, I say ten a day and the doctor tells me to cut down by half. Fine, so I go on smoking my five a day. It's the same with drink. How many whiskies? I say, 'Four a day.' 'Cut down by half.' Thank you very much.

I wouldn't go so far as to guarantee it as a recipe for a long life but I am now in my eighty-second year and still going strong.

The disappointment of the Royalty at least had the virtue of reminding the West End that I was back. It was soon known that I was in the market for new shows and new talent to match the already detectable change of tempo from the dull fifties to the swinging sixties. A queue of young hopeful writers, composers and directors formed outside my office at the Prince of Wales. First in line was Anthony Newley. After breaking into films as a child actor (he was the Artful Dodger in David Lean's version of *Oliver Twist*), Tony Newley had made a respectable if not spectacular living. He was one of those performers who was recognised in the street but rarely by name. 'Aren't you Mr Um Um Um?'

The turnaround came in 1959 when he starred in a low-budget movie called *Idle on Parade*. Tony played a frustrated pop singer called up for his national service, a spoof on the Elvis Presley experience in the American forces. The joke fell flat but the film was a great success nevertheless. Tony's singing, not previously heard by teenage audiences, put him into the charts and into the big league of popular performers. In some quarters *Idle on Parade* was better known as *Idol on Parade*.

My idea for Anthony Newley was to build a fourteen-week summer show around him but, discussing it with his agent, I could not meet his terms. It was then suggested that I should talk directly to Tony who made a strong sales pitch for the high fees he was demanding. I was not persuaded. We shook hands and said goodbye.

At the door, he turned back. 'There is one thing I'm keen to do. I've been working on a musical. You might be interested.'

I was talking only for the sake of having something to say. 'How much will it cost to put on?'

He must have already thought it out. 'Not much. Seven or eight thousand. It's a small musical.'

On the spur of the moment, I couldn't think of a safer investment. 'All right,' I said. 'We'll do it.'

The musical was *Stop the World, I Want to Get Off*, a title I chose from a long list of curiosities including *False Teeth for Everyone* and *Up and Down the Ladder*. Co-written with Leslie Bricusse, the rise and fall of Littlechap, the Everyman figure played by Tony, was imaginatively staged by Sean Kenny in a symbolic circus ring. It was a fantastical view of life, reduced to clownish simplicity but it exactly caught the mood of the times – cynicism founded on hope. A clutch of big numbers led by 'What Kind of Fool Am I?' put Tony back at the top of the charts and boosted the appeal of the show. *Stop the World* ran for nearly five hundred performances. After its London run it went to New York where I co-produced with David Merrick. It was the first Bernard Delfont production to make a million. But *Stop the World* was also very much the musical of its day. Recently revived in the West End, with Tony again in the lead, it failed to catch on. Littlechap was trapped in the sixties.

I had great ambitions for Newley and Bricusse. I put their musical teamwork in the same category as Lerner and Loewe and promoted them accordingly. But the triumph of *Stop the World* was not to be repeated. For their next effort, *The Roar of the Greasepaint, the Smell of the Crowd* (they seemed to favour these elongated titles), Tony wanted to take what was, for him, a back seat, directing but not starring. As a worthy substitute for the Newley presence on stage I suggested Norman Wisdom. After the success of *Where's Charley?*, Norman was on the lookout for another musical and having identified with Littlechap, his liking for the Newley-Bricusse style could be taken for granted. But the chemistry did not work. Whatever the qualities of the show, and its subsequent two-year run on Broadway with Tony in the lead suggests that it had something going for it, in this country it fell victim to two strong wills working against instead of with each other. I was at the first night when *The Roar of the Greasepaint* opened on tour in Nottingham. It failed to take off. Even the hit song 'Who Can I Turn To?' faded miserably.

All was not yet totally lost – miracle recoveries had been known – but I thought I should make clear that on present form the West End was not remotely in prospect. Tony urged patience.

'Give us a chance. We're working on it. It'll be a different show next week, you'll see.'

The changes turned out to be largely cosmetic, a progressive reduction of the clutter on stage. Having started out with an over-elaborate set, by the time they got to the Palace Theatre, Manchester, the last stop before London, they were performing on what was virtually a bare stage. I put away my cheque-book and we all went home to think again. Afterwards, I was told that one of the girls in the chorus showed great promise but at that early point in her career, I cannot say that I noticed Elaine Paige.

In the press, Tony as co-writer and director took most of the blame. I consoled him with a story passed on to me by Alan Jay Lerner about a long-dead musical called *My Dear Public*. It was produced by Irving Caesar, co-authored by Irving Caesar, had lyrics by Irving Caesar and was co-composed by Irving Caesar. The notices were dreadful. The following day, Caesar called Oscar Hammerstein. 'All right,' he said, 'they didn't like it. But why pick on me?'

We did a little better with *The Good Old, Bad Old Days* which settled into the West End for a year. For this, the third Newley-Bricusse collaboration, we returned to the formula Tony liked best – starring and directing. He was undoubtedly the strongest feature of the show. Watching the early run-throughs I urged him to take on more of the singing. It was his voice that customers would come to hear. Finally, with nearly all the big numbers pushed his way, we were left with 'Yesterday, Today and Tomorrow', a melody at the end of the first act which Tony shared with two other members of the cast, one following the other.

'Why don't you do "Yesterday", then you can begin and end the number?' I suggested.

That worked quite well but it left the girl who was 'Today' in a weak position.

I threw in another idea. 'Try singing all three parts.'

Tony was embarrassed. 'Aren't I doing enough? Anyway, who's going to tell her?'

He indicated the actress whose role had already been chipped to near-extinction in earlier revision sessions.

'Don't worry. I'll break the news. It's for the good of the show.'

141

And so it was, even if the growing prominence of Anthony Newley started tongues wagging. Backstage after a performance, I heard two boys from the chorus camping it up like mad.

'Well, dear,' said one, 'just be grateful we don't have to do "God Save the Queen" at the beginning of every performance, otherwise he'd be singing that too.'

After *The Good Old, Bad Old Days*, the Newley-Bricusse partnership faded and Tony settled in the States where his earning power on the cabaret circuit guaranteed him an enviable living. Still the number everyone wants to hear is 'What Kind of Fool Am I?' and Tony belts it out with undiminished vigour. I fancy he has already chosen it as his epitaph.

With activity, and competition, hotting up in the West End, I was in need of someone to hold together the production side of the business, leaving me free to chase after new shows here and in the States. The ideal I had in mind was an unflappable manager with a head for figures and an instinct for what makes a profit – the last a rarity in theatre people who are more inclined to believe that somehow it will be all right on the night, even when the evidence to the contrary is overwhelming. I was running out of possible candidates on the short list when I met Richard Mills. He was working on *Come Blow Your Horn*, the first play from Neil Simon which I co-produced with Frederick Granville for the Prince of Wales. (Incidentally, the play was also a first for the twenty-one-year-old Michael Crawford whose stage career got off to a good start with 'a most promising newcomer' award.)

What impressed me so much about Richard was that he always had the essential facts immediately to hand – not simply how many customers were in that night but projections on how much business we still had to do to cover our production costs and the likelihood of achieving that break. Moreover, I never had to ask him for the figures; he anticipated what I had to know and a bit extra, like the mood of an audience to changes in a show when it was out on the road and beyond my immediate control.

The only obstacle to making Richard an offer was that he already had a job, with Freddie Granville. I decided to talk to Freddie but knowing that I was asking him to lose his right hand, I approached the subject obliquely, leading up to the big question as gently as I knew how. This led to a little misunderstanding. As I waxed keen on the future of Bernard Delfont Productions, my ambition to expand

and my exhaustive efforts to find the right person to accompany me on the great adventure, Freddie settled into his chair and assumed a fixed and happy smile. It dawned on me, the way I was presenting my case, that he expected me to make *him* an offer. I had to break the illusion.

'Freddie, I'll come to the point. I want to ask Richard Mills to join me.'

The smile vanished.

That's it, I thought; a classic mishandling of a delicate negotiation.

But Freddie was a great sport. He took only a moment to recover. 'Be my guest,' he said.

Then he went straight off to see Richard Mills to tell him the whole story – against himself. Richard came on to the payroll a few weeks later, though for the first year or so he sat in with Billy Marsh to learn what there was to know about the agency. After all these years, Richard is still with me. We work closely together and have become good friends.

In the sixties we set out on a range of productions as wide and as varied as the West End could handle. We put on a dozen musicals and twice as many straight plays. As for variety, I've lost count of the shows though I do recall the big crises such as the night Sammy Davis Jnr refused to appear in *Golden Boy* out of deference to the late Martin Luther King. I could understand his concern at the murder of the civil rights leader but equally I knew how the paying fans were liable to react when they heard that their idol had retired to his hotel. I threw him the oldest cliché in the business.

'The show must go on.'

He shook his head. 'Bernie, how can you say this to me? You should know how I feel. Don't forget, I'm Jewish too.'

As an appeal to my better judgement it had at least novelty value. There was no persuading him. The Palladium went dark for one evening and there was much grumbling at the box-office where the cashiers had the galling experience of handing money back to the audience.

Golden Boy was expensive in another way. Sammy Davis brought over his American producer who installed himself in the office next to mine. When he asked if he could use the telephone, of course I said he could help himself. It was only when I got the bill that I realised he had been ringing New York and Los Angeles non-stop for a week. Those were the days when you thought twice about transatlantic calls. The charges were horrendous. By current values I was out of pocket by more than five thousand pounds. But such incidental expenses paled into insignificance against the sums I was investing in musicals. It amuses me nowadays to read that the West End is dominated by musicals as if such a phenomenon has been known only since the advent of Andrew Lloyd Webber. In fact, the turnaround came in the sixties when British talents like Newley and Bricusse and Lionel Bart came to the fore. If the big difference between Lloyd Webber and his forerunners is their failure to sustain their early success, no one can doubt the impact on the popular imagination of shows like *Stop the World* and *Oliver*, great musicals in their own right but, more to the point, great musicals born not on Broadway but in the West End.

Sadly for me, *Oliver* was staged without my help but I did manage to work out a deal on Lionel Bart's next but one musical, *Maggie May*. This was by no means a sure bet. Lionel's follow-up to *Oliver*, a semi-autobiographical tale of the East End at war called *Blitz*, had received a severe mauling from the critics. *Maggie May* had the advantage of a strong book by Alun Owen, one of the most gifted writers of his generation made popular by his television plays, but the setting, in and around the Liverpool docks, gave the show a parochial feel, and the score was missing that essential big number, a contrast to *Oliver* in which every song was a winner.

In the event, the show got off to a splendid start. With Rachel Roberts and Kenneth Haig leading the cast, we opened at the Palace, Manchester to standing ovations.

The favourable buzz brought a run of film people eager to follow up on the triumph of *Oliver* which had been sold to Columbia for a gigantic sum. Some encouraging offers came in but United Artists trumped the lot with a bid of a quarter of a million pounds and a share of the profits. This was enough to cover all outgoings and make a modest profit even if *Maggie May* failed in the West End. In fact, *Maggie May* ran at the Adelphi for just over a year and just about covered its production costs. I had every reason to be grateful to United Artists.

As with all my shows, I regularly popped in to the theatre to see how *Maggie May* was progressing. In Manchester I had only one major criticism. I put it to Richard Mills.

'That singer who opens the show; the one who does the "Oh

Maggie Maggie May" lament. He's dreadful. He's never on cue, he can't get the words right and he looks as if he's the worse for drink.'

For once, Richard was in a forgiving mood. 'He did very well as Sowerberry in *Oliver*.'

'I can't help that. I can't open with him in London.'

And that was how Barry Humphries, alias Dame Edna Everage, came to leave the cast of *Maggie May*. After the move to the Adelphi I made another change in the company. When the deputy stage manager caused havoc by bringing down the wrong curtain, he had to go. He was a keen lad and I felt a little sorry for him.

'Never mind,' I said. 'You'll get another chance.'

His name was Eddie Shah.

I was sufficiently encouraged by *Maggie May* to try again with Lionel Bart. This time it was a musical based on the Robin Hood legend. *Twang* cost between eighty and eighty-five thousand pounds to stage and every penny went down the drain, though on this occasion my involvement did not extend to putting up any money.

The problem with *Twang* was that it lacked any sort of structure. From the very beginning it looked a mess. I put great faith in the director Joan Littlewood who had worked with Lionel Bart on his first musical *Fings Ain't Wot They Used T'Be* and, as proved by that unlikely success, had the capacity to pull together strands to make an original and satisfying whole. But Lionel was no longer the theatrical novice sensitive to Joan Littlewood's obsession with doing things her way. He had ideas of his own and when they clashed with those of the director, he fought his corner. The rows were long and furious, culminating on the day before the Manchester opening with Joan Littlewood walking off the show and out of our lives. A newspaper quoted me as saying that I was not a happy man.

I toyed with the idea of bringing in a script doctor. Bert Shevelove, author of *A Funny Thing Happened on the Way to the Forum*, came to mind. The two shows had in common an anarchic humour which can so easily become self-indulgent. Shevelove might have imposed the discipline of an experienced outsider but he needed more than twenty-four hours to work the magic. Meanwhile, we did a hatchet job on forty minutes of the three-hour show and hoped for the best.

It was no good. At one point in the show Barbara Windsor had to say, 'I don't know what's going on here.' As one, the audience responded, 'Neither do we.' I got the message. I told Lionel Bart and his writer Harvey Orkin that I wanted out, expecting them to follow suit by putting up the white flag. Not a bit of it. After a huddled negotiation they decided to go on without me. Would I still let them have the Shaftesbury Theatre in London? I could hardly say no though it occurred to me that it wasn't much of a favour. I gave the London run a week at most. It exceeded my expectations by a few days with audiences who presumably had not read the appalling notices. The débâcle was a punishing blow to Lionel's career; his stage future was to be heavily dependent on revivals of *Oliver*.

It depends on how you add up the figures but if strict accounting suggests that I just came out ahead on Lionel Bart, I must add a bonus for setting the trend in Dickensian musicals. It was the huge appeal of *Oliver* which sparked my enthusiasm for *Pickwick* which I co-produced with Tom Arnold. Our star was Harry Secombe, a veteran of several of my Palladium shows who was then shaking off his Goon image and proving, with his fine tenor voice, that it was no joke when he proclaimed his early ambition to be an opera singer. He put heart and soul into the role and delivered the obligatory big number, 'If I Ruled the World', as if his life depended on cracking the rafters. *Pickwick* opened at the Saville in July 1963 and kept the box-office busy for eighteen months.

Immediately I saw the first favourable notices I started thinking about a Broadway transfer. David Merrick gave a lift to my hopes when he asked if he could co-produce. Right up until the last moment before the Broadway opening I smelled success. It was only when I read the first night reviews that I knew the wind had been blowing in the wrong direction.

It was my first practical experience of the huge difference between American and British audiences. And it was not just a one-way problem. Two years later I watched *Roar of the Greasepaint* die here only to be reborn in New York. Thereafter, in all my transatlantic dealings, I made a much greater allowance for the uncertainty factors. Someone has called us a people divided by a common language. Having discovered the truth of this in the theatre, I was to go on to find that the aphorism applied with just as much force in film production.

We followed Harry Secombe as Pickwick with Harry Secombe as D'Artagnan in *The Four Musketeers*, technically the most ambitious production mounted at Drury Lane since Noël Coward's pre-war extravaganza, *Cavalcade*. Sean Kenny's set made use of the entire stage, from front to the back wall. So elaborate and so heavy was the set that we had to reinforce the stage with ten tons of steel scaffolding. Even then it didn't work, at least not first time. Initially, the show itself had the same problem of overweight. The run-through was timed at five and a half hours. A crash diet was called for. In the end, we cut ninety minutes to make a presentable show which played for a year without covering our production costs. It is possible that I could have spent less to earn the same amount but audiences were demanding spectacle and it was already an established rule in the business that whatever the cost of a musical, the next one would be twice as expensive.

One mistake I did not make with *The Four Musketeers* was to try it out on American audiences. But that did not mean I had lost interest in the American connection. There were Broadway shows that could do well in London, that I knew, if they could be got on the right terms. To put myself in a stronger position to negotiate I joined up with Tom Arnold and American producer and director Arthur Lewis to buy Dorchester Productions from its joint owners EMI, Capitol Records and producers Feuer and Martin. This gave us access to several shows waiting for a London home, notably Neil Simon's first musical, *Little Me*, directed by Arthur Lewis whose long list of credits included the first British production of *Guys and Dolls* at the Coliseum. *Little Me* starred Bruce Forsyth, then best known as the master of ceremonies of the popular television show *Sunday Night at the London Palladium*. I had first seen Bruce in a summer season at Eastbourne and had mentioned to Lew, who was then at Associated Television, that he would be ideal as a variety compère. But it was Arthur who chose Bruce for *Little Me*. There was some concern when our star was propelled into a widely publicised divorce but in the event we had no need to worry. *Little Me* was a triumph and played to packed houses for seven months. It would have gone on much longer but when Bruce went down with a horrendous attack of flu and was out of the show for several weeks, interest faded. It was sad but we couldn't keep going without him.

Another first was *Our Man Crichton*, this one for Kenneth More who had not appeared before in a musical. *Our Man Crichton* occupied the Shaftesbury for six months, a disappointment to us all, not least to Herbert Kretzmer who wrote the lyrics and adapted the book from J. M. Barrie's *The Admirable Crichton*. Herbert set great store by this show, hoping that it was to be his big leap from popular singles to a full musical. Never doubting his talent, I urged him to go on.

'These things take time.'

I was right there. He had to wait another twenty years for his triumph. But he can now afford a luxurious retirement on the proceeds of his contribution to *Les Misérables*.

With the backing of Dorchester I went over to the States with my cheque-book open. The two musicals everyone was talking about were *Mame* and *Sweet Charity*, both controlled by Joe Harris and Bobby Fryer. In London it was said that *Mame* was a flier but that *Sweet Charity* would hit the deck on opening night. Producers were lining up for a one-show deal but Harris and Fryer insisted on two or nothing. I intended making my own judgement. I saw *Mame* in the afternoon, followed by an evening with *Sweet Charity*. The next day I went to see Joe Harris. He started talking before I was halfway into his office.

'Don't even think of it. You can't have *Mame* without *Sweet Charity*.'

We shook hands.

'Joe,' I said, 'I've got news for you. The show I want is *Sweet Charity*. I'll take it with or without *Mame*. It's your choice.'

In the end, I did take both shows which I co-produced with Harold Fielding, a great friend and a true professional who agreed with me on the relative prospects of the two musicals. Our instinct was right. *Sweet Charity* was the greater success. It had verve and style and pace, not to mention a star in Juliet Prowse who combined a generous measure of all three qualities. By contrast, Ginger Rogers as *Mame* was colourless on stage and none too sparkling off stage either. When told that it was usual at Christmas to show appreciation to the boys in the orchestra, she gave them each a jar of boiled sweets.

By far the most frustrating musical of this period was *Funny Girl* which launched Barbra Streisand's career on Broadway. The show came to me via Arthur Lewis who made the deal with Ray Stark in New York.

I was anxious to present Barbra's first show in this country but she would only agree to come for sixteen weeks. I reckoned that if we played to capacity I could just about break even. Knowing that Barbra was strong box-office and that *Funny Girl* would be a good image-builder for the Prince of Wales, I took the gamble. We started well with Barbra on top form, a desirable state I attributed to the influence of her husband Elliott Gould who combined the roles of lover, friend, comforter and confessor. But after the first few performances she seemed to lose interest. After a third lacklustre evening I went backstage to find out if she was ill. No, she said, it was just that she hated doing the same thing twice. That set me wondering why, if she was bored with her stage role, she had agreed to do *Funny Girl* in London, though all became clear when I was told that the West End was part of a wider deal guaranteeing her the lead in the film version of the musical.

And that was only the first surprise. The next revelation came when Barbra invited me to her dressing-room for a private chat. She was in euphoric mood.

'Bernie,' she cried, 'I've got great news. I'm pregnant.'

I tried hard to contain my lack of enthusiasm. 'But Barbra, you must have known before you came to London.'

'I wasn't certain,' she sighed, not realising for a moment what she was saying. 'It must be an act of God.'

I counted up to ten. 'No Barbra,' I said. 'It's not an act of God; it's an act of Elliott Gould.'

My star departed from *Funny Girl* after six weeks. We struggled on with understudies but it was Barbra the public had paid to see and we were forced to pay back most of the advance bookings.

For other lost opportunities in the musical theatre I had no one but myself to blame. David Land came to me with a great idea.

'What's it called?'

'*Jesus Christ Superstar.*'

'You have to be kidding.'

'No, seriously. It's about this guy who . . .'

'Enough. Get out of here!'

Having struck unlucky with me, David took the idea to Robert Stigwood who was so impressed by the young composer Andrew Lloyd Webber and his lyricist Tim Rice he agreed to put up the money. When I heard he was looking for a theatre I told him the Palace would soon be available. So, after turning down *Jesus Christ Superstar* as a producer, I became its landlord – for nearly eight years.

It was much the same story with *Hair* which I was prepared to back until I heard the language on the record and was told about the nude scene. I was urged not to worry. Censorship in the theatre was about to end. There was no limit to what could be shown on stage. Maybe not, I thought, but this is not what I call a Bernard Delfont show. I bowed out, thinking I had heard the last of it. But then I was asked if I would rent out the Shaftesbury. What was the show? Of course, *Hair*. It ran for close on two thousand performances and only stopped short of the magic figure because the roof fell in. It was generally held that the heavy beat of the music night after night loosened the plaster. This was certainly my story though I was asked more than once if I had taken a crowbar to the ceiling, just to get *Hair* out of my hair, so to speak.

Chapter 10

While I was busy in the theatre, my brothers were pursuing their own fortunes, Leslie with the Grade Agency, Lew with Associated Television. I was closer to Leslie but did not see much of him or Lew. In so far as we had a relationship, it was based more on mutual respect than on any need to socialise with each other. The strongest link between us was our mother, then well into her seventies, who fussed over us but recognised the competitive streak which made for some edgy family reunions.

In these circumstances, I could hardly complain when Lew took the leap into television without thinking to involve me. Yet I had to confess to feeling a little hurt that, unlike Leslie, I had not been given an opportunity to buy shares in ATV. As a producer I was naturally attracted to the medium everyone spoke of as the future. I could even claim to have played a small part in its early development. In the late twenties, I was paid two pounds to dance in front of a camera made and operated by John Logie Baird. My image was transmitted to an audience of City types, potential backers I assume, who were gathered round a bulbous screen a few hundred yards down the road.

After the war, when the BBC television service was beginning to make its mark, I had my second experience of television, this time as a producer. I had to cast one of the earliest variety shows to go out from Lime Grove studios. *Carefree* was broadcast on 24 June 1950. Viewers (the few who had television sets) were treated to the varied talents of eight performers supported by a sixteen-piece orchestra conducted by Eric Robinson. The budget for the lot, including scenery, wardrobe and make-up, was three hundred pounds. I was rapped for going over the limit by twelve pounds.

I did more ambitious TV shows, live variety, from the Pigalle and the Talk of the Town but these were one-off and were contributed,

151

as it were, from the outside track. Lew, meanwhile, was in a secure position on the inside track. I had an urge, if not to join him, at least to prove that I could take on the front runners.

The first opportunity to show my mettle came, incidentally, as part of a grand scheme to expand my theatre interests. Both the leading theatre owners, Moss Empires and Stoll, were having trouble filling seats and both, it seemed to me, were in defeatist mood, ready to offer live entertainment as a sacrificial victim to the small screen. The two companies were joined by interlocking share ownership and directorships but the one I fancied, Moss Empires, was open to a skilful takeover. The prize was some of the finest theatres in the country headed by the Palladium and the Victoria Palace. Moss also owned the biggest single stake in Associated Television; two-thirds of the voting shares. All I was short of to mount a coup was five million in stake money. I thought of Charles Clore.

Though I had met him on and off over the years, it was as my landlord at the Prince of Wales and the Royalty theatres that I got to know Charles Clore well, if not entirely to understand him. He was wealthy – enormously so after his alliance with Jack Cotton, the other leading property developer of the time. But though he had come from a poor background (like me he was an East Ender), his riches did not make him happy. In his personal life there was a streak of meanness which showed in his dealings with his wife, Francine. When their marriage was breaking up he rang me early one evening to invite me to dinner. 'Francine is coming round,' he explained. 'I don't have to go through all that. If you're there, she won't talk about the divorce.'

On another occasion, he told me about a friend of his who was down on his luck.

'I can't do anything for him. Can you help? You might give him some money.'

He came alive only with the prospect of a deal. Making money excited him. It was like this when I put up the idea of winning control of Moss Empires. He had a strategy worked out in five minutes. After a preliminary skirmish on the Stock Exchange to pick up any stray shares, we, meaning Charles, me and Jack Cotton, would make an outright bid. The big question was whether to go for surprise or try to prepare the way with a friendly approach to Prince Littler, joint chairman of Moss and Stoll. I thought there was a good chance Prince would regard us sympathetically. He was getting on in years but he was not on good terms with his brother Emile who was his likely successor. The money he stood to make from selling his own shares would ease his retirement.

As the one who knew about theatres, I was deputised to test the water with Prince to find out how he would react to a hypothetical offer to take over his business. The only way I could think of doing this without giving away the whole game was to create the circumstances for an informal chat, over dinner, perhaps, when we might naturally turn to speculation about our business futures. The trouble was, although I knew him well in a business context, I had never before invited Prince to dinner. If I did so now, he would immediately smell a rat. The only possibility I could think of was to take advantage of the coincidence that we were holiday neighbours in the south of France. When I heard that Prince was about to take a break, I rearranged my diary accordingly, hoping to bump into him accidentally on purpose.

One evening I spotted him in the casino bar at Juan les Pins. A few drinks later I had sussed what I already suspected, that he was not happy with the existing set-up at Moss. He implied he would welcome ideas for giving the theatres a new lease of life. I duly reported back to Charles Clore that the signals were favourable. We decided it was time to come out into the open.

A lunch was arranged for Charles to put across to Prince Littler the arguments for a takeover. I had no doubt that he and Charles would get on but as the meal progressed I could see that Prince was holding back on us. Whenever the conversation moved from generalisations to specifics, he countered repetitively: 'I'll have to think about that.'

Later in the afternoon, when Prince had departed and we were still no closer to divining his real intentions, Charles said, 'I'm sure we'll be able to do a deal with him. He's just waiting to see how much we'll offer.'

That was our first mistake. Prince did not wait for us to make the first move. The next thing we knew, he had bought in, as chairman of Stoll, all the preference shares in Moss Empires that were not already in his hands. Curiously, Charles Clore had completely overlooked this possibility. But he was still confident we could win. So too was Val Parnell who had stayed on the board of Moss Empires while moving in with Lew to run ATV. He put out a statement saying that he would be willing to remain a director of Moss if control passed to the attackers. This much publicised split with Prince, who was also a major shareholder in ATV, did no harm to our case though Val later tried to minimise the impact by claiming that all along he had assumed Prince was in favour of the takeover. The press did not believe him.

Our counter-bid made clear that while Val was welcome to stay on the board, Prince would have no further say over the running of the theatres which, along with the other entertainment interests, would come under my control. We were off and running and I could not think of anything to stop us. I had reckoned without Jack Cotton. Having so far stayed in the background he now felt bound to make his contribution by sounding off to reporters on what he would do with the Moss theatres once we had moved in. In his view, they would make wonderful office blocks. Tear them down and start again, was his motto.

I could only close my eyes to shut out the horror. The Palladium, an office block. Unthinkable.

I rang Charles Clore and told him how disgusted I was with Jack Cotton's outburst.

He told me not to worry. 'Jack talks too much. He doesn't mean half of what he says.'

'It's more important what other people believe,' I said. 'This could wreck our chances.'

I put on a brave face when reporters tracked me down.

'Is it true you plan to convert theatres into office blocks?'

I told them there was no question of losing the theatres. Jack Cotton was talking nonsense.

But the press made much of the difference of emphasis between me and Jack Cotton, shifting attention away from Prince's difficulties in maintaining a united front. The initiative slipped away from us. Before the week was out Charles conceded defeat. For me, it was a foregone conclusion. As soon as Prince Littler bought in the preference shares, I feared the worst.

'A bad day,' Charles confessed philosophically. 'On top of everything, my horse lost at Ascot.'

I did not ask Lew how he would have reacted if the bid had succeeded and as an inevitable consequence I had joined him as a senior director of ATV. But when, two years later, I passed on to Lew a strong rumour that Stoll Moss was again on the market, he was quick to move. With ATV backing he put together an offer

154

Entering the Palladium for the Royal Variety Performance, 1964.

Punch cartoon, 1968.

Punch cartoon, 1975.

The Royal Variety Performance at the Victoria Palace, 1984.

With Lord Shawcross (*left*) and Lord Peddie at my introduction to the House of Lords, 1976.

'Dear Bernie – Your belief in *The Jazz Singer* helped us all through and made the dream a reality – Thank You! Love Neil, 1980.'

which delivered all the Stoll Moss theatres into his domain, just getting in ahead of Emile Littler who expected to take over. Prince Littler joined Lew on the ATV board. As for me, though naturally disappointed at the failure of my bid, I was pleased the theatres were in the family. Now they were Lew's problem. I had other pressing matters to attend to.

Having failed in one takeover, I succeeded in another, only this time I was on the receiving end. To add a further twist to the story, the man who wanted to buy part of my business was my own brother – Leslie Grade.

It has been said often enough that Leslie was the brightest of the family. Certainly, I believe it to be true. He was not well known to the public because he was essentially a backroom boy whose organisational skills made ideas work. He was also a great salesman. As an agent, he was known to every producer by his opening pitch, 'Have I got an act for *you*.'

Backing his judgement on the quality of a performer was a safe bet. He had an eye for talent and an uncanny ability for presenting it to best effect. As partners, Lew and Leslie thrived on their shared ambition to create the number one entertainment agency in the country. But when in 1955 Lew went off to run ATV, there was a general assumption that without the front man the business would develop at a more leisurely pace. Not a bit of it. If anything, Leslie accelerated the rate of growth, not least by shrewd purchases of rival theatrical agencies such as London Management and London Artists who counted Laurence Olivier, Noël Coward, Rex Harrison, Albert Finney, Sir John Gielgud and Dame Peggy Ashcroft among their clients.

In the early sixties, the Grade Organisation, as it was now known, branched out into film distribution with the acquisition of the cinema chain Shipman and King, which accounted for thirty-two cinemas and Elstree Film Distributors.

The next step was into film production, spearheaded by the urbane Robin Fox, now best known as the father of the theatrical triumvirate of Edward, James and Robert. Trained as a lawyer, Robin had worked in the London office of the Music Corporation of America, then the world's biggest show business agency. One of Leslie's clients he knew well was Cliff Richard and it was through this mutual contact that together they were able to produce two of the singer's early movies – *The Young Ones*, which the critics welcomed as a creditable effort to revive the British screen musical and *Summer Holiday*, a directorial début for Peter Yates. Both made money, the first achieving something of a record by going into profit within a month of its opening.

They went on to produce *Sparrows Can't Sing*, directed by Joan Littlewood from a play first seen at Stratford East. A warm portrayal of the working-class cockney, it revived so many memories of our own upbringing that Leslie decided on holding the première in an East End cinema. It turned out to be a marvellous publicity stunt attracting more crowds and column inches than an opening in one of the Leicester Square showcases. But the real money was made on another variation of the cockney theme. As that energetically amoral Alfie, Michael Caine was confirmed as a major star and Cilla Black had a great hit with the title song.

None of us knew it at the time, but the next production for Leslie and Robin Fox was to be the last of their joint efforts. It says much for Leslie's trust in Robin that he ever gave the go-ahead for the project. The subject matter – the sexual corruption of a wealthy playboy by his sinister valet – was not much to the liking of a man who had dedicated his career to family entertainment. But the talents that were brought together for *The Servant* – book, Robin Maugham; screenplay, Harold Pinter; director, Joseph Losey; star, Dirk Bogarde – subdued any fears he might have had of a moral backlash though he was always self-conscious about his association with the production. His proudest boast was that he brought it in under budget. Critics and audiences voted *The Servant* an outstanding film of its time and though nowadays the theme has lost its shock value, it is still appreciated and rightly so, for launching the career of the young James Fox, who gave an outstanding performance.

Early in 1964 Leslie announced he had a business proposition he wanted to discuss. Usually he would have told me outright on the telephone what was on his mind but this time he was uncharacteristically reserved, saying only that he thought we should get together. Intrigued, I fixed a time to go round to his office in Regent Street. When we did meet, he took his time coming to the point. He wanted to know how many shows I had on, what the prospects were for more American deals, whether I was making enough of a profit to carry on feeding a musical-hungry West End. Such brotherly interest! Then he came out with it.

'Wouldn't you like to concentrate on what you do best? I know you love presenting shows. So why don't you sell me the agency?'

In principle, the idea appealed. My heart was not in the agency. Selling the business would release cash, though how much I had yet to discover, and would free my hands to concentrate on the tricky problem of making my theatrical productions pay. On the other hand, I was used to the agency as the one stable element in an increasingly erratic world. And it had some blue-chip performers – Norman Wisdom, Frankie Vaughan, Morecambe and Wise, Leslie Crowther, Dickie Henderson and Harry Worth among them. I had no intention of letting them go cheaply.

'How much are you offering?'

'A hundred thousand.'

I thought that was much too low and said so. 'Apart from any cash, I'll want shares in the Grade Organisation.'

Leslie said he had to consider that one. I assumed he wanted to talk to Lew before committing himself to a firm bid. We agreed to meet again by the end of the week. I went away to work on a few figures.

The revised offer was quite attractive – one hundred thousand pounds in cash and two hundred thousand shares. Since the Grade Organisation had lately entered the list of publicly quoted companies, I was able to put a precise value on my stake: one pound twenty a share, according to the FT Index.

The news of the deal caused a certain flurry in the press. In some quarters the link-up with my brothers was seen as a planned move towards a family monopoly of the British entertainment industry. With Lew as a TV mogul, Leslie as a top agent and me as a producer with more shows than I could remember to count, it was easy to see how suspicions were aroused. The *Sunday Times* published an elaborate graph apparently showing how we all interlocked to mutual advantage.

But the idea of us trying to dominate show business was clearly preposterous. Quite apart from the rivalry that was known to exist between us (it could be said, for example, that when I was running the Casino, Lew actively worked against me by sending his best acts to the Palladium) the monopoly argument was only valid on the unlikely assumption that powerful organisations like the ITV companies and the BBC would tolerate such a state of affairs. In fact, as we all knew, if there had been a hint of unfair competition we would have suffered a severe backlash – and rightly so.

On the surface, little changed after the merger of the Delfont Agency with the Grade Organisation. Leslie's style was to give everyone in the company the freedom to do their own jobs in their own way. He interfered only when he saw a threat to the bottom line. Billy Marsh and his team had no problems on that score and so were left to carry on as usual. It was a reasonably steady period of my career. I joined the board of the Grade Organisation but strictly in a non-executive role. For me, the biggest impact of the merger was on my bank manager who ventured the thought that, at last, I was making good. If by that he meant that I was settling down, he and I both should have known that it couldn't last.

But taking advantage of the natural break in my career, perhaps this is a good moment to sidetrack on to a part of my show business life that was devoted entirely to other people.

Chapter 11

I've had my ups and downs with the critics but there is one part of my career where, from the word go, I have been able to do no right. In choosing the line-up for the *Royal Variety Performance* the press has attacked me for favouring too many old-timers or too many unknown youngsters, for overloading the bill with American acts or ignoring the transatlantic contribution to variety, for making the show too long or ruthlessly cutting artistes short. If there is a format for satisfying all the show business writers, I have yet to find it.

Never mind. I am grateful for the interest. It confirms what I have always maintained, that the *Royal Variety Performance* is more than a charitable event. It is the top date in the light entertainment calendar. No doubt the format will change, as it has in the past. In 1990, for instance, in special celebration of the Queen Mother's ninetieth birthday, the BBC will be showing a compilation of past Royal Variety high spots. The break gives us the chance to rethink the programme in time for the next Royal Variety, an opportunity I welcome after the embarrassment of 1989 when there was at least one act that was totally unsuitable for the occasion. But whatever is decided, I am sure the young royals will carry on the tradition.

My run with the Royal Variety started in 1958. It was Prince Littler, chairman of Stoll Moss, who rang me to ask if I would take over from Val Parnell. Val felt it was time for a break. He had been doing the job for several years and was feeling the strain. Maybe I wouldn't have been quite so thrilled if he had stressed a few of the problems, like finding stars who were prepared to commit themselves in time for the programmes to be printed and then making sure that they got on with each other long enough to bear the inevitable frustration of over-hasty rehearsals and improvised settings. But no doubt he assumed I knew all this. After all, I had been helping out with Val Parnell for several years. It was therefore not exactly in a

159

spirit of sweet innocence that I approached the thirty-second *Royal Variety Performance*. I took comfort from the triumphs of my predecessors. The first *Royal Variety* was in July 1912 at London's Palace Theatre. It should have been held a year earlier in Edinburgh to coincide with the coronation of George V but the Empire Palace Theatre burned down a few weeks earlier, killing some of the performers who were due to take part. Understandably, the spirit went out of the enterprise. Still, 1912 was a palpable hit. Harry Tate did his motoring sketch and Harry Lauder sang 'Roamin' in the Gloamin''. Sadly, the great Marie Lloyd was not invited. It was thought that her songs overreached the bounds of royal propriety, though for my money George V would have enjoyed a spirited rendering of 'One of the Ruins That Cromwell Knocked About a Bit'. Maybe Queen Mary was the stumbling block, though if she was as strait-laced as she was made out to be, I assume the double meanings would have passed straight over her head.

For the benefit of those who think that today's *Royal Varieties* are over-long, I can't resist pointing out that 142 named artists were on the 1912 programme. Of these, at least a dozen are numbered among the greats, including Harry Tate, Vesta Tilley, Little Tich, Wilkie Bard, Harry Lauder, Anna Pavlova, Harry Champion, George Robey, Harry Weldon and Lupino Lane. Proceeds from the show went to the Variety Artistes Benevolent Fund (which I changed to the Entertainment Artistes Benevolent Fund to cover artistes in all spheres of entertainment) to help maintain Brinsworth House in Twickenham, a nursing home for retired performers opened the previous year.

And that was it until 1919 when the second *Royal Variety* was held at the London Coliseum and Harry Marlow, a one-time stand-up comedian who now ran Brinsworth House, thought of instituting an annual *Royal Variety*. The cycle started in 1921 with only occasional gaps up to the war. We were back again in 1945 and have suffered just one interruption since then, in 1956, the year of the Suez crisis.

Val Parnell was in charge and I was his first lieutenant that year. We had a marvellous cast including Gracie Fields, Liberace, the Crazy Gang, Winifred Atwell and a novel dance trio – Laurence Olivier, Vivien Leigh and John Mills doing Fred Astaire's *Top Hat* number. Someone suggested a finale with the men in Liberace suits and the women dressed as Mom. I had my doubts that Liberace would approve. I should have remembered that his entire act, though played with deadly seriousness, was a merciless send-up – of himself. He was delighted with the proposal and even offered to pay for the costumes. But then, four hours before curtain-up, Val called me into his office. He was so tired he looked as if he was about to fall down.

'Dreadful news,' he said. 'We have to cancel tonight's show.'

I was thoroughly confused. 'Why? What's happened?'

Val shook his head. 'I've just had a call from Buckingham Palace. Because of the landing at Suez and the fighting, the royals won't be coming.'

It was a huge disappointment but I could well understand the reasoning behind the decision. Winifred Atwell gave an impromptu party to try to lift our spirits, without much success. It was the only year the show has lost money.

For my first venture as *Royal Variety* supremo I had at least three great advantages: Robert Nesbitt, Billy Marsh and Keith Devon. Robert agreed to direct and continued to do so for twenty years while Billy Marsh and Keith Devon started pulling every string imaginable to get the best possible line-up. I wanted this to be the *Royal Variety Performance* to beat all *Royal Variety Performances*.

I don't know whether I succeeded but I did introduce a few changes, not all of them greeted with unanimous approval. For a start, I felt it was about time we did more to encourage young home-grown talent. This meant cutting back on the American presence (we settled for two imports, Eartha Kitt and Pat Boone) and on the safe, established acts, the old favourites addicted to the old routines. So in came Roy Castle, Max Bygraves, Harry Secombe and Bruce Forsyth and out went the Crazy Gang.

The press seized on this act of temerity. The Crazy Gang was a *Royal Variety* institution with an unbroken run of post-war appearances to prove it. Individual members of the team could claim an even longer association. Nervo and Knox made their début in 1930. Two years later they were on again, this time sharing the bill with Flanagan and Allen. George Black thought of overlapping their acts with Bud Flanagan giving a commentary on a Nervo and Knox burlesque of *Swan Lake*. It was the beginning of the Crazy Gang, later joined by Naughton and Gold and 'Monsewer' Eddie Gray.

I never tired of their routines but I thought it was time to give younger performers a chance. We were into the age of television and the public expected the *Royal Variety* to recognise the fact by making room for TV names like Charlie Drake, Bernard Bresslaw (then best known for *The Army Game*), the conjuror David Nixon and the wildly energetic thirty-year-old compère of *Sunday Night at the London Palladium*, Bruce Forsyth. Elsewhere on the bill, as one or two critics were quick to point out, Delfont shows and Delfont stars figured prominently – Norman Wisdom in an excerpt from *Where's Charley?*, the 'good old days' number from the Palladium show, the 'girls and boys' from the Talk of the Town, Frankie Vaughan. But this was a year in which my name appeared in fourteen show-bills, five in London and nine more in the provinces, more than any other impresario. Presumably this was the reason why I was asked to take over after Val Parnell.

Every *Royal Variety* is controlled chaos. Just think of it: more than twenty acts and countless ensembles to meld together and less than two days to do it. In 1958 we were in the London Coliseum. Rehearsals started on Sunday morning with Robert Nesbitt plotting every move down to seconds. Timing, I soon discovered, is vital otherwise a projected two-and-a-half-hour show can easily stretch to four hours. It has happened – too often, I'm afraid.

Once, when we overran wildly, the line-up of stars at the end of the show seemed to last for ever. I couldn't help noticing the Queen glancing at her watch. It was 12.40 a.m. The Queen's next engagement, just eleven hours away, was the state opening of Parliament. Renowned for her impatience with bad time-keeping, I could well understand if this day of all days she felt miffed by my failure to stick to schedule. But she remained charming, if a little cool.

'Thank you, Mr Delfont,' she said as I escorted her to her car. 'Don't be surprised if you see me wearing the same dress to open Parliament.'

I muttered something about the politicians being delighted because it was such an attractive dress. The following week I had a polite letter from her private secretary asking me in future to keep tighter control of the running time.

I tried. Goodness knows, I tried. The problem is that top entertainers who are giving their services free are not always amenable to the discipline of a commercial show. When Rex Harrison led the *My Fair Lady* company he didn't even turn up for rehearsal. Half an hour before the show Harrison appeared, urbane as ever, while the rest of us were close to nervous breakdown.

Then again, with so much talent on the same bill, a certain amount of upstaging is inevitable. Singers who promise faithfully to limit themselves to three numbers (equal to ten minutes at most) then feel compelled to compliment the audience, declare what a privilege it is to appear in a *Royal Variety* and rabbit on about how they have always wanted to play the Coliseum or Palladium or wherever the show happens to be. By the time they have said their piece, ten minutes has become twenty minutes. What can a producer do? Dropping the curtain in mid act is hardly suitable for a royal show, less so the long-handled hook favoured, as legend tells us, by the Victorian master of ceremonies. I settled for looking fierce if there was any hint of excess. Much good it ever did me.

The record for overrunning is held by Ken Dodd who went on for twelve minutes and stayed for forty. (He was a great hit.) But the classic story of outstaying a welcome has to do with Max Miller. He kept going in defiance of Val Parnell who was standing in the wings shouting to him to come off. Those of us in the front stalls had no trouble in detecting the famous Parnell temper about to break. Max Miller turned it into a joke using Parnell as an unseen stooge.

'He wants me to come off. Do you hear that, lady? I ask you, is that fair?'

Up to this point, the audience was with him but then he took a crack at the American performers led by the much loved Jack Benny. 'They get all the time they want. Isn't that right, my love? So why shouldn't I have a bit of extra?'

In any other show the cheerful leer signalling an intended double meaning would have earned him a laugh. But not at the royal show. The audience was embarrassed. Max knew when he was beaten. He quickly wound up and made his exit. Val Parnell was waiting for him as he came off stage. He should have left well alone but instead he gave Max the chance of the last word.

'You'll never work for me again,' Val shouted. 'Do you hear? You'll never work again in one of my theatres.'

Comedian and producer stood eye to eye.

'Val,' said Max. 'You can forget it. You're four hundred thousand pounds too late.'

Nowadays, there is the added pressure of the television companies – not to keep the time down but to lengthen the show. That way, they have more choice in editing. My response has been to cut the number of acts, from an average of twenty-two to sixteen.

In spite of the loss of the Crazy Gang (they were back in 1960 and, finally, in 1961) my first *Royal Variety* had an enthusiastic reception. The Queen and the Duke of Edinburgh were there. I was so nervous for the first half, I stayed out in the foyer keeping the doorman company. Thereafter I kept an eye on the royal party, trying to gauge if they were laughing and applauding for real or whether it was feigned politeness. I settled for it being the genuine article only when Carole was presented and I overheard the Queen saying, 'We loved every moment of it. It was a wonderful show.'

As they departed, Prince Philip took me aside. 'You look haggard,' he said. 'Go and have a good week's sleep.'

If I had to choose the low point of the show it was Tony Hancock in his budgie sketch. He was the bird in the gilded cage having to listen to the mindless chatter of his doting mistress played by Hattie Jacques. It was a brilliant idea and I did not need to be persuaded that Tony Hancock was a most talented comedian, but having seen him once or twice in the West End, I felt that he was not comfortable in live variety. He was heavily dependent on his script and could be easily thrown by unexpected laughter. It was on radio and television that his genius flourished. At the Coliseum the nervousness showed.

In subsequent *Royal Variety Performances* there have been many other disappointments, nearly always unexpected. The first time Frankie Howerd appeared he was a flop and he was the first to admit it. But he came back fighting and was such a hit the second time around he was adopted as a *Royal Variety* institution, like the Crazy Gang. His running joke – from year to year, that is – was the horror of working for Bernie Delfont. I was 'him, up there', Frankie pointing aloft to an imaginary sanctum above the Palladium stage where I was supposed to exercise my power, largely at Frankie's expense. According to his favourite insult I was 'common as muck'. Sympathisers sent me kind letters saying that Frankie should not be allowed to say such terrible things. What they did not know was that a week before the show he called by my office to agree all the jokes.

Nineteen sixty-three was the year of the Beatles, then starting off on their phenomenal career. Me, I had never heard of them. My daughter Susan was a fan and when I asked what they did, she said they were somehow – well, you know – different, which was all I was permitted to know until Billy Marsh told me that the Beatles were doing a Sunday concert for our organisation at the Princes Theatre, Torquay. I rang the theatre.

'How's business?' I asked the manager.

'We're sold out,' he said. 'There are fans sleeping on the street, waiting for returns.'

That was good enough for me. I made the booking. As the year progressed, so did the fame of the Beatles so that by November they were the biggest name on the programme. This upset Marlene Dietrich who thought, reasonably enough, that the kudos should be hers. I anticipated a clash of temperament but I should have known that Miss Dietrich would not stoop to a vulgar brawl. Instead, she fought back with all the subtle ruthlessness of Lady Macbeth. Whenever the photographers gathered for the Beatles, there she was pushing her way into the picture. The boys, who were still a little unsure of themselves, accepted the intrusion as a compliment. Not so the production team who recognised scene-stealing when they saw it. To win them round, she went straight for the jugular – in the nicest possible way. She turned up to rehearsals with two crates of champagne and a lot of glasses. She then proceeded to give us a one-woman concert accompanied by a free handout of bubbly. The orchestra loved her. So did we. At the end of two hours we were convinced she would take the Prince of Wales by storm. She did too, with a little help from Burt Bacharach at the piano, though the Beatles, all innocent charm, scored their own triumph with a well-turned phrase from John Lennon, 'Don't bother to applaud, just rattle your jewellery.'

Without doubt, the Beatles were going places. Later, I found out that the Delfont Agency might have gone with them. Brian Epstein, their manager, had offered Keith Devon the chance of representing the Beatles but Keith had decided they were too expensive.

The real stars of the *Royal Variety* are the guests of honour, the Queen one year, the Queen Mother the next, with whoever they wish to include in their party. One of the fascinations of producing the show has been to see an evolving relationship between the Royal Family and the rest of the audience. When I started, it was all very formal which could make it difficult for performers to break through the atmosphere of reserve.

The Crazy Gang helped to lighten the occasion with their then outrageous jokes aimed at the royal box.

'Will the owner of car number HR1 please remove it from the front of the theatre. It's double parked.'

Then a bunch of keys was thrown up to the royal box.

Harmless enough today but in the fifties the stalls would look anxiously aloft to see how the royals were taking it before deciding whether to laugh. That the Queen and Queen Mother were relaxed and smiling made all the difference.

Tommy Steele was another performer who extended the limits of the *Royal Variety* though probably he did not realise his contribution when he asked the audience to clap to the rhythm of one of his rock and roll numbers. The reaction was muted until the Queen Mother leant forward in her box to lead the way in audience participation. After that the clap along was a regular feature of the *Royal Variety*.

Since I had no wish to end up in the Tower, my inclination as producer was always to play safe. If in doubt, cut it out, was my motto.

I said as much to Maurice Chevalier when he told me he intended singing 'You Must Have Been a Beautiful Baby' to the Queen Mother.

'You can't do it,' I pleaded. 'It could be very embarrassing.'

He gave me a friendly squeeze on my arm. 'You must not worry. The way I do it will be fine. I promise.' His squeeze tightened. 'I will do it,' he said in a tone which suggested that if I did not agree he might walk out.

I went on arguing for half an hour but in the end I had to take a chance on Gallic charm.

The gamble paid off. In the climax to his act, Maurice Chevalier turned to the royal box, went down on one knee and sang the entire song finishing with, 'You must have been a beautiful baby, cos Majesty look at you now.'

I held my breath. So too did the audience. The Queen Mother smiled and led the applause. The audience went wild.

More palpitations were caused when we took the plunge with *Till Death Us Do Part*. No sooner had we announced the programme than there was an outcry at an episode in the television series that was said to be sacrilegious. My post-bag was full of protest letters. How could I possibly think of exposing the Queen Mother to such profanity? I spoke to Johnny Speight, the writer and creator of *Till Death*, who evidently felt that I was fussing about nothing. I went over his script so many times looking for double meanings, he must have thought I had taken training with the Lord's Day Observance Society. The inevitable compromise was just about all right. I let through a couple of bloodys. Afterwards, the Queen Mother said to me, 'Well, that wasn't too bad, was it?' I think she was a bit relieved.

One of the most taxing *Royal Varieties* started with Duke Ellington and his orchestra turning up without their instruments. At rehearsal the band threw themselves into a sing-song, led by Duke Ellington at the piano. The instruments finally arrived but without the arrangements. No matter: the audience was treated to happy improvisation.

Every year brings its own crisis. In 1966, Gilbert Bécaud, one of the top French singers, arrived with less than two hours to spare before the customers took their seats. He made it but his voice didn't. When I went to see him in his dressing-room he could barely whisper, 'Hello.' He was a sad and disappointed man but I made sure that he did not miss out entirely. He enjoyed the show from a seat in the stalls.

It was after a *Royal Variety* that I found myself in trouble with Elton John. He was quoted in the press as saying that he would never go through such a horrible experience ever again. His chief complaint was my apparent lack of respect. During rehearsals he had felt like giving me a punch on the nose. I wrote to him saying he could punch me any time he liked as long as he made a donation to the Benevolent Fund. He sent a cheque for fifteen hundred pounds by return.

Maybe I was a little hard on him. But when you are trying to meld up to a couple of hundred performers, musicians, designers, technicians, the only way is to treat everybody on an equal basis. The stars usually understand this.

Nowadays, the *Royal Variety* is very much in the hands of the boys from television: the BBC and ITV take it in turns to present the show which always makes the top ratings and brings in much needed extra revenue to the Entertainment Artistes Benevolent Fund. But the virtues of letting in the television cameras were not always apparent. Until the end of the fifties, theatre owners were nervous that too much exposure would deter audiences from paying to see live variety. Then, as the music hall continued its decline, the argument reversed itself. Television, it was said, might actually revive interest in the real thing.

The exclusive rights were snapped up by Lew at ATV who quickly proved that the *Royal Variety* could attract a huge fireside audience. Inevitably, the BBC asked to be let in on the act, arguing that such an important event should alternate between the two channels. I agreed; Lew did not. We had a first-class row, one of our loudest and rowdiest, which echoed across to every show business editor in Fleet Street. But, in the end, he had to concede. Never again was I to be accused of being in cahoots with Lew.

The television fee to the Entertainment Artistes Benevolent Fund has crept up over the years but I have always felt that it is tremendous value for money. Today, the show brings in between four and five hundred thousand pounds from television at home and overseas. And I *still* think it is cheap at the price.

After the first cameras appeared, it was not long before US television showed an interest which encouraged us to put in more American acts. The exception was Jubilee year, 1977, when Lew clinched a deal with NBC worth a cool two million dollars. I should add that the television version of the *Royal Variety* is an annual event in all the Commonwealth countries.

We first agreed to a live television broadcast in 1976. If I had had my way, it would have been the last. We had a great programme with Shirley Bassey, Max Bygraves, the Dance Theatre of Harlem and other top-liners. But disaster followed us at every turn. A mike was knocked flat in the opening number, the lights went out on the ventriloquist Roger de Courcey who was plunged into darkness a full minute before the end of his act and a sound fault allowed the orchestra to drown out the voice of Mike Yarwood. Not surprisingly, the reviews were poor.

Against my better judgement, we relived the tension of a live broadcast two years later. This time the gremlins stayed away but we only had to reflect on what could have gone wrong to decide, never again. For the last twelve years the *Royal Variety Performance* has been recorded and edited for television. I cannot imagine it ever being any other way.

My biggest and, I believe, best *Royal Variety* was for the Silver Jubilee in 1977. Bob Hope was the compère with, among others, Shirley MacLaine, Harry Belafonte, Cleo Laine, Tommy Cooper and Julie Andrews competing for honours. By common consent, it was Shirley MacLaine who stole the show, whipping off her black diamanté trousers to whirl into a dance so electrifying as to send half the audience into a trance. Later that night at the celebration dinner Shirley sat between me and Prince Charles. He complimented her on her performance. 'I wish I could take my trousers off as fast as you can.' On stage, the competition for Shirley came from Miss Piggy of the Muppets ('Kissy wissy to the Queen') and her sidekick, Kermit, who spent the entire act making eyes at the royal box.

There was one sadness. We all missed Bing Crosby who was to have shared the stage with Bob Hope. He had died suddenly five weeks earlier. It says much for his widow Kathy that she was there, in the audience, an encouragement to Bob Hope who was clearly missing his old sparring partner.

My Silver Jubilee duties did not end with the *Royal Variety*. I was asked to join the London Celebrations Committee, chaired by Lord Drogheda. One of my tasks was to organise street parties hosted by popular entertainers (it didn't help that on the day the rain fell) and to put on a Thames firework display with full musical accompaniment.

The entire royal family with their full contingent of children watched the event from the top of the Shell building. Earl Mountbatten expressed his satisfaction with the entertainment. 'Look at that, Bernie,' he said, as the last rocket burst in the sky, 'it's better than one of your shows.' I think he meant it as a compliment.

In some years there are two *Royal Variety Performances*, the second out of London. I always worried about these extras simply because they were so difficult to get together – and, on occasion, highly sensitive. When the Queen was invited to open the new Mersey Tunnel and asked for a royal show celebrating Merseyside culture, the Liverpool authorities turned to me. At first I refused but when no one else would take it on, I had to give way. The big problem was that some of the brightest of the local talent were, not to put too fine a point on it, so far on the political left as to qualify for a hammer and sickle. I was lucky to escape with just one anti-monarchist sketch which the Queen took in her stride. She was more concerned about the time. The royal train was scheduled to depart at 11.30 p.m. She mentioned this when, at the end of the show, she hurried down the line of performers. A member of that wonderfully anarchic pop group Scaffold overheard her. 'Don't worry, Ma'am. You can always catch the twelve thirty.'

After twenty *Royal Variety Performances* and at least another ten royal shows, I decided to call it a day. That was in 1978 when I was sixty-nine. It was a good moment to depart. The Silver Jubilee programme was one of our best ever and with the opening of a new wing, Brinsworth House was entering a new phase of development. My last *Royal Variety* was 'A Tribute to the Queen Mother'.

169

During rehearsals I heard that the Queen Mother had asked for a personal message to be read out during the show. David Jacobs did the honours for what turned out to be a fulsome tribute to me. While the Queen Mother was applauding I stood up to take a bow. It was a very happy moment in my life. Later, someone asked me to describe the experience of producing a *Royal Variety Performance*. I said it was like being in a car crash and only suffering from shock.

Louis Benjamin took over from me to do an outstanding job while I became Life President of the Fund. This means that I am still closely involved in the difficult business of selecting applicants for places at Brinsworth House and whenever I hear a hard-luck story I am quickly on to Reg Swinson, the General Secretary of the Fund who, somehow, keeps the machine working smoothly. There are many old-timers who rely on us to make ends meet, not only the forty or so residents of the home but also some four hundred elderly performers spread throughout the country. For obvious reasons we do not advertise their names but I can say that past entertainers who have benefited from the Fund and who now are no longer with us include Hylda Baker (who appeared in one of my earliest shows), Wilson Kepple and Betty, the bandleader Roy Fox and, most recently, Terry Thomas.

Of all the royal visits to Brinsworth House my fondest memory is of the sixtieth anniversary celebrations. It was the turn of Princess Margaret whose style was such that she could easily have been mistaken for a star of stage and screen. In fact, that is precisely how she was seen by one elderly resident.

'Hello, dearie,' she said as the Princess approached. 'It has been a long time. What are you in nowadays?'

I can think of only one story to beat that. It has to do with the big show we held at the Talk of the Town in aid of the World Wild Life Fund. The royals were out in force, not just from this country but from overseas, many of them attending, I couldn't help noticing, in their finest furs. Throughout the evening I sat next to the Queen whose first visit it was to the Talk of the Town or, I guess, to any cabaret. Of all the illustrious guests, the most colourfully turned out was Barbara Cartland. As the novelist swept past our table, the picture of mature glamour, the Queen twinkled. 'Who's that?' she asked. 'Danny La Rue?'

Chapter 12

Leslie was just forty-nine when he had his stroke. Though the youngest of we three brothers, he had suffered indifferent health ever since he had come back from the war in the Middle East where he had caught typhoid. But his illnesses were never so serious as to prepare us for this blow.

The first I knew of it was a telephone call from his wife Audrey to say that he had been taken to Guy's Hospital. He was in a coma and no one knew when or if he would come out of it. The next call was from Lew. We had to meet, urgently.

Our first concern was for Audrey and her two young children, Anita and Antony. Two days earlier, on 19 April 1966, they had moved into their dream home, a flat in Kensington Palace Gardens, otherwise known as Millionaires' Row. Having looked forward to the change, now all they could sense was the strangeness of the place, the half-lived-in feel, which made the uncertainty the more difficult to bear. Audrey coped marvellously and after making sure she had everything she wanted, we could do little else on the personal level.

But when it came to business, Lew and I did have a part to play. Taking the most optimistic view, Leslie would not be back in the office for a long time. Recalling my own heart trouble, I concluded that for every month Leslie was in hospital he could assume a year away from work. That left a serious gap in the upper reaches of the Grade Organisation. When last anyone had thought about the problem it was assumed that Lew would take over. But Lew was now boss of ATV, no longer his own man, free to take off to run another company. Outside the family, the obvious successor was Robin Fox but he too was ill and, as we were soon to find out, mortally so, with lung cancer.

That left me: not entirely a free spirit, but an independent who was used to adapting his working day to a variety of circumstances.

171

And I was a senior director of the company. I felt bound to take over as head of the Grade Organisation while hoping that Leslie would make a complete recovery. I did not want to go back to agency work long term.

I had an idea. Michael, Leslie's son by his first marriage, was one of the brightest of the younger generation of Grades. At twenty-four he had already made a name for himself as a sports journalist (his byline appeared in the *Daily Mirror*) and while he had never expressed a strong desire to follow in his father's footsteps, I knew that he had ambitions to set up his own business as a sports promoter.

When we met for lunch, I pressed him as hard as I dared on the virtues of the agency. I would never have done so had I not believed that he could carry the job. My confidence in him was further boosted by the knowledge that Billy Marsh was on hand to teach him the ropes.

While Michael was thinking over his future we heard that Leslie was out of danger but still critical. He had suffered a cerebral haemorrhage. The doctors did not expect lasting brain damage; they did expect Leslie to be frail for a long time to come. Though no one voiced the thought, we all knew that the chances of a full recovery were remote. The good news was that Michael was ready to keep the Grade flag flying. In spite of his frequently expressed worries about living up to his father's reputation, he became an outstanding agent, nurturing, among others, two brilliant comedians – Larry Grayson and Freddie Starr.

Meantime, I was preparing the way for another big change in the Grade Organisation. A short while before Leslie went into hospital seductive approaches had been made by the music giant EMI whose chairman, Sir Joseph Lockwood, and managing director, John Read, were keen to diversify their business. One could well understand their point of view. EMI was the world's leading music record company, responsible for marketing top-line entertainers like Frank Sinatra, Nat King Cole and, in Britain, the musical phenomenon of their age, the Beatles.

But fashions can change quickly and in the volatile sixties they were changing faster than ever before. It did not take an astute accountant to recognise the fragile base on which the record business was founded. The strategy of the company was thus to use its very considerable cash resources to branch out into other sectors of the leisure industry. No single investment was totally secure but there was thought to be safety in numbers – it was unlikely that all of them would go to the wall at the same time.

It soon became clear that the Grade Organisation was high on the EMI list of prospective acquisitions. Well regarded in the stock market, what was now the largest agency in Europe had itself led the way on diversification with Leslie's entry into film production and distribution. It was, I believe, this policy as much as anything that protected our share value against the full impact of Leslie's illness; that, and our rapid moves to bolster the top management. Though, for a company our size, we had little in the way of solid assets (the cinemas were about all we could claim in freehold property), the Grade Organisation was worth a lot of money. Quite how much I was soon to discover.

Leslie was still in hospital when I first heard from Sir Joseph Lockwood himself. He came straight to the point. If EMI made a bid for our company would it be sympathetically received? There was only one answer. Yes, if the price was right and it benefited our shareholders. In the back of my mind was the knowledge that we were enjoying an outstanding year, thanks to Michael Caine and *Alfie*. But I doubted that we could keep it up. If there was an ideal time to sell, this was it. When I reported my conversation with Sir Joseph Lockwood to Leslie and Lew, they reacted in the same way. If the offer was sensible we should put it to our shareholders.

There followed two months of weighty negotiations, leading off with EMI's bid well above the market value of Grade shares but not quite enough to secure our enthusiastic endorsement. We put out a statement to the press that we were after two pounds a share, almost twice the going price before EMI appeared on the scene. While EMI was thinking about this (by taking their time they started a round of press speculation, which was doubtless their intention) parallel talks started on the delicate matter of who would actually run the Grade Organisation if it happened to be taken over by EMI. Leslie was insisting that he would soon be as good as new but he was realistic enough to know that the state of his health was a great worry to EMI. The message came over loud and clear: if the sale was to go through, I had to be part of the deal, going in to run what they hoped would become a leading leisure company.

I made no secret of my reservations. I was not an agent but a producer; I was not a company man, but an independent and, as Carole was fond of pointing out, I was not a youngster starting out on his career but a middle-aged businessman who, some might think, had left it a bit late to start life as a corporate executive.

The counter-argument was put by Sir Joseph Lockwood and John Read. If I joined EMI I would enjoy unrivalled opportunities to build up the leisure division into a major company in its own right. There was no shortage of investment money and I would have virtually a free hand on how to spend it. It was an offer I could not resist.

Having nodded acceptance in principle to being part of the takeover (in the event, both Leslie and I signed five-year service contracts) EMI responded with a price for the company that matched our expectations – twelve million pounds, of which the major portion was shared between Leslie, Lew and myself. Thanks to television, Lew was already in the front row of high earners but now Leslie and I had enough money to make us feel secure. I had to pinch myself to remember that a few months earlier I had been worried sick by the loss on a West End show.

But I was still jealous of my independence. To make clear that I was not in the usual run of corporate executives, I resisted a move to the EMI headquarters in Manchester Square. Instead I kept on my office in the Prince of Wales, while telling anyone who cared to listen of my continuing commitment to the theatre.

Many of the shows which give me greatest pride were presented at my time with EMI: plays like John Osborne's *The Hotel in Amsterdam* which I brought into the West End from the Royal Court; Joe Orton's comedy, his last as it happened, *What the Butler Saw* with Ralph Richardson and Stanley Baxter (a more unlikely acting team it was difficult to imagine); *Kean* with Alan Badel and, in her first West End role, Felicity Kendall; *Harvey* with James Stewart and *Emperor Henry IV* with Rex Harrison.

Vanessa Redgrave appeared in a revival of *The Threepenny Opera* at the Prince of Wales and Claire Bloom in *A Doll's House* at the Criterion, followed by *A Streetcar Named Desire*, also with Claire Bloom, at the Piccadilly. I could go on listing West End shows, summer shows and pantomimes but I must mention the longest-running pantomime which starred Danny La Rue. It ran from December to early June – the longest ever, so I believe. I have no doubt we could have booked through the following Christmas but Danny had to break for a television series.

By no means all these productions were money-spinners. Star names were no guarantee of success as I found with Ralph

Richardson. (I can't say he didn't warn me. 'Rum play,' he told me when we discussed *What the Butler Saw*. 'Are you sure you want to do it?') Critical acclaim had its limitations too. Harold Hobson, the doyen of critics, gave *The Hotel in Amsterdam* his highest accolade. 'The best English contemporary play in London,' he called it; 'the richest in wit, the most arresting in mood, the most accomplished in presentation.' But that did not stop the crowds from staying away in their thousands. Some were simply bad plays; it was just that we didn't know it until it was too late. I should never have started with *Caligula* but I did and that's all there was to it (except the twenty-thousand-pound write-off).

And as for *Gomes*, after seeing the dress rehearsal Richard Mills gloomily described it as a cross between *Titus Andronicus* and *Sleuth*. It opened on a Tuesday and closed before we had had a chance to see the Sunday notices. It must have been round about this time that we installed an answering machine for the office telephone.

'What message should we record?' asked Richard.

I thought for a moment. 'What about, "The cheque is in the post"?'

I had a near miss with *The Soldiers*, a controversial play which was brought to me by Kenneth Tynan. I found the unfavourable portrayal of Churchill hard to take and thought the script contained too many hostages to fortune. I said so. The next thing I knew, I was being pilloried in the press as the bad guy who was threatening artistic expression, which was a little unfair bearing in mind that the play had already been rejected by the National Theatre. I simply did not believe that it would work, an opinion confirmed when Ian Albery stepped in to produce what turned out to be a crashing failure.

I started off at EMI in pursuit of a love affair. I had always had a soft spot for Blackpool. There was, I know, much to be said against the place. At worst it was seedy and decrepit but then so too was every other popular seaside resort. Cheap charter holidays to the European sun-spots had hit hard at domestic tourism and many once-prosperous coastal towns looked to be in terminal decline. But Blackpool was exceptional. Though it had suffered a downturn in trade that made investors think twice before sinking more money into hotels and entertainments, the resort was held in enormous affection by millions of holidaymakers. I was certain that, given an imaginative face-lift, Blackpool could reassert its claim to be the fun capital of Europe.

I had proved the point to my own satisfaction a few years earlier when, on behalf of Charles Forte, I had put in a bid for the North Pier. I found it in a sad state of neglect. There were a few elderly people staring out to sea (I guessed that they had to be there early in the morning to bag a deckchair that wasn't broken), a solitary fisherman and a smattering of seagulls. That was it. I walked to the theatre which was perched out at the end of the pier. A show was in full swing playing to a near-empty house. I began to wonder if I was misusing Forte's money.

But within months, the North Pier was transformed. We abolished admission charges and did away with those formidable turnstile barriers which only serve to irritate customers who have to wait in a queue. On the forecourt we built new shops and restaurants. The theatre was restored and we mounted a succession of first-class summer shows. Business thrived. I paid one hundred thousand pounds for the North Pier. Today, it must be worth many millions. Charles Forte was so impressed he wanted more of the seafront attractions. A little while later we obliged by buying the Central and South Piers. Both turned in an early profit.

Knowing all this, when EMI gave me an open cheque to build up their leisure interests, my thoughts immediately turned to Blackpool. Clearly, Charles Forte had no wish to surrender the piers but there were other potentially valuable properties which, if not actually on the market, might shift in response to a good offer. The prospect that caused me greatest excitement was the Blackpool Tower Company. One only had to glance at their property portfolio to realise that their shares were much undervalued. In addition to the tower, at five hundred and twenty feet, a worthy rival to its Parisian counterpart, the company owned the Opera House and Grand Theatres and a choice selection of promenade shops. Housed in the tower was an aquarium, a zoo, a circus, a ballroom and a famous organ.

The chairman of the Blackpool Tower Company was as far re-moved from the world of popular entertainment as it was possible to imagine. Dr Ted Badman was an anaesthetist, a highly respected local resident who had inherited a financial interest in the business. I felt sure that his commitment to his part-time job was less than wholehearted. At any rate, when I called him to mention the possibility of a bid, he was immediately interested. Almost too interested.

'We must keep this to ourselves,' I warned him. 'If the news gets out that we are meeting it will start a speculative run on your shares. That could wreck any deal we might agree on.'

Ted Badman agreed but suggested that the mere fact of us getting together would not pass unnoticed. 'How on earth can we keep it a secret?'

I had already considered the problem. 'We must meet out of Blackpool and out of London, somewhere neither of us are known. What about choosing a point midway between us?'

Opting for security over comfort, we settled for holding our summit in the tea-room of Crewe station. Four times we met there, four times we justified our presence by selecting the best of the worst from the self-service counter. The experience made us both eager for a settlement.

The figure we agreed on was four million, six hundred thousand pounds. Fortunately, both of us were empowered to shake on the deal there and then, though in ordinary circumstances we would have referred back to our financial advisers. I was against this, as I explained to Ted Badman.

'I worry about the experts. They try to score points. I listen to them but in the end I make my own decisions. In this case, I'm sure the deal is good for both of us. How do you feel about us going back to our bankers and saying, that's it, we've made our decision, there's nothing you can do about it?'

Ted Badman thought that this was a very good idea indeed. As we shook hands over the formica table-top, EMI became the proud owner of the Blackpool Tower and all its satellites.

One of my first changes was to install Dickie Hurran as director of the Tower Circus with instructions to go out and find new talent. But there were two resident acts he could not improve on. Charlie Cairoli was the best-loved clown in British circus, Norman Barnett the supreme ringmaster. When he first went into the ring at the age of twelve, Norman wanted to be a lion trainer but his father advised against. 'They get the most money but ringmasters live longer.' Last year, Norman featured in the 'Experts' Expert' section of the *Observer Magazine*. I was delighted to see that in the near unanimous verdict of his peers, he was the best ringmaster of them all.

As for Charlie Cairoli, his long run at the Tower Circus took him well beyond retirement age. Years after his death he is still remembered with love and for a new generation there is, in the entrance to the Tower Circus, a reminder of his greatness, a dedication to 'The happy memory of Charlie Cairoli, who, for thirty-nine years, filled the Tower Circus with the joyous sound of children's laughter'.

Having scored early with the Blackpool Tower deal for EMI I was naturally eager to press home my advantage with my fellow directors. A yet more ambitious project attracted my interest. The Associated British Picture Corporation (ABC) was second only to the Rank Organisation as a film producer and distributor. But that was not saying very much. With fifty per cent of Thames Television, London's new midweek channel, three hundred and fifty cinemas, Elstree Studios and the Pathé News film library, not to mention bowling alleys, squash courts and other worthwhile assets, the company was so unadventurous as to be almost comatose. As an interested outsider, I could think of many ways of hoisting ABC's low-lying profit margin.

The first chance to test my views on how ABC might polish up its act came with the rumour that Warner Brothers, who had a twenty-five per cent stake in the company, was anxious to sell their shares. I put my idea to John Read, arguing for a deal with Warner as a preliminary to a bid for the whole of ABC. John caught on quickly to the opportunities. In property values alone, ABC had to be worth a generous dollop of investment.

Encouraged by John, I rang Elliott Hyman, head of Warner Brothers in California and fixed for the two of us to meet him and his right-hand man, Alan Hirschfield, a financial wizard and future boss of Columbia Pictures and, subsequently, of Twentieth Century Fox. On the same reasoning which led to the successful acquisition of the Blackpool Tower, we planned our get-together on neutral territory, though a private suite in a small luxury hotel on New York's Fifth Avenue was a far cry from Crewe station at peak travelling hours.

On the flight to New York, John was in bullish mood, convinced that we were about to relieve Warner of an unloved property at a bargain price. I had no reason to doubt his judgement. The film industry was still suffering the after-effects of its war with television and there were powerful voices in the business community who gave it no chance at all of recovery. It seemed unlikely that our ambitions for ABC would be met with serious competition.

At the same time, Elliott Hyman knew very well that we could not get much further with ABC without the Warner shares. He adopted a tough approach. The courtesies over, he announced that there was one price and one price only for what we wanted – twenty-five million dollars. I played for time, hoping that if we talked round the subject for long enough, the Americans might soften their attitude. We talked and talked, about anything that came to mind; matters which had little or nothing to do with ABC. To lighten the mood, I told a joke.

An English couple visiting New York were in the back of a cab. Their driver, in typical manner, threw forthright questions at them. 'Where ya from?'

The man said they were from England.

His wife, who was hard of hearing, asked him to speak up.

'I TOLD HIM WE'RE FROM ENGLAND, DEAR.'

The driver demanded more. 'Where in England?'

'From Suffolk.'

The wife wanted another rerun.

'I TOLD HIM WE'RE FROM SUFFOLK, DEAR.'

'Where in Suffolk?'

'Lakenheath.'

The driver spat out the stub of his cigar. 'Lakenheath, you say. I knew a girl in Lakenheath. Was she the pits? She couldn't cook, she couldn't sew. And in bed, you wouldn't believe it. She got a headache just by switching off the light.'

The wife leaned towards her husband.

'What did he say?'

'HE SAYS HE THINKS HE KNOWS YOU, DEAR.'

This got a big laugh from Elliott Hyman.

'I'll tell you what I'll do,' he said. 'I'll make it twenty-four million dollars. That's as far as I go.'

I didn't believe him. I searched my memory for another joke. A few laughs later, Elliott dropped to twenty-three million. I tried again but with less success. Elliott had stopped laughing. We settled on twenty-three.

Back home, the announcement of the deal brought a call from Sir Philip Warter, chairman of ABC, inviting John and me to join his board. It was not the happiest of associations. He and Robert Clark, the chief executive, were never less than polite but they knew that ABC was under threat.

Relationships were further strained when EMI failed in its first bid for control. In retaliation, ABC set off on its own expansionist course with a proposal to buy a company called Tele Bingo which supplied prizes for bingo halls up and down the country. In principle there was nothing wrong with this but our suspicions were aroused when, instead of paying cash for Tele Bingo, the board approved an increase in share capital to finance the venture. This had the effect of reducing the EMI holding as a percentage of the whole. The difference was not great but it revealed one way in which Robert Clark and his allies were hoping to cut us out of their deliberations. It made sense to mount another and, this time, decisive bid before they could think of other companies to buy.

Our offer of sixty-three million pounds for seventy-five per cent of the company brought howls of protest from the ABC directors but rather more encouraging sounds from the shareholders. We scraped home with a narrow majority on our side. Robert Clark rang me to concede victory. A little to my surprise, there was no rancour in his voice. Meeting him a short time later to discuss the handover, I could see that he was upset. I made it clear I was happy for him to continue with the company but he insisted on standing down. I knew then what a shock it can be to lose a top job. Yesterday: colleagues lining up for words of wisdom, secretaries at beck and call, the chauffeur waiting at the door. Today: nothing. Fortunately for Robert Clark he had other interests. I kept in contact with him over the years to the point where we became good friends. He even bought shares in EMI.

Acquiring ABC raised some unexpected complications with the Independent Broadcasting Authority, the ITV watchdog. To begin with, there was concern that a major holding in Thames Television, or in any other independent television company for that matter, could be sold to the highest bidder in defiance of the merit principle of awarding television contracts. With hindsight it is staggering that no one had thought of this earlier but it was not the only example of muddled thinking caused by the attempt to combine commercial with public service broadcasting.

In the end, the IBA decided that EMI was a fit custodian of London's weekday channel but to be quite sure on the matter they wanted us to sell some of our shares to reduce our holding to under fifty per cent. I also disposed of the Grade Organisation. The reasoning behind this decision harked back to the old argument that I might be tempted to operate a cartel of theatre, television and agency interests. How I could have worked this extraordinary trick

180

was never adequately explained but I was not inclined to argue. I devised a scheme whereby Billy Marsh with Michael Grade and Laurie Evans and Dennis Van Tahl could stage a management buy-out of the various parts of the agency at a modest price. The Shipman and King cinemas were merged with the ABC chain.

I had a new title to celebrate – chairman and chief executive of EMI Film and Theatre Corporation. Now I had to justify it. I made a start by resolving to be more of a company man. I moved my office from the Prince of Wales to Golden Square where my formidable secretary, Mrs Lena Gaston, put all my callers through a rigorous vetting process.

Mrs Gaston had uncompromising views on what was proper. I had a chauffeur called Ron until Mrs Gaston decided it would be more fitting for him to answer to the name of William. And, still my chauffeur, William he remains to this day, at least in his professional context.

I never knew Mrs Gaston as anything but Mrs Gaston, but her assistant, Mary Connor, I was allowed to address in more familiar terms. Mary is still with me, having taken her vows as a fully fledged personal secretary. But such is the vital role she plays in my life, to describe her duties as secretarial is less than adequate. The chief executive to the chief executive might be nearer the mark.

Even after settling in at Golden Square I still felt a little awkward at board meetings. A lifetime of making my own decisions and taking my chances did not prepare me for the trials of committee in-fighting. But I soon learned a few tricks of the trade.

The sharpest of my fellow directors was Lord Shawcross whose legal and political background (he was a former Attorney General) made him an awesome interrogator. I sat next to him at board meetings. He was in the habit of circling those items on the agenda which attracted his critical interest. Peering over his shoulder I could see where I was on the black list. I then made sure that I got in first, stating my case before he had the chance to mount an attack. It took a little time for him to catch on but after a few months he moved his place to the opposite side of the table.

There was a second politician lawyer on the EMI board, younger, more reserved but no less ambitious. His name was Geoffrey Howe. The characteristic that impressed me most about him was his resolute honesty. There was the occasion when he asked his fellow directors' approval for a 'bed and breakfast', that is, selling shares and rebuying them soon afterwards. When thousands of shares are involved a declaration of intent is entirely proper but Geoffrey Howe owned so few shares as to make the exercise virtually meaningless. Still, he was obviously keen to make the best use of his money. I was not at all surprised when he became Chancellor of the Exchequer.

To keep the IBA happy, Thames Television was hived off from the rest of the company though EMI retained a large shareholding. Lord Shawcross became chairman with a brief to manage the channel as he thought fit. As a director of EMI, he reported back to the main board on any contentious issues but rarely in any detail. He didn't have to: he did an excellent job.

My main interest was the cinemas: film production and distribution. Starting in Edinburgh, we launched a programme of tripling and quadrupling those ABC cinemas on prime sites. Others I closed or turned into supermarkets or surrendered to the apparently insatiable public demand for bingo. I did not enjoy doing this. I wanted above all else for the film industry to thrive but there was no way this could happen without a dependable supply of movies audiences would pay good money to see. Production was in the doldrums. For years, Rank, ABC and British Lion, the only three British production companies of any note, had been content to cruise along on tired ideas and cheap budgets. Of course, there were exceptions to the boredom rule but the difficulty of bringing more than a few to mind just shows how little effort went into attracting audiences back into the cinemas.

To reverse the downward trend in output and revenue, I enlisted the services of a producer whose company, Anglo Amalgamated Films, was already partly owned by ABC. Nat Cohen was the sort of film maker who knew all there was to know about popular demand. Starting in cinema management (in his time at the Mile End Empire he had once had the good sense to hire Delfont and Toko as a warm-up act for the big feature) he had moved into production in the early fifties with a long-running succession of low-budget Edgar Wallace mysteries. They still pop up on late night television to the indignation of mature actors who kick themselves for having worked on the series without insisting on repeat fees.

Nat followed up on Edgar Wallace by buying the script for a failed stage play and turning it into a film comedy called *Carry on Sergeant*. He went on to back a dozen *Carry On*s, making a pile of money in the process while mystifying younger producers who, never having been near a music hall, could not begin to appreciate the universal appeal of lowbrow humour.

But I noted another side to Nat Cohen. Whatever his reputation in Wardour Street for appealing to downmarket audiences, he was quick enough to spot the talents of John Schlesinger. He co-produced all that director's early films such as *A Kind of Loving*, *Billy Liar*, *Darling* and *Far From the Madding Crowd* – quintessentially British films which introduced a new generation of actors (Alan Bates, Julie Christie, Tom Courtenay) who quickly achieved international appeal. Nat's track record was strong enough to make one believe that he was just what we needed to beef up our production schedule. I bought up the rest of his company (a twenty-five per cent share) and put him on to the payroll as chief executive of EMI Films.

There was a limit to what one man could achieve. It occurred to me that a way of bringing forward the delivery date for a marketable slate of movies was to split the productions. All I had to do was to appoint a head of Elstree Studios who could work independently of Nat Cohen. For this critical job I appointed an all-rounder with strong views on what was wrong with the British film industry and equally strong views on how it could be put right. Well known to cinema audiences as an actor, Bryan Forbes had a fast-growing reputation as a screen writer and director. He was on record as claiming he knew how to make quality British films for mass audiences. I thought it was time he had the chance to put his ideas to the test.

Towards the end of 1969 we were far enough ahead to announce the start-up on thirty British films over eighteen months, all to be backed exclusively by British money. The industry had for so long been dominated by American finance that we had trouble in persuading some critics that we really were serious in our intentions. British films *and* British money! Was Bernie Delfont out of his mind? When they were convinced that I meant what I said, I was fêted as the saviour of the industry while Bryan Forbes was credited with almost magical powers to light up the big screen. Wisely perhaps, Nat Cohen kept his head down. He had his plans but he wasn't prepared to go for broke by delivering all his goodies in a single package.

Aiming squarely at the family, Bryan started encouragingly with *The Railway Children*, a first for director Lionel Jeffries who was more accustomed to appearing in front of the cameras; and with his own film, *The Raging Moon*, which starred Mrs Bryan Forbes, better known as Nanette Newman. Both films were praised by the critics but this time their enthusiasm did not carry through quite so strongly to the paying public. Perhaps there was a message here I should have picked up but my attention was diverted by the real dodos belly-flopping out of Elstree – *And Soon the Darkness*, *Hoffman* and *The Man Who Haunted Himself*, a time-warp story in which Roger Moore was chased by his alter ego in ever decreasing circles. I should have put a stop to that one as I did to *The Breaking of Bumbo*, a messy and unwatchable piece of military hokum which remains on the shelf to this day.

Bryan was naturally upset by these failures (he was not alone) but defended himself as the promoter of family values against the cheap purveyors of sex and violence. This did not go down well with Nat Cohen whose own contribution to the EMI production output began with *Up Pompeii*, a television spin-off in which Frankie Howerd transported *Carry On* jokes to ancient Rome and continued with *Get Carter*, a gangster movie starring Michael Caine as the avenger with a novel line in disposing of his rivals.

Nat resented the implication that his films were somehow less worthy than those appearing under the Elstree banner, the more so because his films made a lot of money. In Wardour Street, where Nat had his power base, the talk was of Bryan Forbes enjoying the luxury of spending what Nat and his friends earned.

But the differences between the two production chiefs went deeper. Bryan took the view that British films should be made for British audiences and that overseas sales should be treated as a bonus. Knowing well that the cinema-going habit had lost its power to television, he came to me with plans for strengthening the marketing of our films, to bring audiences back to the cinema to generate the revenue to keep Elstree going.

The counter-argument from Nat Cohen was to accept the limitations of the domestic market but to overcome the problem by concentrating resources on big-budget movies which would appeal to audiences on both sides of the Atlantic.

I was split between the two. My heart was with Bryan Forbes: I wanted him to succeed. But as a director of EMI, with a responsibility to shareholders and the workforce, I had to accept that Nat Cohen was talking practical common sense. The trouble with Bryan's argument was that to succeed it would have taken an investment of time and money which was out of all proportion to the likely return. He wanted new cinemas, luxury conversions, a massive advertising campaign and an accelerated production programme to meet the anticipated rush of public support. I could not see it happening, at least not for a very long while. I was rather more inclined to back the market I knew to exist, in other words, to go the way of Nat Cohen, than to chance all on a long-odds bet.

As Bryan came to realise that he would not get all that he demanded, his relationship with the company deteriorated still further. To make matters worse, a whispering campaign against Bryan was fed by the Fleet Street gossip columnists. It was said that he was remote and aloof (though his defenders at Elstree argued the opposite, that he was the first studio boss who was prepared to listen to problems) and that in picking his wife to star in *The Raging Moon* he was guilty of nepotism. It was so much nonsense but hard to ignore.

In my conversations with Bryan he often hinted at the prospect of resigning if the job became unmanageable. By early 1971 I could see that we were close to that point. EMI film production was losing its sense of direction and morale was low. After talking long and hard about how to resolve the crisis, Bryan agreed that he would have to go. Since his departure one year ahead of the completion of his contract was bound to attract press attention, we went to great trouble to produce a statement making clear that my regard for Bryan as a film maker was in no way diminished by his resignation. As evidence of this Bryan was to remain a director with the EMI Film and Theatre Corporation.

The announcement was circulated to the press on 25 March. I expected some reaction in the evening papers, a paragraph or two on an inside page, perhaps. I was not prepared for the banner headline in the *Evening News*: FAMILY FILM MAN FORBES IS SACKED.

The story was written up by Felix Barker, a leading film critic and an old friend of Bryan. It was clear where the information had come from.

'This afternoon when I asked Mr Forbes if he knew why he had been asked to leave, he replied: "Perhaps you could put it that one reason is that I have not been prepared to join them – to pander to the lowest common denominator." '

I rang Felix Barker. 'You know this is nonsense. Bryan resigned. He was not sacked. I happen to believe he is an excellent film maker.'

Felix did not comment but gave me the gist of his conversation with Bryan. After he had finished I was left with no doubt that Bryan had fed him a tarnished version of the truth. But I was not prepared to argue. I was annoyed with Bryan for having broken the spirit of our agreement but I could see no point in prolonging the agony by engaging in a public row.

The next day Bryan was all over the papers: the white knight of the film industry who had ridden forth at the head of his little army only to be cut down by the savages of Wardour Street. One did not have to look very hard to identify the chief of the barbarians. But Nat Cohen had the last laugh. Holding to his belief as to what made a good picture, he bought the rights to one of the bestsellers of all time and hired a platoon of famous actors, as famous in America as in Britain, to bring the story to the screen. *Murder on the Orient Express* was the first British film ever to top the list of dollar earners on the American cinema circuit. It grossed over two hundred million pounds worldwide and was arguably the most successful wholly British-financed film ever produced.

The signing off of Bryan Forbes's reign at Elstree was *The Go-Between*, an English story in an unmistakably English setting directed by an expatriate American, Joseph Losey. For some reason, the treatment came to me initially and I passed it on to Bryan with a heartfelt recommendation to give it priority. The film was sheer joy, evoking in its clever use of flashback the famous opening sentence of the novel: 'The past is another country, they do things differently there.' Closer to the European than to the American style of film making, *The Go-Between* was not by any means a blockbuster but it was lavishly praised by the critics and warmly received by the sort of audiences who had almost given up their local cinema as a lost cause. It won the top award at the Cannes Film Festival though by then Bryan had left the company.

With Russ Abbot during his summer season in Blackpool, 1986.

With Ken Dodd and Carole at the centenary of the Winter Gardens, Blackpool, 1989.

The family at a Variety Club Luncheon in October 1988 to celebrate sixty years in show business.

Standing, left to right: my daughter Susan, my nephew Andrew Freeman, Carole, my nephew Ian Freeman, my sister Rita Freeman, my nephew Michael Grade, my sister-in-law Lady Grade, my son David and my niece Anita Land.

Sitting: myself and my brother Lew Grade.

My eightieth birthday celebration in 1989. *Left to right*: David, his wife Sarah, Carole, myself, Jenny and Susan.

The cartoon that appeared in the *Daily Mirror* on the announcement of the first-year profits of First Leisure.

Chapter 13

In August 1975 I was invited to be one of eighteen members of a working party on the future of the British film industry, chaired by the prime minister, Harold Wilson. I was flattered to be asked to join such luminaries as Richard Attenborough, Carl Foreman, Alasdair Milne, Lord Ryder and Brian Tesler and to meet lesser known but emerging figures in the industry like David Puttnam.

We were unanimous that the film industry was in a bad way. The decline in cinema attendances, which had been pretty well continuous since the peak year of 1946, had deterred all but the bravest, or perhaps the most foolhardy, of backers. What little money the government pumped in was discounted by a tightening of the tax laws which succeeded in driving out the American film makers who had done so much to keep the major studios going. Now there were only two studios in operation – Pinewood and Elstree.

But having agreed that something had to be done, there was a shortage of ideas on what exactly we had to do. One of the few positive suggestions came from my fellow committee member, Alan Sapper, boss of the film union, the ACTT. He suggested nationalising the whole industry. The rest of us wanted to know how this would guarantee audiences. No answer. Another idea was to push the television companies into investing in the film industry. This was endorsed enthusiastically as a general principle but we had trouble in thinking of ways to translate the ideal into reality. We fell back on gentle persuasion which must have had some effect because nowadays there is a big overlap between television and film investment. But at the time, we were not confident.

The lack of substance to the working party debate confirmed my fear that the domestic market was not set for an early recovery. To succeed, our business had to be international or it was no business at all.

Among those who shared this view were Barry Spikings and Michael Deeley, the partnership who had taken over British Lion, the third-largest production company in Britain. British Lion could claim an illustrious history. Once the power base for Sir Alexander Korda, the company had made ends meet after the war by drawing on government money provided through the National Film Finance Corporation. It is interesting to reflect that old favourites like *The Third Man*, *The Wooden Horse* and *The Happiest Days of Your Life* would not have reached the screen without state finance. But in the early sixties British Lion was put up for sale to the highest bidder, since when output had stagnated. Now, under Spikings-Deeley ownership, and with a little help from the NFFC, the objective was to make films with world appeal, like the David Bowie science-fiction extravaganza, *The Man Who Fell to Earth*.

Expectations were high but it was clear that British Lion would have to be extraordinarily lucky to keep up its momentum. It simply did not have the resources to compete with the Hollywood studios. On the other hand, British Lion and EMI working together might achieve wonders. My idea was for British Lion to merge with EMI, freeing Barry Spikings and Michael Deeley to head the American offshoot I proposed setting up. Cash would be released for the big-budget movies they wanted to make but could not afford with British Lion working in isolation.

I squared it with Nat Cohen. Unlike the appointment of Bryan Forbes, there was no risk of the deal cutting across his interests. As chairman and chief executive of EMI Film Distribution he was kept happy with a revolving fund of six million pounds for a series of productions including the inevitable sequel to *Orient Express* – another popular Agatha Christie, *Evil Under the Sun*. The British Lion deal went through on the nod. Shortly afterwards, Barry Spikings and Michael Deeley left for Hollywood.

It was three years before I saw the first return on their labours – but it was well worth the wait. *The Deer Hunter* was quite simply a triumph for everyone associated with it. Picking up on a highly topical but, in film terms, a highly original theme – the American involvement in Vietnam – our producers had the good judgement to employ talents that were known but not so famous as to be predictable. This applied most obviously to the star, Robert De Niro, whose roles in

The Godfather Part II and *Taxi Driver* confirmed him as one of the most promising young screen actors of his generation, his co-star Meryl Streep who had made her film début a year earlier in *Julia* and the director, Michael Cimino who had earned his spurs writing and directing for Clint Eastwood (*Magnum Force*, *Thunderbolt* and *Lightfoot*).

With all the praise that has been lavished on *The Deer Hunter*, few will admit now that they ever had any doubts as to its commercial value. But the fact is we had a hard time persuading Universal, who distributed the movie, not to mangle it out of all recognition. The objection was its length. At three and a quarter hours Universal argued they would be forced to reduce the number of screenings and as a consequence lose a pile of money. They wanted to cut a minimum of twenty minutes and would have been happier if the running time could be brought down to two and a half hours.

Predictably, Michael Cimino threw a fit, claiming a conspiracy to destroy his work. Lew Wasserman at Universal was equally forthright with his views on temperamental artists who had not the first idea about making a film pay. As the dispute hotted up, the man in the middle, Barry Spikings, appealed to me to act as arbitrator. I did not relish putting on Solomon's robes but I knew that if *The Deer Hunter* was not to remain on the shelf, a decision had to be made soon. Moreover, as the one who had most to lose financially, I was clearly in the strongest position to make that decision.

Before flying to Los Angeles I prepared the way with Lew Wasserman. 'I'm only willing to do this if what I say is taken as final.'

Believing, with some justification, that I was more likely to be for him than against him (I too wanted the maximum number of screenings) Lew accepted the condition. More to my surprise, Michael Cimino also agreed. I guessed he had reached the stage where he simply wanted to be put out of his agony.

For my first viewing of *The Deer Hunter*, I sat in splendid isolation at Universal Studios in a thousand-seater cinema. At the rear of the auditorium, out of sight but an intruding presence none the less, was Michael Cimino, pacing up and down, willing me, a mere producer, to measure up to his achievement.

I had a fair notion of where Lew Wasserman intended wielding his scissors. Could anyone justify half an hour on a wedding scene? (At one of the previews, it was said by a wag that the couple took so long to get married the audience felt like giving them a present). But it seemed to me that the wedding was one of the key scenes. It showed us the lead characters in a way that gave a meaning to the rest of the story. If it went, the core of Michael Cimino's film would go too. What I had to consider was the possibility of another film – or, if you like, another level of film: mark two Michael Cimino instead of mark one, which would lose subtlety and depth but appeal to a wider audience. If I wanted to minimise the commercial risk, it made sense to go with Lew Wasserman.

When the house lights came on, I walked slowly from the auditorium. Michael Cimino was waiting for me in the foyer. He looked as if he could do with a long sleep.

'Michael,' I said, 'I have to tell you. It's a great film.'

'Yes?' He was clearly pleased though still apprehensive.

'We'll leave it just as it is. I'll not allow a single frame to be cut.'

Never before had I seen a grown man jump for joy. Michael did it; a clear two feet off the ground, not once but several times. He was still jumping when I left the cinema to break the news to Lew Wasserman.

The Deer Hunter more than justified my faith. The film was nominated for nine Oscars and won five – best picture, directing, supporting actor, editing and sound. It also made an early profit for EMI, a welcome shot in the arm at a time when the rest of the company was not feeling at its best.

The triumph of *The Deer Hunter* was offset somewhat by the reception for the next Spikings-Deeley effort, a John Schlesinger film called *Honky Tonk Freeway*. Those like Alexander Walker who criticised me for making British films in America were strengthened in their argument by this disaster. With hindsight, they may have been right. As a home product on a modest budget *Honky Tonk Freeway* might have worked but as a big money Hollywood movie (up to then, the Americans had still not heard of modest budgets) it was inflated way beyond its capacity and, predictably, it burst.

Sometimes I lost money out of choice, which suggests that overall I was not doing too badly. First off I was enthusiastic when Barry Spikings wanted to put two million pounds into the latest *Monty Python* film. Then at the height of their collective popularity I did not see how any venture of theirs could possibly fail. But when I was handed the script I had second thoughts, not about the safety of the investment so much as the wisdom of getting involved in a project which seemed likely to put us in court on a charge of blasphemy. I said I was sorry not to be able to back a British movie but *The Life of Brian* would have to be made without EMI. I was prepared to write off our initial investment.

I was told not to be so stuffy: of course there was no sacrilegious intent. I remained sceptical and I have no reason to regret my decision. Though, as far as I know, the film never fell into the hands of the lawyers the script went through some major revisions. When I saw the finished product, as a paying customer, my biggest laugh came at the end with the credits and a voice-over, 'Bernie told us this would never make money.' Of course, the film did make a great deal of money for all the participants including the eventual producer, George Harrison of Beatles fame. When he spotted me on a transatlantic flight he came over and shook my hand warmly. 'Thank you so much for turning down *The Life of Brian*.'

My potential for trouble was greatest when I was wearing my film distributor's hat. I did not want to act like a censor but I reserved the last word on films to be shown on the ABC circuit. To have done otherwise would surely have made nonsense of my duty as the EMI director in charge of two hundred and eighty-eight cinemas. As it happened, I made a fuss on only two occasions.

Banning the Alec Guinness film, *The Last Ten Days of Hitler*, led to great falling out with Lew who asked me along to a charity performance. I came out of the cinema fuming with anger at having watched a film which, in my judgement, portrayed Hitler in a sympathetic light.

'Can't you think of a better way to raise money?' I asked Lew. 'How can you lend your name to this?' I made no attempt to hide my emotion.

Lew shouted back. 'What about you? The film will be showing in your cinemas next week.'

I didn't know that. As soon as I got back to the office I checked the schedule. Lew was right. *The Last Ten Days of Hitler* was due to open in twenty-two cinemas. I gave the order to cancel. My colleagues warned that it might be hard finding a replacement movie at such short notice and, anyway, it would hurt our relationship with our distributors. I told them that was the least of my worries.

The story made the front pages. Sir Joseph Lockwood, EMI chairman, put out a statement saying that I was an emotional person. I agreed, adding that an unemotional person had no right to be in the film or theatre industry. Alec Guinness called me a dictator, a view endorsed by others in the film world who feared a sort of back door censorship. But for the life of me I could not see that I was acting irresponsibly. If I had declared open house and pledged to show any film whatever its subject or content, *that* would have been irresponsible.

In any case I did not have the power to act as censor. My competitors made sure of that. No sooner had I dropped *The Last Ten Days of Hitler* than along came Rank to offer the splendid consolation of a nationwide Odeon screening. I took some satisfaction when the public reaction proved to be lukewarm, bordering on the tepid. Some time later when I talked to Sir John Davis, head of Rank, he told me, 'You made the right decision for the wrong reasons.'

I wasn't having that. 'No,' I said. 'I made the right decision for the right reasons.'

It was much the same story with *Hennessy*, a melodramatic thriller about an IRA attempt to blow up Parliament. The objection here was the use of newsreel footage of the state opening of Parliament which made it look as if the Queen was part of the action. At best, the film was guilty of bad taste; at worst, it invited retaliation in the courts. It also happened to be a very tedious movie which earned a thorough panning from the critics when eventually it did secure a release. This did not stop some of them from pointing the finger at me as the enemy of free speech though, again, I assumed they did not expect me to offer a blanket guarantee to screen any film that was delivered to my office. The muddled thinking showed up most obviously in a Sunday paper where an attack on me by the film critic was immediately followed by a theatre notice for a revival of *What the Butler Saw*, in which the reviewer referred to the first West End production of the Joe Orton comedy, praising those who had the courage to present the controversial play 'before its time'. That was me, too. So there I was, a split personality: the enemy or the champion of free speech. The reader could take his choice.

On top of making and distributing films, I also invested in other people's films. By happy accident this turned out to be the most profitable of my activities. At one of EMI's board meetings we were told that Columbia wanted to sell its music publishing house called Screen Gems. Although I had nothing to do with the publishing side of the company, I was asked to go to New York to see if I could make a deal with Alan Hirschfield, boss of Columbia, who was well known to me. I was told I could go to around twenty-five million dollars. But Alan wanted much more and, however hard I tried, he would not budge. I came up with a possible compromise. What if I linked twenty-five million dollars for Screen Gems to an investment of ten million dollars in the next four Columbia films? The condition was that we would be guaranteed to get back at least fifty per cent of our outlay. If the films were successful then EMI would have a share of the profits which could be set against the cost of buying Screen Gems.

I could see that Alan was taken with the idea. He asked for an hour to think it over and I left him in a huddle with his financial boys. When I returned it was to hear that we had a deal. After much hand-shaking and back-slapping I was preparing to leave when a thought struck me.

'By the way, what are the films we're talking about? I'd like to know where I'm putting my money.'

Alan reeled off the list. '*The Cheap Detective* with Peter Falk.'

'Fine,' I said. 'I'll put two million into that.'

'Then there's *The Deep*.'

I felt secure with the sequel to *Jaws*. 'OK. I'll put two million into that. What next?'

'*The Greatest*, a screenplay on the life of Muhammad Ali.'

'I'll put two million into that.'

'There's only one more,' said Alan. 'A science-fiction movie. Spielberg is directing.'

Again the connection with *Jaws*, Steven Spielberg's first big success.

'What's it called?'

'*Close Encounters of the Third Kind*.'

'Right. I'll put four million into that.'

The EMI stake in those movies, *Close Encounters* and *The Deep* in particular, made Screen Gems a real bargain. I have long since lost count of just how much money *Close Encounters* has made. Suffice to say, in its first year, it grossed over two hundred million dollars. It amused me to read the press reports of how astute I had been. In reality, it was sheer luck that I scored three out of four. The only failure was the Muhammad Ali picture.

The first cheques arrived just in time to compensate for the bruising I took from the Associated Film Distribution Company. The idea started with Lew, who was convinced that British films were given a raw deal by American distributors. Instead of paying them thirty to thirty-five per cent of revenue, argued Lew, we should set up our own distribution company to do a better and cheaper job. I could understand his interests. As head of Associated Communications Corporation, the film-making offshoot of ATV, Lew was, like me, heavily dependent on the American market. But I did not fancy an all-out fight with the established distributors. In the end Lew went ahead on his own with me taking a one-year option on shares in the new company. When I could delay no longer I went over to New York to see how Lew was making out. What had been achieved in such a short time was impressive. Lew had established a working relationship with the cinema chains and he was on the verge of leasing a showcase cinema in New York. Why not? I thought. Lew and I shook hands on a fifty-fifty partnership.

Maybe we made too much of it. In any event, the fanfare announcement of our alliance, made at a press reception at Hollywood's Beverley Hills Hotel, was interpreted by our American rivals as a declaration of war. Suddenly there were problems at every town. If our film output had been stronger we might have withstood the pressure, but while we were big on our home ground, our combined output could not outclass the Hollywood studios. We needed *The Deer Hunter* ten times over to do that. Consequently, we were not taken seriously by the other distributors. With them having first choice of screenings we were left with whatever they did not want. It was no way to run a business. We made a deal with Universal to handle our films and pulled out of distribution. Ironically, Lew soon followed up with some outstanding film successes – *On Golden Pond*, *Sophie's Choice* and the *Muppet Movie*. With products like these we might easily have made a go of our distribution company.

I had better luck with my efforts to break into American television. Barry Spikings set up the operation which made an encouraging start with *The Amazing Howard Hughes* and followed through with several smaller-scale successes. Next in line was a film called *SOS Titanic*. It had all the ingredients of popular drama but the costs were two million dollars, too high to be balanced by television revenue alone. Although experience had taught me that films made for television rarely work in the cinema, I was persuaded to go along with a selected cinema screening to recoup part of the budget, followed by eventual television release.

We were well into production when I had a call from Lew. 'I hear you're making a film about the *Titanic*.'

'That's right.'

'You know I've been working on *Raise the Titanic*. Why are you doing this to me?'

He had it wrong. 'I'm sorry, Lew. I had no idea. What do you suggest?'

'Well, it's obvious, isn't it? You've got to stop yours.'

I told him that was impossible. If anyone withdrew, it would have to be him.

This caused a bellow of rage. 'I can't do it, I'd lose a fortune.'

I wish I had said, 'You'll lose a fortune anyway and so will I, so why don't we cancel both movies?' But lacking the gift of prophecy, I chose the obvious route forward, consoling myself with the thought that the market was big enough for both of us.

It was an expensive miscalculation. *SOS Titanic* and *Raise the Titanic* were disaster movies in every sense. Lew's own view of his extravaganza was that it would have been cheaper to lower the Atlantic.

By now so much of EMI film production originated in the States it made sense to acknowledge the fact by moving our head office to Los Angeles. I found myself on the transatlantic commuter run, picking up on deals where there was a chance of profitable overlap between different parts of the leisure division. One such was the remake of *The Jazz Singer*, a long-cherished ambition of Neil Diamond which he had almost, but not quite, sold to MGM. I went to see Neil backstage at the Maple Leaf in Toronto to tell him that we were ready to make the film, on one condition: EMI was to handle the record singles and album sales for this one production. When I made the offer I was not at all sure that such an arrangement was feasible. Neil was under contract to CBS who were naturally reluctant to hand over one of their top recording stars even on a short-term basis. But they must have reckoned there was more to lose by holding out and possibly antagonising their star, because the next I heard everybody was giving *The Jazz Singer* their blessing. For a one-million-dollar fee, Laurence Olivier agreed to share the top billing.

It was not enough to inspire a great film (though it did well in some countries) but with world record sales to our credit we could afford to go down on cinema attendances and still make a handsome profit. Not for the first time was I grateful that EMI leisure had several strings to its bow.

195

Chapter 14

The fame of an entertainment mogul, as the newspapers insisted on calling me, had its disadvantages.

The seventies opened with a foretaste of what I could expect when a well-organised bunch of toughs raided my Hampstead home. As it was a Friday evening Carole and I were in the country. In the ordinary course of events, the rest of the family would have been with us but on this occasion our son David had wanted to stay up in town. He returned latish in the evening to find the place being ransacked. He was coshed, tied up and threatened with a sawn-off shotgun to force him to say what he did not know: where I kept the keys to the safe.

It was an unnerving experience for an eighteen-year-old. David and his fellow captors, the housekeeper and a friend, behaved with great courage. They were locked in a linen cupboard and it was not until early the next morning that they managed to break free and telephone the police.

After that, security was tightened up all round and then, in 1975, tightened again when my name appeared on a death list found by police in a raid on a Bayswater flat. Much to the irritation of the police part of the list was revealed to the *Guardian* and then spread over the other papers. Why I was chosen as a prospective victim by the leader of a Palestinian assassination squad was a mystery to me. But I was in good company. 'Carlos', as he was known (and is still known because, as far as I know, he has never been identified), had compiled what looked to be a guest list for a top table of intelligence – Lord Drogheda, John Osborne, Sir Keith Joseph, Yehudi Menuhin and Lord Harewood among others. When reporters asked me why I was on the hit list, I said it was probably Carlos's way of telling me he didn't like one of my shows.

For a time, being part of what was headlined an 'assassination conspiracy' was quite a status symbol and I could not help noticing

196

that Lew was insisting that he too was on the list. But the excitement soon passed. Treated like the president of a foreign country here on a state visit, I felt suffocated by those who were trying to protect me. I accepted the alarms and security locks but drew the line at having minders following me everywhere. I took the view that if they really wanted to get me, they would get me.

Other trappings of fame were more appealing, though, in their own way, just as difficult to handle. I was lately into my sixty-first year when the possibility of an honour was first mentioned. It was not an offer from on high but a passing reference by a friend who had studied the New Year's honours list and was surprised, so he said, not to see my name. 'It's about time, Bernie. You deserve one.'

The thought had never occurred to me. But when the subject came up again – and again – I began to wonder, should I be taking this seriously? I know how it must sound when I say that the prospect of some sort of recognition for my charity work did excite me. But however desirable in the abstract, humility is not part of the make-up of the competitive businessman. I could not get the thought out of my mind: why not me?

The first nod of approval came from a totally unexpected direction. A letter from the Italian Ambassador informed me I had been awarded the Commendatore, making me a Commander of the Italian Order of Chivalry. The justification was the money I had helped to raise for the Italian Hospital in London though I had no doubt that Charles Forte had put in a word for me. There was a delightful lunch in my honour from which I departed with a most handsome medal and ribbon.

Not long afterwards I had another official-looking letter, this one couched in the unmistakable phraseology of the British establishment. It asked, would I be prepared to accept a knighthood? I was delighted and very proud. I showed the letter to Carole.

She said, 'Are you sure you want this? Honours should only go to people who do really outstanding work.'

There is no one quite like a straight-talking wife to bring you down to earth.

But it was an excuse for another wonderful party, this time at the Savoy with Earl Mountbatten presiding. He apologised for Lew's absence, saying he was in Rome (which was true) working out a deal with the Pope (a slight exaggeration).

And there, I feel, it should have stopped. I was happy enough to continue with my public service. I took it as part of my job at EMI to be one of the advisers to the prime minister on the future of the film industry and as a natural extension of my charity work with the Entertainment Artistes Benevolent Fund to help raise money for the Attlee Memorial Home in the East End and for other good causes.

I did get to know Harold Wilson quite well; also Marcia Williams (Lady Falkender) who was on the film committee and was my chief link through to the prime minister when I wanted to involve him in fund-raising and other special events. I was therefore not altogether surprised when I returned from a lunch to be told by Mrs Gaston that the PM wanted to see me. I immediately assumed it had something to do with the film committee, though I could not understand the urgency. I remember thinking, as my car turned into Whitehall, I do wish I could have more notice of these get-togethers.

I had always enjoyed Harold's company but that day he was in a particularly jovial mood. He offered me a sherry and chatted about film and theatre. Then he said, 'How would you like to go to the House of Lords?'

I was not at all sure what he meant. Was he asking me to listen to a debate? If anyone else had been speaking I would have assumed that the House of Lords was a pub. But it seemed unlikely that he was inviting me out for a drink.

He saw my puzzled look. 'I'm offering you a peerage.'

I made a totally inadequate response. I felt flattered and, yes, a sense of pride that someone from my background should be so honoured. 'Thank you. That's very kind.'

Even now, over fifteen years on, I feel faintly guilty at not asking for time to think. What was I taking on? I really had no idea.

But Harold Wilson was still talking about my work in the entertainment business and for charity. Eventually, he asked, 'What's it to be for? Services to charity or entertainment? You can choose.'

I said I thought it should be for charity.

'Good. Have another sherry.'

Five minutes later we had shaken hands and I was on the way out. It was then, with exquisite timing, that the prime minister dropped his second bombshell.

'Oh, by the way. You're not the only member of the family who's been here today.'

I wanted to ask the obvious question but he had already turned to welcome his next visitor. Back in the office, I rang Lew.

'Were you in Downing Street earlier today?'

'Yes.'

'Did he offer you what he offered me?'

'Yes.'

For a moment it crossed my mind that Harold Wilson, who had already announced that he was standing down as prime minister, intended a dramatic exit by declaring a wholesale elevation to the Lords of everyone he had ever met.

I held off telling Carole the news until I had received the official letter.

She was not enthusiastic. 'You must be mad. What on earth do you want that for?'

My son David was equally dismissive. When I told him I was about to be made a lord, he burst out, 'Don't be so bloody ridiculous, Dad.'

I rang my mother, then almost ninety, for a more encouraging response. She was enormously proud of having two sons at the pinnacle of respectability. Her only sadness, and ours too, was that Leslie, through no fault of his own, was out of the running. With more robust health, he would have outshone us both.

Harold Wilson's resignation honours list did cause a stir. It was known as the Lavender List, a reference to the supposed influence of Marcia Williams. I have no way of knowing why I was especially favoured but it is true that I was one of an unusual selection, mostly self-made men who had made their reputations less by background and inheritance than by their wits. It was characteristic of Harold Wilson not to toe the conventional line.

Having gained the distinction of a life peerage, I hardly ever go to the House of Lords and have still not made my maiden speech. This apparent contradiction is easily explained. The political scene is not for me. I am not at my best in public debate, either speaking or listening. I would rather be at the coal-face.

My happiest association with honours has been helping to get them for other people. I am not sure I could do it now but there was a time . . .

Shortly before I was elevated, when I was still Sir Bernard, I met up with Vera Lynn and her husband Harry Lewis at the Cannes Film Festival. We have been great friends for many years and were used to talking openly. When the subject of honours came up, I said to Harry, 'When you think of how much Vera means to Britain I wonder why she hasn't been made a Dame.'

The more I thought about it, the more convinced I became that something should be done.

Having to return to London for a meeting of the film committee, I found myself seated next to Harold Wilson at dinner. With the publication of the spring honours list barely two months away, it was a bit late for a recommendation. But it was worth a try. I slipped Vera Lynn into the conversation.

'I'm surprised she's never received her due.'

Harold Wilson's memory, as ever, was faultless. 'What do you mean? I gave her the CBE.'

'Yes, but is that enough? In the war, she was famous across the world and she still has a huge following.'

I told of my experience in Amsterdam when, as a recording artist for EMI, Vera Lynn came along to an opening of one of our new businesses. Whenever Dutch people saw her they started applauding. I asked one fan, 'Why do you think so much of her?' He said, 'Because she gave our people courage in their darkest years.'

The prime minister pondered. 'Marcia is always telling me I should get more glamour into the list.'

Nothing more was said.

When I returned to Cannes I mentioned the conversation to Harry Lewis while playing down its significance. 'I don't think anything will come of it. But you never know.'

A few days later I had a call from Mrs Gaston. There was a message from the prime minister's office. Harold Wilson wanted me to know, 'that the lady you spoke about the other evening will be all right'.

I kept the secret, of course. But I was among the first to congratulate Dame Vera Lynn. The award was acclaimed in the press and there is no doubt it was one of the most popular honours of the period.

Having started and continued on a high note, the seventies ended depressingly with the death of Leslie. We had all been expecting it for some time but the shock was none the less great. Our mother found the loss of her youngest son particularly hard to bear.

For ten years or more, Leslie, Lew and myself had shared the cost of her home, a three-room apartment in Park Lane's Grosvenor House Hotel. The idea was that she should have every comfort she deserved but she could never rid herself of the habit of frugal living. When she had visitors, they were entertained in her flat, never in the restaurant.

'See how much they charge for a cup of tea? Better we have one upstairs, where I can make it myself.'

We lied about the room prices at the Grosvenor House, telling her we had a special deal which made her flat a bargain. If she had ever discovered the truth she would have moved straight back to the East End.

Just before Christmas 1980, she fell and strained her left wrist. Even when the doctor said she should go into hospital we didn't think it was too serious. But on one of my last visits, after she had returned to Grosvenor House, she made it clear she did not want to go on.

'It's so hard to die,' she told me. 'It takes so long.'

On the night of 15 January I had a most vivid dream. I heard a loud voice, like an echo. 'Your mother is dead.' When the telephone rang, I knew what the message would be. The tributes were fulsome, and rightly so. She was an extraordinary woman. We owed everything to her.

By 1979, the leisure division of EMI was turning in a pre-tax profit of nearly twenty million pounds compared to just one million pounds when the Grade Organisation was taken over. The defence division and alarm systems were also doing well. That was the good news. The downside, as widely reported in the financial press, was the disappointing results turned in by some other parts of the company. The contrast in performance, which had been showing up for some time, was now so great, it was widely assumed in the City that if separated from EMI, the leisure division could have a bright future as an independent company. I should have been flattered but instead I was more worried about the general health of the company. A hostile takeover bid, and several were rumoured, was unlikely to favour the interests of shareholders or staff.

The weakness of EMI, once the favourite of the stock market, showed up particularly in the medical electronics division where investment in a revolutionary diagnostic scanner had run into trouble. In charge was John Powell, a technical mastermind but it was really John Read (now Sir John) who was the cheerleader for the medical division. When he took over from Sir Joseph Lockwood as chairman of EMI, merging the job with his own as chief executive, he gave Powell everything he wanted. For a while, the gamble looked to be paying off with what was known as the 'scanner boom' lifting EMI shares from fifty pence to two hundred and fifty pence in less than a year. But then we made the mistake of rejecting an American franchise deal on the grounds that we wanted a British invention to stay British. This prompted our competitors to lobby Washington for import restrictions to give them time to produce a superior scanner. Before we knew where we were, the barriers went up on the American market, which up to then had been one of our strongest earners.

I have no doubt that in the short run we could have supported the medical division if every other sector of EMI had been performing to full strength. But this was not the case. The music division, once assumed to be a licence to print money, was going through a difficult period. In this respect, at least, EMI was not alone. The record business is notoriously volatile. Other record companies were experiencing a sales dive that was the equivalent of a free-fall parachute jump – with the parachutist forgetting which cord he had to pull. The causes of the disaster were many and various – a failure to cope with home pirating (for every LP sold three were taped), the flood of cheap imported discs from the Far East, rising production and marketing costs and, top of the list, the dearth of talent to follow in the wake of the Beatles, the Rolling Stones and all the other trail-blazers of the sixties and early seventies. In May 1979 John Read had to announce that the slump in records meant that the group would make a loss for the second half of the year.

By now there was gathering pressure in the City for changes at the top of EMI. If the company was to survive, more of it had to be sold to reduce the mountain of debt. But the directors were unable to agree on which part of EMI should be sold. I said that I was prepared to do whatever was necessary to put EMI back on course. Then I went away to ponder my strategy. As the head of the only division in EMI to be performing at all respectably, I was in a strong position to impose my views. Though this was not the way I liked to do business, it was clear that I could not hold back for much longer waiting for the board to decide on a strategy.

In mid May I went to Cannes for the Film Festival. I had barely arrived at my apartment when I had a call. I was needed back in London for an emergency board meeting. This was not necessarily as desperate as it sounded. The lead item on the agenda was the confirmation of a new managing director. Roger Brooke, formerly of Pearson Longman and one of the rising stars of service management, was John Read's best hope of beefing up the image of EMI and silencing the critics. I was in favour of his appointment but, without doubting his talents, I did not think he could do the job on his own. It was time to speak up.

Leaving Carole to enjoy the spring sunshine, I caught the next plane back to London. On the flight I made elaborate notes on what had to be done to save EMI. First of all we had to cut overheads to create a slimline administration. There were too many desk men at EMI, not enough business getters. Then we had to slim the company itself by selling whatever brought in the highest bids. There were to be no let-outs on this exercise. Everybody had to take their chances, including the head of the leisure division.

Then I came to the crunch: John Read would have to stand down as chief executive. I made only one nomination for his replacement. From Heathrow, I made straight for the office where the notes were transformed into an imposing memorandum addressed to all my fellow directors. The pages were still warm from the photocopier when I presented myself for the board meeting. At reception I saw Roger Brooke waiting to be called in. He was looking perfectly relaxed and why not? For him, the summons was a mere formality. He could have had no idea that he was at the centre of a boardroom drama.

It was a near full attendance. The only absentee was Lord Shawcross who I knew was abroad. John Read took the chair and got the meeting under way with the usual preliminaries but before we started ticking off points on the agenda, I asked if I could make a short statement. John sensed the challenge, I am sure. He did not say anything; he simply leaned back, gesturing with both hands as if to suggest that it was up to me to dictate the proceedings.

I started by recapping on the crisis the company was in, how we had reached the stage where confidence could be restored only by drastic remedies. Any delay would make us yet more vulnerable to a takeover. I went on to say that my memorandum offered detailed proposals which the board would need to study. But the rescue plan turned on one essential: while remaining as chairman, John Read would hand over to me as chief executive. I knew I would face a huge task in pulling the company back into shape but, rightly or wrongly, I believed I was in the best position to deal with any hungry predators and to achieve the best terms for our shareholders. The alternative was my resignation.

When I had finished, there was a long silence. I remember a sense of ease at having at last said what I had to say and also a feeling of slight surprise that I had summoned the boldness to do it.

Then John Read was speaking. He was in perfect control, not a hint of tension in his voice. 'I feel we should study Bernie's memorandum.' He turned to me. 'Would you mind leaving us for a while?'

Mind? I was delighted. Outside I had another glimpse of Roger Brooke. He was still at peace with the world though maybe wondering a little why he was being kept waiting. I thought it best not to get into conversation.

I kicked my heels for an hour before a secretary came to find me. When I went back into the meeting I saw a lot of serious faces. John Read was standing at the far end of the table. As I made for my place, he walked towards me, his hand outstretched.

'Congratulations,' he said. 'You've just been made chief executive.'

Chapter 15

I flew back to Cannes thinking of how I might break the news to Carole that, at nearly seventy, I was proposing to launch off on a new career as chief executive of the EMI group. Only a week earlier she had been telling me how much she was looking forward to my retirement.

Fortunately, the press was ahead of me. By the time I arrived at the hotel, several reporters had tracked down Carole to record her sheer disbelief. When she got round to me her irritation had given way to weary resignation.

The newspapers made much of the story. There were the usual jokes; references to the *Titanic* ('Delfont can't sink this one') and digs at my age; John Read, who was nine years my junior, was said to be 'giving way to an older man'. But most of the editorial comment was on a positive note. In the view of the City commentators, the changes at the top showed that EMI was determined to fight its way out of trouble. Having survived, even prospered as a theatrical producer, I was credited with powers to work miracles.

It was a great help that John Read had declared his support. He was to stay on as chairman. Roger Brooke was also with us. He became my right hand, not the easiest of jobs but one that seems to have stood him in good stead. Today, he runs Candover Investments, a highly successful company handling management buy-outs.

At Cannes, I paid little attention to the new films and even less to the polite conversation at parties. Everybody wanted to know my plans. I was tempted to say that I was open to all suggestions. This may not have inspired confidence but in one sense was very close to the truth. Having declared my readiness to sell one or more parts of the company, I wanted to see who would come forward with offers. I could hardly wait to return to London but undue haste would, I knew, suggest panic and start a run on the EMI shares.

Our first nibble came from Japanese companies interested in acquiring our medical scanners. This brought General Electric, the world's largest electronic company, into the game. Arnold Weinstock (Lord Weinstock) was interested in taking on medical and defence and any other part of the business if this helped to secure a deal. We even talked of GEC buying the whole of EMI and then floating off the leisure division as a separate company with me as its chairman. The same plan in reverse order appealed to Sir Maxwell Joseph of Grand Metropolitan who wanted our hotels and chain of bingo halls (the latter obtained by me at a modest price from two gentlemen whose entrepreneurial energy outpaced the toleration of the Inland Revenue). However appealing in strict financial terms, these proposals were a last resort leading to the break-up and virtual annihilation of EMI. I was more interested in a rescue package which would leave EMI intact.

I had nearly given up on this ideal solution when I was contacted by Charles Bludhorn, the head of Gulf and Western. This US conglomerate owned Paramount which, in turn, had an interest in music publishing through a small subsidiary called Famous Music. Bludhorn put to me the idea of merging Famous Music with EMI's music division to create a new company to be run on a fifty-fifty basis. Since at that time EMI was the world's largest record and music company, while Famous Music was a small subsidiary of Paramount, it was accepted that they would have to inject a large amount of cash to make up the difference.

Now this did sound interesting. I agreed to meet Charles Bludhorn in Paris at the George V hotel. Before setting out I had a long session with Dick Watt, our financial director. We would keep it simple, we decided, by offering a one-price deal that would lift the pressure from EMI without scaring off Gulf and Western. The figures were set out on a single sheet of paper.

Charles Bludhorn was not an easy person to deal with. He came on like the old-style Hollywood mogul, aggressively sociable – all back-slapping, arm-squeezing and 'have a cigar'. I felt more comfortable with Barry Diller, the chief executive of Paramount. I had known him for some time and trusted his judgement. But it was Charles who led the negotiations and it was Charles who would have the last word.

After talking round the subject at length, I weighed in with the vital question. If Charles Bludhorn wanted to buy in to EMI Music was he prepared to pay the price?

'Tell me the figure,' he said.

I pushed over a sheet of paper. Seventy million pounds was heavily underlined. Barry Diller played with his calculator to come up with the dollar equivalent. He was tight-lipped for a while, implying that the price was too high and Charles tried to argue me down. But I was not prepared to budge and Charles knew it. He smiled.

'We're still in the same ball game.'

We shook hands. I was relieved and delighted.

The deal was a three-way triumph. We had our much needed cash injection with the bonus of a stronger foothold in the US music market and both achieved without any loss of control. Bhaskar Menon, who ran our music operations, was to become head of the joint venture.

We still had some way to go but as we had already signed heads of agreement, I felt confident enough to make a press statement. EMI was in urgent need of favourable publicity.

In the following weeks, Dick Watt threw up a few warning signals. He discovered that Gulf and Western had problems with the American revenue departments: a team of accountants was hacking its way through a warehouse of documents to assess how much the company owed in back taxes. But as far as I could see there was no crisis of confidence. Seventy million pounds was what we had agreed and seventy million (less the value of Famous Music put at about five million pounds) was what I expected to get.

When I flew to New York in August, I was in good spirits. I was given a rousing welcome at the Gulf and Western headquarters, a skyscraper office block in east side Manhattan, before being shown in to a vast office where Charles Bludhorn's team of wheeler-dealers were gathered round a glass conference table. I sat opposite Charles. He looked enormously pleased with himself.

There were the usual courtesies. Then Charles said, 'We've worked out how we can arrange the finance.'

I said I was delighted to hear it.

'Yes,' he went on. 'We've done some creative accounting.'

I glanced sideways at Dick Watt who was nervously tapping his fingers on the table-top. Now I was worried. 'There's no problem is there?' I said.

'No, no.' Charles was keeping up the cheerful front. 'It's just that we'll need to borrow on the assets of the company to pay you the full sum. You'll get the money all right.'

I looked directly at Charles Bludhorn. 'This isn't what we agreed in Paris. You're telling me there's no deal.'

He appealed to his audience. 'Did I say that?'

I felt my voice rising. 'If you can't pay from your own resources, there's no deal,' I told him. 'That's all there is to it.'

I got up from my chair and walked out.

Barry Diller followed me. 'You can't talk to Charles like that.'

'Barry,' I said, 'I don't like the way this has been handled. As far as I'm concerned, we shook hands on a deal. This is not the way I'm used to doing business. I'm going back to London.'

When the news got round that Gulf and Western had fallen out of bed, there was the inevitable blip in EMI shares and renewed interest from companies powerful enough to mount an outright takeover bid. In one case, interest hardened into action.

It was not the first time that Thorn had been mooted as a likely partner for EMI. That company was heavily involved in television manufacture and rentals. With the uncertainties of a market coming to terms with video players and compact discs, it made sense to link with a software manufacturer like EMI. When Sir Jules Thorn had been in charge, talks had foundered on his worry of losing control of the business he had built from nothing, but his successor, Sir Richard Cave, was not deterred by tradition. He was after the best deal he could get and with EMI he saw the chance of a very good deal indeed.

The first approach came in a telephone call.

Dick Cave wanted a meeting with me and John Read. Could he call round later that evening? Oh yes, and he would like to bring his finance director.

I did not need a crystal ball to predict the subject of conversation. It was brief and to the point. After declaring his aim of merging Thorn and EMI, Dick Cave handed over a letter, saying, 'The contents will be made known to the Stock Exchange before trading opens tomorrow morning.'

I glanced at the letter, taking in the figures, before passing it across to John Read. I said, 'I would like to have a word with John in private.'

The two of us found an empty office and sat down to mull over the offer. It was a share bid without any cash element and, anyway, it was not high enough. But this was only the start of the game.

We went back to Dick Cave with a counter-proposal. If he withdrew the challenge and gave us a few days' grace we would come up with a plan to suit both sides. The alternative was an expensive and damaging fight which we would do our damndest to win. We were not to be rushed, Dick Cave could see that, and he accepted the peaceful option with good grace.

It took two weeks to work out a strategy. On the return to the negotiating table Thorn supplemented their share offer with cash up front. Our shareholders were enthusiastic; so too were our employees who welcomed an end to uncertainty. To reassure them that they were not losing their identity, I insisted on the new company having EMI in its title.

I refused to discuss my own position until the merger was formalised. It was then that I was asked to join the Thorn EMI board and to return to my old job running the leisure division.

But as we settled in under the new régime, I did begin to feel a little isolated. Leisure was not a core activity. The fact was emphasised at a board meeting when Dick Cave rejected a carefully reasoned proposal to buy in a rival business.

'We haven't yet digested EMI. I feel we should wait before we launch on another expansion.'

The director who had pushed hard for the acquisition was understandably irritated. As he gathered together his papers he spoke directly to the chairman. 'This was not what we agreed six months ago. Taking over EMI was supposed to help us expand, not stop us in our tracks.'

I understood his frustration and felt partly responsible. Having pushed Dick Cave not to break up EMI, save in exceptional circumstances, I was seen as an obstacle to expansion in other areas. Selling parts of EMI that were peripheral to Thorn EMI would have freed resources for growth in core activities.

I decided to break the deadlock. I told Dick Cave that he should not let our understanding on the future of the EMI divisions inhibit him from disposing of unwanted properties. This evidently came as welcome relief, for within days he was asking me to find a buyer for our hotels which I eventually sold to Scottish and Newcastle Breweries. In doing so I had to fend off an attack from Sir Maxwell Joseph of Grand Metropolitan who tried to wreck the deal by declaring that he wouldn't touch the hotels with a bargepole. Since this was a reversal of his earlier position I could only assume that, in fact, he was trying to get them on the cheap.

It was a short step from Scottish and Newcastle to a sell-out of all leisure activities except the film and music divisions. I was sad to think of losing my empire but, as I was soon to find out, my own time at Thorn EMI was running out.

On holiday in France, I had a call from Dick Cave. 'I see you've turned seventy,' he said. 'I'd no idea that you were that age.'

I thought he was about to offer congratulations but he had something else on his mind.

'You're up against the retirement rule, I'm afraid. Directors have to retire at seventy.'

I was not too pleased at this. Dick Cave must have had some idea that I was close to a critical age. But he had given no warning. Still, if it was company policy, I had to go along with it. I started thinking of how I might spend the rest of my life. As a born-again producer, perhaps, with my own West End theatres?

It did not turn out that way.

I was asked to stay on at Thorn EMI long enough to sell off other parts of the leisure division.

Having put out a few feelers it did not take me long to think of Sir Charles Forte (soon to be Lord Forte) as a likely purchaser. We had been close friends and business associates since the birth of the Talk of the Town twenty-one years earlier. I had made some recompense for all the help Charles had given me at that critical stage in my career by supporting him in the mid seventies against a hostile takeover by Allied Breweries. By borrowing quite heavily to increase my Trust House Forte holding and persuading friends to do the same, I played a small part in preserving THF as an independent concern. Of more immediate relevance, I had helped to build up the leisure side of THF by snapping up three Blackpool piers and other entertainment properties. It made sense to merge our leisure interests to create a stronger entity with excellent prospects for growth.

Charles was interested but, naturally, he wanted to know the price. I told him he could have the lot – the Blackpool Tower, the Leicester Square Empire, three West End theatres, restaurants, amusement parks, show bars, ballrooms, sports centres, the Chichester marina – all for fourteen million pounds, a figure Thorn EMI was happy to accept. After some debate Charles accepted the asking price. But there was a condition attached to the deal. Charles wanted me to be chairman and chief executive of the company which would merge with his own leisure division to become Trust House Forte Leisure.

I thought, here we go again. Not that I was in any way reluctant to take on the job. The very idea of retirement appalled me and while I knew that Carole harboured a desire to see me slow down, I also knew that she would go mad if I was around the house smoking cigars all day long.

The handover went smoothly. When I asked Charles about my own contract, he gave me a sheet of blank paper.

'Set out your terms. I'll sign whatever you suggest.'

I could not have asked for a stronger vote of confidence. I moved my office and immediate staff from number thirty to number seventeen Golden Square for what I imagined was to be the last move of my career. Not a bit of it. The best was yet to come.

After little more than a year at THF I was pulled in for an informative chat with Eric Hartwell, the long-standing business partner of Charles Forte, who was known for his blunt delivery of bad news. He told me there were soon to be changes in the top management of THF which would upset the balance between catering and leisure. Charles's son Rocco, who was about to take over as chief executive, wanted to concentrate on the business he knew best. The message was clear. The hotels and catering came first, a policy I could not disagree with.

Eric softened the blow by stressing that THF would not try to dispose of the leisure group without my agreement; and that even if leisure was sold I was invited to remain with the company. I was grateful for the compliment but, still, the sudden change of policy caught me totally by surprise. I told Eric I needed time to think.

A day or so later I talked to Charles Forte who repeated Eric's promise that if I was against selling the leisure division, he would not do so. But while I had no doubt he would keep his word and allow me to make my own choice, I worried that if, later, leisure did not prosper for some reason, it would look as if I had put my own interests before that of the company. There was no doubt in my mind that the search for a new business home was about to begin all over again.

That weekend Carole and I visited our son, David, in the West Country. Stopping overnight at the Imperial Hotel in Torquay, I had a quiet evening to myself to contemplate the future. On the plus side, I controlled a successful company with sales around the thirty-million-pound mark with profits over three million and rising. It was a secure investment with great potential. The glimmer of light came as I was enjoying a drink on the terrace. Why was I even thinking of finding another purchaser for the company? Why didn't I buy it?

211

I went to see Charles first thing Monday morning. Would he agree to a management buy-out? I promised a smooth transition with no redundancies.

He asked, 'Can you raise that sort of money?'

The truth was, I didn't know. But I was ready to try. 'Give me a little time.'

We discussed the price and Charles said, 'The deal must satisfy our shareholders. There's only one price – thirty-seven and a half million pounds.'

And I had only six weeks in which to do it.

Where to start?

I told Carole of my plan. She was appalled.

'You must be mad to even think of this at your age.'

But, as ever, when she saw I was determined, she gave me her full support.

Having jumped that hurdle, I went to see Jacob Rothschild who had the money and the contacts. He made encouraging sounds but gave the impression that he did not want to be too closely involved. He was the friendly adviser who would suggest likely backers for me to meet. His first suggestion was to talk to Gerald Ronson which sounded like a good idea but turned out to be a disappointment – he told me rather curtly that he could see nothing in it for him. I began to worry that I was wasting my time. Then I remembered Bill Thompson who was the specialist in film finance at the First Bank of Boston. Since we had worked together to mutual advantage at my time at EMI I felt no qualms in ringing him to say that somehow or other I had to put my hands on thirty-seven and a half million pounds plus working capital within the next month.

To his everlasting credit, Bill flew over to London the next day, bringing with him three of his top-line advisers. Together we constructed a deal whereby the bank would put up twenty million pounds, leaving eighteen and a half million to be raised by equity; or rather, seventeen and a half million because I declared my intention to borrow against my assets including my houses to put one million into the kitty.

Bill had a link through to Hill Samuel who agreed to present our case to the City institutions. To show good faith I borrowed a million pounds against my assets to buy the same number of shares.

Armed with a smart sales pitch I chased after likely contacts, starting well with Sir Dennis Mountain of Eagle Star who committed half a million. His example encouraged several other insurance companies to follow suit.

By now we were over the first wave of enthusiasm and still at least eleven million short. I thought of Lord Rayne, head of London Merchant Securities. Though he had made his money in oil and property, there was another side to Max Rayne which surfaced with his chairmanship of the National Theatre. I knew him well enough to interrupt his holiday in the south of France. He invited me over for a meeting.

After listening to my lengthy and, by now, well-practised spiel without interruption, he asked, 'How much do you want?'

'I was hoping you'd put in a million.'

He thought for a moment. 'No, I don't think I'll do that.' And while the look of disappointment was still on my face: 'But I will put in five million.'

Now I really was on my way.

Max introduced me to Sir John Woolf who roped in Anglia Television and the *Guardian* and when I went back to Charles Forte to report progress, he too wanted to invest to the tune of one and a half million. It was an astute move. Not long ago he sold his shares at a profit of ten million pounds.

Totting up the figures, I was just two million short. Hill Samuel had run out of suggestions and I had run out of contacts. I was sitting in my office searching for inspiration when Max Rayne came on the line. For a terrible moment I thought he had changed his mind – by then, I was ready for anything. But in fact he was about to extend another great favour.

'I hear you're in need of a little support. You can count on me for the two million.'

So, through his company, London Merchant Securities, Max Rayne was in for seven million. Without him, I could not have completed the deal. As it was, THF was happy, and the City was marvelling at one of the biggest management buy-outs yet seen in Britain. The new company was to be called First Leisure Corporation. By 1 January 1983 we were open for business.

Chapter 16

We raised thirty-eight and a half million to buy First Leisure. Today, seven years on, the Stock Exchange value of the company is just at close on three hundred and thirty million. In other words, every pound invested in First Leisure in 1983 has grown eleven-fold. I think I can say the shareholders are happy, particularly those who invested in the early stages.

Not everything has worked out quite the way I had hoped. At one time I was reasonably confident of bringing in Andrew Lloyd Webber and his Really Useful Company. My links with Andrew went back a long way to the days when having turned down the opportunity to produce *Jesus Christ Superstar* (we all make mistakes) I helped to get it staged at the Palace Theatre. That was in 1972. Even then, his ambition was to buy a West End theatre. In fact, it was an obsession. When he failed to get The Old Vic I sold him the lease of the Palace which I controlled with Emile Littler. Later, he was able to buy the freehold and did a magnificent job in renovating the building. Six years after the opening of *Jesus Christ Superstar*, *Evita* started its triumphant run at the Prince Edward, another of my theatres. At around this time, Andrew came to see me about the New London.

As it happened, this theatre was not a direct interest of mine though I acted as chairman of the controlling body on behalf of the then owners, the English Property Company. The New London was a brave experiment. Built on the site of the Winter Garden Theatre, the idea was to combine a highly versatile theatre (stage, seats, orchestra pit, even walls could move at the flick of a switch) with the sort of facilities customers had come to expect on their nights out such as a decent restaurant and easy underground parking. The development was started in 1971 and we opened in early 1973 with Peter Ustinov starring in and directing his own play, *The Unknown Soldier and His Wife*. What money we made on this production was

214

quickly lost on its successor, the musical *Grease*, which, appropriately enough, ran until the oil crisis of 1974 caused havoc in the tourist market and put paid to any marginal West End shows. Unable to find a replacement we used the New London for conferences and television studios while hoping, as I thought, that the right production would eventually come along.

This brings me back to Andrew Lloyd Webber. He wanted the New London for his latest musical. More than that, the New London was the only theatre that could measure up to his needs – an auditorium that could easily convert to theatre-in-the-round. I had doubts about the appeal of a show in which all the performers were dressed up as cats but I was not about to argue with a composer of Andrew's track record. I came to a satisfactory deal with a tough young producer called Cameron Mackintosh (who today is probably the most successful theatrical producer in the world) and told the theatre owners the good news. Except they didn't think it *was* good news. They were happy to go on with the New London as a conference centre. I had Andrew, his director Trevor Nunn and Cameron Mackintosh in one room while I held a separate meeting with my fellow directors. I argued strongly for giving live entertainment another chance. 'I don't know whether *Cats* will be a hit or not but we must keep faith with our promise to run the New London as a theatre.'

When it looked as if they might still hold out I told them that if the New London was to continue as a conference centre, my position would become impossible. That, if anything, did the trick. Trevor Nunn has been kind enough to say that without Bernard Delfont, the show would not have happened. After opening night Stanley Honeyman, the managing director of English Property, paid me another compliment. 'I'm so glad,' he said, 'that I will not be known as the man who turned down *Cats*.'

Clearly, the industry that was growing up around Andrew Lloyd Webber had great potential – though just how much was beyond anyone's imagination. I was convinced that Really Useful would make a good fit with our theatre division. I put the scheme to Andrew with an offer of five million pounds for seventy-five per cent of his company.

In principle, Andrew was happy to accept and we began drawing up contracts. But since he was in the throes of a divorce he worried that if the deal went through too quickly he might face financial problems. He asked for time; I was content to wait. Meanwhile, he talked to his merchant bankers. They told him that Really Useful should fetch around fifty million if it went public. Andrew rang me with the news.

I told him he should go ahead and wished him the best of luck.

In retrospect the valuation was not unreasonable. *Phantom of the Opera* and *Aspects of Love* have proved that. For me the consolation is that my business connection with Andrew has continued. *Aspects of Love* has found a home in the Prince of Wales, my favourite theatre and the flagship of First Leisure. Long may it stay there.

Another favourite building is the Empire, Leicester Square, a première entertainment centre incorporating cinemas and disco. I was still at EMI when I secured an option on the Empire from Eric Morley at Mecca, then part of the Grand Metropolitan group. I had sold Eric twenty-five of our surplus cinemas on condition that I could buy the Empire for one million seven hundred thousand pounds at any time up to ten years. My idea was to convert the Empire from a ballroom to a West End showcase cinema for EMI. I don't think for one moment that Eric imagined that I would exercise my right and when I did, he resisted.

His argument was that I no longer wanted to use it as a cinema now that I had converted the Saville theatre into a triple cinema. If I pressed my option he threatened to strip the Empire of all furnishing, even the chandeliers and other lights.

'It'll cost you two million to put it all back,' he warned.

I could see this was liable to be a long battle. I decided to cut it short by talking to Sir Maxwell Joseph, chairman of Grand Met. I told him that Eric was simply intent on hurting me for no better reason than disappointment at the prospect of losing a favoured property. To overcome the problem I offered to pay a premium of three hundred thousand pounds 'on condition you finish trading as Mecca dancing on Saturday night and we take over the next day'.

We had a deal.

Now, as part of First Leisure, the Empire was high on my list of investment priorities. We started on an ambitious refurbishment programme which was only recently completed. I think of it as the pride of Leicester Square and it gives me added pleasure to reflect that it is right next door to the little office where I started my business all those years ago.

After thirteen months of operating First Leisure as a private company, we decided to go public. This was much earlier than anticipated but with growth well ahead of forecast, I was confident of a successful launch. We offered six million shares at one hundred and eighty pence each to raise ten million pounds. In some quarters it was said that the leisure market was too volatile to support such an ambitious flotation and that, in any case, my age was against me. But at seventy-four I certainly did not feel too old to do the job. I believed very strongly that I still had something to give. The public evidently agreed because applications for shares totted up to a massive three hundred and thirty million pounds. In other words, we were oversubscribed thirty-two times, which is probably a record for the leisure industry.

By 1986 I was beginning to think it would be in the interests of the company to bring in someone to take over as chairman with me remaining as president. Michael Cottrell came to us from Courage where he was managing director. He struck me as a most charming man and we immediately hit it off. But despite a carefully orchestrated handover the plan did not work out. Why, I am not best placed to say. One theory is that Michael assumed the presidency to be a nominal job whereas I saw a more active role for myself. In any event after a brief absence from the hot seat the board asked me to come back as chairman, an invitation I was pleased to accept.

Fortunately, these internal manoeuvrings did nothing to harm the profitability of the company which has been consistently excellent. This has meant that we have not been forced to chase growth by acquisition but instead have generated our own expansion. A first-rate team led by John Conlan as chief executive, Nick Irens as finance director and Richard Mills in charge of theatre operations has made a success story of a whole range of leisure activities. In seven years the full staff has grown from two thousand seven hundred to five thousand, proving to my satisfaction that youth and ambition, coupled with the wisdom of age, is a winning combination.

As for me, I am happy to go on as long as I am able and as long as I am needed. My first love remains, as ever, the theatre. One of my great joys is to know that our two West End theatres, the Prince Edward and the Prince of Wales, are more than holding their own in a hotly competitive market. And the New London is still going strong with *Cats*, now almost into its tenth year.

I believe I will know the right time to give up. On the other hand, the elderly are not necessarily the best judge of their own faculties. If mine do begin to fail without me noticing, I hope my colleagues will give me a gentle hint. In that event and, assuming reasonable health, I fancy going back into production with my own West End theatre.

I would start my new career with the virtue of experience. I know enough not to spend more than a day worrying about failure – or more than half a day celebrating success. I know that going backstage after a hit is riskier for a producer than going backstage after a flop. It is when the show triumphs that the star begins to feel hard done by. 'My dressing-room is too small; I don't like the wallpaper; where's the champagne?' But when the show is a disappointment, the producer, as the leader of the home team, is seen as the protector of the innocent. 'What a marvellous company to work with; I so love this dressing-room; the critics had it wrong, didn't they?'

I have also learned a thing or two about myself. One trait that has stood me in good stead is my ability not to get rattled by events, however outrageous or infuriating. I am essentially an easy-going character, a slow burner who will take so much . . .

Many years ago, when Benny Hill was starting out, I was keen to get him for a summer show at Yarmouth. His agent Richard Stone agreed terms on the understanding that the billing would read, 'Bernard Delfont presents in association with Richard Stone'. I had no objections. When the show was a hit, Richard suggested a follow-up with him taking a twenty-five per cent share of the profits. I said yes. The next year, he wanted the billing changed to 'Bernard Delfont and Richard Stone present . . .' No problem. But then I happened to be in Yarmouth and I saw that all the scenery – my scenery – had Richard Stone Productions stamped on the back. That was it. I told Richard our business association was at an end.

My toleration goes a long way but there is a limit.

I have not made many enemies, at least not deliberately and I owe a great debt to friends who have believed in me in times of adversity.

I am blessed with a loving and supportive wife who is mad on animals, doing her best to help with all charities connected with them and with gardening and all 'green' issues. And I have three lovely children who, on the whole, have not been too much of a problem, even if David did worry his mother a little when he first discovered girls.

Following through on a resolution to encourage the children to travel (they covered America by Greyhound bus and Jenny spent nine months on an Israeli kibbutz) we sent David to Paris to learn the language. Not long after he had settled in, I returned home one evening to find Carole in fighting mood.

'Do you know what's happened? Your son has a girl living with him in his apartment.'

My reaction was mixed relief that he was normal with happy memories of the freedom of youth and perhaps a tinge of jealousy.

Carole took a different line. 'You must ring him immediately. Tell him if the girl is not out by Friday, you'll go over there and bring him back to London.'

I made the call.

By Friday I had forgotten all about it. But Carole had greater persistence. She stayed close while I dialled the number in Paris.

'David, is that you? Have you done what I asked? Has the girl moved out?'

My son was suitably contrite. 'Yes, Dad. But I can't see what you're so pleased about. I've moved her into a hotel down the road. You've just doubled your expenses.'

Back home, David again incurred his mother's anger when she heard from a friend that he had misbehaved at a party. A ruffled bed was offered in evidence.

Carole was inconsolable. 'The shame is too much,' she declared. 'He must go to Australia.'

I passed on the message.

'Australia?' asked David innocently. 'Does the feeling go away there?'

David is now happily married. He and his family have settled in Devon on the edge of Dartmoor. The new house is almost finished!

Sue, our eldest, has two lovely children, Tom seven and Lydia four – our only granddaughter. Sadly, she is just divorced but still very friendly with her ex-husband. She is the only one who ever wanted to go on the stage: she has a good voice but was petrified when confronted by an audience and had to give it up. She is now taking a break from her career as a stills photographer for films in order to look after the children. As they live in London we see a lot of them.

Jenny was the first to get married and has our two eldest grandsons, Jamie fifteen and Sam eleven. She studied art and became a potter until her marriage when the family went to live in North Devon. Now she does magnificent batik work, mostly pictures on silk. She and her husband parted several years ago but they live only a few houses away from one another in Bath and the boys divide their time between their parents.

Both the girls' husbands are always welcome to come and stay with their children at our house in the country during the holidays and often do so. The children all seem to get on famously together but as they have abundant energy we can generally do with a holiday after we wave them goodbye!

Of my own family generation, Lew is as busy and as exuberant as ever. We don't see much of each other socially – Lew has never been a great party-goer – but we talk often on the telephone and we are never averse to exchanging advice, sometimes in loud voices.

My sister Rita was devastated when her husband Joe died. That was in 1979. It was one of the happiest marriages I have known and Rita has never quite got over the shock of it ending though, thankfully, she has found some solace in a new career as a radio presenter. I joke with her that she owes her performing skills to me, having once appeared in a Bernard Delfont production of *No, No Nanette* as Betty from Bath.

My main relaxation is watching racing on television – or any kind of sport for that matter. Carole and I have an understanding that on Saturday afternoons I am left undisturbed in my study with absolutely no interruptions until tea-time. By then the smog from my cigar has filled the room and being a fresh-air fiend, Carole promptly opens the door to the garden. That is when I freeze. But I suppose it is more healthy.

At my age I think of myself in a mile race. I have covered seven furlongs and have lived through most facets of life – the ups and the downs. Now I am looking forward to that last furlong. Who knows what it will bring?

I am a most fortunate man.

Theatrical Productions which Bernard Delfont presented or was associated with:

YEAR	THEATRE	PLAY	STAR(S)
1941	Tour	*Room for Two*	Gene Gerrard
1942	St Martin's	*Jam Today*	Beatrix Lehmann Olga Lindo Frank Pettingell
	Piccadilly	*Sleeping Out*	Gene Gerrard Winifred Shotter Irene Prador
	Ambassador's	*Other People's Houses*	Mary Clare Phyllis Dare Clarice Mayne
	St Martin's	*Rookery Nook*	Ralph Lynn
	Stoll	*Rose Marie*	Phyllis Monkman Marjorie Browne George Lacy
1943	Princes	*Old Chelsea*	Richard Tauber Carole Lynne
	Tour	*The Duchess of Danzig*	Fay Compton Charles Heslop
	Comedy	*The Fur Coat*	Henry Kendall Jeanne de Casalis
	Tour	*The Man in Dark Glasses*	Mary Glynne Cathleen Nesbitt Kenneth Kent

221

	Phoenix	*The Wingless Victory*	Mary Merrall Andre van Gyseghem Rachel Kempson
	Tour	*The Count of Luxembourg*	George Gee Victoria Hopper
	His Majesty's	*The Admirable Crichton*	Barry K. Barnes Diana Churchill
	Winter Garden	*Where the Rainbow Ends*	Italia Conti Michael Medwin
	Whitehall	*The Moon is Down*	Paul Scofield Lewis Casson
1944	Coliseum	*Something for the Boys*	Daphne Barker Evelyn Dall Leigh Stafford
	Stoll	*The Student Prince*	Bruce Trent Marion Gordon
	Saville	*Her Excellency*	Cicely Courtneidge Billy Dainty Austin Trevor
1945	Saville	*Big Boy*	Fred Emney April Stride Richard Hearne
	Winter Garden	*The Gaieties*	Hermione Baddeley Walter Crisham Leslie Henson
	Palace	*Gay Rosalinda*	James Etherington Ruth Naylor Cyril Ritchard Peter Graves
1946	Saville	*Here Come the Boys*	Bobby Howes Jack Hulbert
	Saville	*The Wizard of Oz*	Ellen Pollock Claude Hulbert Walter Crisham

1947	Palace	*The Bird Seller*	Douglas Byng Adèle Dixon George Howe
	Saville	*Noose*	Michael Hordern Nigel Patrick Campbell Singer
	Saville	*Honour and Obey*	Ursula Howells Naunton Wayne Mona Washbourne
1948	Saville	*Four Hours to Kill*	Jack La Rue Thelma Ruby
	Princes	*Hellzapoppin'*	Ole Olsen Chic Johnson
	Saville	*Ram Gopal and his Indian Ballet*	Ram Gopal
	Saville	*Liliom (Grenier-Hussenot Co)*	Yves Robert
	Saville	*Bob's Your Uncle*	Leslie Henson Vera Pearce Austin Melford
	Tour	*The Chocolate Soldier*	Fred Emney Jessica James Roy Royston
1949	Tour	*Bless the Bride*	Valerie Lawson Edmund Goffron
	Saville	*Belinda Fair*	Adèle Dixon John Battles Jerry Verno
	Saville	*Roundabout*	Bobby Howes Pat Kirkwood Jerry Desmonde
1950	London Hippodrome	*Folies Bergère Revue*	Tommy Cooper Dickie Henderson

	Prince of Wales	*Touch and Go*	Carole Lynne Sidney James Bill Fraser
	Saville	*Spring Song*	Meier Tzelniker Yvonne Mitchell
	Saville	*The King of Schnorrers*	Meier Tzelniker Yvonne Mitchell Warren Misell
	Saville	*Awake and Sing*	Meier Tzelniker Harry Towb Alan Tilvern
	Saville	*The Schoolmistress*	Madge Elliott Cyril Ritchard Fred Emney
1951	St James's	*The Madwoman of Chaillot*	Martita Hunt Richard Johnson Angela Baddeley Marius Goring
	Stoll	*Bless the Bride*	Valerie Lawson Edmund Goffron
	London Hippodrome	*New 1951 Folies Bergère Revue: Encore des Folies*	Igor Barczinski Tommy Cooper Annette Chappell
	Tour	*Don Juan in Hell*	Charles Laughton Sir Cedric Hardwicke Agnes Moorehead Charles Boyer
1952	Prince of Wales	*Paris to Piccadilly*	Norman Wisdom
	Australia	*Folies Bergère*	
	New Zealand	*Folies Bergère*	
1953	Prince of Wales	*Anna Lucasta*	Isabelle Cooley Erroll John
	London Hippodrome	*Champagne on Ice*	Belita Joe Church

	Prince of Wales	*Pardon My French*	Frankie Howerd Winifred Atwell
1954	South Africa	*Folies Bergère*	
1955	Prince of Wales	*Paris by Night*	Benny Hill Tommy Cooper
1956	Palladium	*Rocking the Town*	Harry Secombe Alma Cogan Winifred Atwell Beryl Reid
	Tour	*Star Maker*	Jack Hulbert Cicely Courtneidge Una Stubbs
1957	Prince of Wales	*Plaisirs de Paris*	Dickie Henderson Sabrina
	Palladium	*We're Having a Ball*	Max Bygraves Joan Regan
1958	Palace	*Where's Charley?*	Norman Wisdom Jerry Desmonde
	Palladium	*Large as Life*	Harry Secombe Eric Sykes Terry Thomas Hattie Jacques Harry Worth Adèle Dixon
1959	Palladium	*Swinging Down the Lane*	Max Bygraves Hope and Keen Elizabeth Larner
	Palace	*Fine Fettle*	Benny Hill Robertson Hare Shani Wallis
	Royalty	*The Visit*	Alfred Lunt Lynn Fontaine

1960	Palladium	*Stars in Your Eyes*	Edmund Hockridge Joan Regan Cliff Richard Russ Conway Billy Dainty Des O'Connor
1961	Queen's	*Stop the World – I Want to Get Off*	Anthony Newley Anna Quayle Marti Webb
1962	Prince of Wales	*Come Blow Your Horn*	Bob Monkhouse David Kossoff Michael Crawford Nyree Dawn Porter
	Saville	*An Evening with Yves Montand*	
	Piccadilly	*The Rag Trade*	Peter Jones Miriam Karlin Reg Varney
	Palladium	*Every Night at the Palladium*	Bruce Forsyth Morecambe & Wise Eve Boswell
	Saville	*Karmon Israeli Dancers*	
1963	Haymarket	*Who'll Save the Plowboy?*	Maxine Audley Harry H. Corbett Donal Donnelly
	Palladium	*Sammy Davis Jr Entertains*	
	Palladium	*Swing Along*	Arthur Haynes Nicholas Parsons Joan Savage Frank Ifield Susan Maughan

Saville	*Pickwick*	Harry Secombe Anton Rodgers Jessie Evans
Prince of Wales	*Never Too Late*	Fred Clark Joan Bennett
Saville	*An Evening with Maurice Chevalier*	
Queen's	*The Seagull*	Peggy Ashcroft Vanessa Redgrave Paul Rogers Peter Finch George Devine Rachel Kempson Peter McEnery
1964 Phoenix	*Caligula*	Kenneth Haig Michael Gwynn
Palladium	*Startime*	Tommy Cooper Cilla Black Frankie Vaughan
Comedy	*A Thousand Clowns*	Roy Kinnear James Booth
Adelphi	*Maggie May*	Rachel Roberts Kenneth Haig
Cambridge	*Little Me*	Bruce Forsyth Avril Angers
Arts	*In White America*	Bessie Love Earl Cameron
Shaftesbury	*Our Man Crichton*	Kenneth More Millicent Martin
Palladium	*Aladdin*	Cliff Richard & the Shadows Arthur Askey Charlie Cairoli
Palladium	*Lena Horne*	
Shaftesbury	*Victor Borge*	

	Palladium	*Variety*	Frankie Vaughan Joe Church Arthur Worsley
	Palladium	*Variety*	Helen Shapiro Matt Monro Billy Dainty
1965	Savoy	*The Night of the Iguana*	Sian Phillips Vanda Godsell Mark Eden
	Saville	*The Solid Gold Cadillac*	Margaret Rutherford Sidney James
	Savoy	*The Circle*	Evelyn Laye Frank Lawton
	Piccadilly	*Ride a Cock Horse*	Peter O'Toole Wendy Craig Sian Phillips Barbara Jefford
	Duke of York's	*The Killing of Sister George*	Beryl Reid Eileen Atkins
	Piccadilly	*Barefoot in the Park*	Daniel Massey Marlo Thomas Mildred Natwick
	Palladium	*Doddy's Here!*	Ken Dodd
	Palladium	*Babes in the Wood*	Arthur Askey Sidney James Frank Ifield Roy Kinnear
	New York	*Pickwick*	Harry Secombe Anton Rodgers
	New York	*The Roar of the Greasepaint, the Smell of the Crowd*	Anthony Newley
1966	Criterion	*The Owl and the Pussycat*	Diana Sands Anton Rodgers

	Globe	*The Matchgirls*	Vivienne Martin Cheryl Kennedy Marion Grimaldi
	Prince of Wales	*Funny Girl*	Barbra Streisand
	Palladium	*London Laughs*	Harry Secombe Jimmy Tarbuck Nicky Henson Thora Hird
	Saville	*Joey Joey*	Ron Moody Vivienne Martin
	Queen's	*The Odd Couple*	Jack Klugman Victor Spinetti
	Prince of Wales	*Way Out in Piccadilly*	Frankie Howerd Cilla Black
	Palladium	*Cinderella*	Cliff Richard & the Shadows Terry Scott Hugh Lloyd
1967	Comedy	*Queenie*	Vivienne Martin Bill Owen Paul Eddington Julia McKenzie
	Prince of Wales	*Sweet Charity*	Juliet Prowse
	Drury Lane	*The Four Musketeers*	Harry Secombe John Junkin Elizabeth Larner
	Palladium	*Robinson Crusoe*	Arthur Askey Jimmy Logan Engelbert Humperdinck
	Palladium	*Doddy's Here Again*	Ken Dodd
	Saville	*Martha Graham* *Dance Company*	

229

1968	Fortune	*You're a Good Man, Charlie Brown*	
	Royal Court	*Time Present*	Jill Bennett
	Palladium	*Golden Boy*	Sammy Davis Jr Gloria de Haven Ben Vereen
	Royal Court	*The Hotel in Amsterdam*	Paul Scofield Joss Ackland Judy Parfitt Isabel Dean
	Royal Court	*Look Back in Anger*	Victor Henry Jane Asher Martin Shaw
	Palladium	*Jack and the Beanstalk*	Jimmy Tarbuck Arthur Askey
1969	Drury Lane	*Mame*	Ginger Rogers Julia McKenzie
	Comedy	*Your Own Thing*	
	Queen's	*What the Butler Saw*	Ralph Richardson Coral Browne Stanley Baxter
	Garrick	*The Giveaway*	Rita Tushingham Dandy Nichols Roy Hudd
	Prince of Wales	*Cat Among the Pigeons*	Elizabeth Seal Richard Briers Victor Spinetti Murray Melvin
	Prince of Wales	*Promises, Promises*	Donna McKechnie
1970	Drury Lane	*Carol Channing With Her 10 Stout-Hearted Men*	
	Palace	*Danny La Rue at the Palace*	Danny La Rue Roy Hudd

	Drury Lane	*The Great Waltz*	Sari Barabas Diane Todd
1971	Globe	*Kean*	Alan Badel Felicity Kendal
	Apollo	*Children of the Wolf*	Yvonne Mitchell
	Roundhouse	*Rabelais*	Bernard Bresslaw Joe Melia
	Apollo	*Lulu*	Julia Foster Edward Petherbridge
1972	Prince of Wales	*The Threepenny Opera*	Vanessa Redgrave Joe Melia Barbara Windsor Hermione Baddeley
	Prince of Wales	*Paris to Piccadilly*	Sacha Distel Ted Rogers Stephane Grappelli
	Her Majesty's	*Applause*	Lauren Bacall
	Prince of Wales	*The Good Old Bad Old Days*	Anthony Newley
1973	New London	*The Unknown Soldier and his Wife*	Peter Ustinov Brian Bedford
	Criterion	*A Doll's House*	Claire Bloom Colin Blakely Anton Rodgers Stephanie Bidmead
	Apollo	*The Wolf*	Edward Woodward Judi Dench Leo McKern
	Queen's	*Gomes*	Roy Dotrice Rachel Kempson
	Prince of Wales	*The Danny La Rue Show*	

	Prince of Wales	*The Val Doonican Show*	
1974	Mayfair	*Brief Lives*	Roy Dotrice
	Her Majesty's	*Henry IV*	Rex Harrison James Villers
	Piccadilly	*A Streetcar Named Desire*	Claire Bloom Martin Shaw Joss Ackland Morag Hood
	Her Majesty's	*The Good Companions*	John Mills Judi Dench Marti Webb
	New London	*Sammy Cahn's Songbook*	
	Casino	*Cinderella*	Twiggy Nicky Henson Roy Kinnear Harry H. Corbett Wilfrid Brambell
	New York	*An Evening with Peter Cook and Dudley Moore*	
	New York	*Ulysses in Nighttown*	Zero Mostel
1975	Prince of Wales	*Harvey*	James Stewart Mona Washbourne
	Adelphi	*A Little Night Music*	Jean Simmons Hermione Gingold Joss Ackland Maria Aitken
	Prince of Wales	*The Plumber's Progress*	Harry Secombe Simon Callow
	Shaftesbury	*Dad's Army*	Arthur Lowe John Le Mesurier Clive Dunn

	Casino	*The Exciting Adventures of Queen Daniella*	Danny La Rue Moyra Fraser
	New York	*Sizwe Banzi is Dead and The Island*	
1976	Prince of Wales	*Mardi Gras*	Nicky Henson Dana Gillespie Marsha Hunt
	Roundhouse	*La Grande Eugène*	
1977	Mermaid	*It's All Right If I Do It*	John Stride Prunella Scales
1978	Adelphi	*Beyond the Rainbow*	Roy Kinnear
1979	Adelphi	*Charley's Aunt*	John Inman Mark Wynter Helen Cherry
	Prince of Wales	*An Evening with Tommy Steele*	
1980	Prince of Wales	*It's Magic*	Paul Daniels
1981	Drury Lane	*The Best Little Whore-house in Texas*	Henderson Forsythe Carlin Glynne
1982	Prince of Wales	*Underneath the Arches*	Roy Hudd Christopher Timothy
1983	Prince of Wales	*An Evening with Paul Daniels*	
1984	Prince of Wales	*Little Me*	Russ Abbott Sheila White

And well over 200 summer shows in British holiday resorts.

Information supplied by the Raymond Mander and Joe Mitchenson Theatre Collection.

Cinema and Television Films made whilst Bernard Delfont was chairman and chief executive of EMI Film and Theatre Corporation.

TITLE	PROD'N YEAR		
Aces High	1976	Demons of the Mind	1972
Alfie Darling	1975	Dr Jekyll and Sister Hyde	1971
All The Way Up	1970	Dove	1974
Amazing Howard Hughes	1977	Driver	1978
		Dulcima	1971
And Soon the Darkness	1970	Elephant Man	1980
Arabian Adventure	1979	Entertaining Mr Sloane	1970
Are You Being Served?	1977	Eye Witness	1970
Awakening	1980	Family Life	1971
Bad Boys	1983	Fear in the Night	1972
Baxter	1972	Fear is the Key	1972
Best of Benny Hill	1974	Final Programme	1973
Best Pair of Legs in the Business	1972	Frances	1982
		Go-Between	1971
Blood From the Mummy's Tomb	1971	Handgun	1982
		Henry VIII and his Six Wives	1972
Body	1970		
Breaking of Bumbo	1970	Hoffman	1970
Can't Stop the Music	1980	Holiday on the Buses	1973
Cat and Mouse	1974	Honky Tonk Freeway	1981
Convoy	1978	Horror of Frankenstein	1970
Coronation '53	1977	House in Nightmare Park	1973
Cross Creek	1983	Howard Hughes	1977
Cross of Iron	1976	I am a Dancer	1971
Death on the Nile	1978	Inside Moves	1980
Deer Hunter	1978	Jazz Singer	1980

235

Keep It Up Downstairs	1976	*SOS Titanic*	1979
Lady Caroline Lamb	1972	*Spanish Fly*	1975
Likely Lads	1976	*Spring and Port Wine*	1969
Love Thy Neighbour	1973	*Stardust*	1974
Lust for a Vampire	1970	*Steptoe & Son*	1971
Made	1972	*Steptoe & Son Ride*	
Man About the House	1974	*Again*	1973
Man at the Top	1973	*Stories From a Flying*	
Man Who Haunted		*Trunk*	1979
Himself	1970	*Straight On Till Morning*	1972
Mirror Crack'd	1980	*Swallows and Amazons*	1973
Murder On the Orient		*Sweeney*	1976
Express	1974	*Sweeney 2*	1977
Mutiny on the Buses	1972	*Take Me High*	1973
Not Now Comrade	1976	*Tales of Beatrix Potter*	1971
On the Buses	1971	*Tender Mercies*	1982
Orphan Train	1979	*That'll Be The Day*	1973
Our Miss Fred	1972	*That's Carry On*	1977
Out of Season	1975	*To the Devil, A Daughter*	1975
Percy	1970	*25 Years – Impressions*	1976
Percy's Progress	1974	*Up Pompeii!*	1970
Raging Moon	1970	*Up the Chastity Belt*	1971
Railway Children	1970	*Up The Front*	1972
Scars of Dracula	1970	*Villain*	1971
Second Thoughts	1982	*Warlords of Atlantis*	1978
Seven Nights in Japan	1976	*Zoltan – Hound of*	
Silver Bears	1977	*Dracula*	1976
Some Will, Some Won't	1970		

Information supplied by Weintraub Entertainment Group.

Index

237